The Geography of Aging

The Geography of Aging

Preparing Communities for the Surge in Seniors

GERALD HODGE

McGill-Queen's University Press
Montreal & Kingston · London · Ithaca

© McGill-Queen's University Press 2008
ISBN 978-0-7735-3429-2 (cloth)
ISBN 978-0-7735-3430-8 (paper)

Legal deposit third quarter 2008
Bibliothèque nationale du Québec

Printed in Canada on acid-free paper that is 100% ancient forest free
(100% post-consumer recycled), processed chlorine free

This book has been published with the help of a grant from the Canadian
Federation for the Humanities and Social Sciences, through the Aid to Scholarly
Publications Programme, using funds provided by the Social Sciences and
Humanities Research Council of Canada.

McGill-Queen's University Press acknowledges the support of the Canada
Council for the Arts for our publishing program. We also acknowledge the
financial support of the Government of Canada through the Book Publishing
Industry Development Program (BPIDP) for our publishing activities.

LIBRARY AND ARCHIVES CANADA CATALOGUING IN PUBLICATION

Hodge, Gerald
The geography of aging : preparing communities for the surge in
seniors / Gerald Hodge.

Includes bibliographical references and index.
ISBN 978-0-7735-3429-2 (bnd)
ISBN 978-0-7735-3430-8 (pbk)

1. Aging – Social aspects – Canada.   2. City planning – Canada.
3. Older people – Services for – Canada.   4. Baby boom generation –
Canada.   5. Barrier-free design for older people – Canada.   I. Title.

HV1475.A3H643 2008   307.0846'0971   C2008-901840-0

Set in 10.5/13.5 Sabon with Syntax
Book design and typesetting by Garet Markvoort, zijn digital

For the grandchildren:
Jehanne, Kosma, Elishka, and Selah.
May they live in communities for all ages.

Contents

Tables and Figures

TABLES

FIGURES

Preface

The popular phrase, "what goes around comes around," is particularly apt both for this book and for me personally. When I became involved in community planning in the mid-1950s, much of the effort in this field was devoted to designing Canadian neigbourhoods to accommodate the burgeoning numbers of families and children emanating from the baby boom which was already well under way. Today, almost three generations later, those children from the baby boom are on the verge of becoming part of another surge of population, this time at the other end of the age spectrum. And I find myself again writing about planning for the needs of the same population group but which is now much older and in which I'm also included. For today's and tomorrow's senior citizens are framing the new challenge for those planning and designing communities and for those managing activities within them.

This challenge, unfortunately, has been too little considered both by the many professions whose actions impinge on the daily lives of seniors and by those elected officials whose policies shape Canada's communities. Seniors desire independence in their lives, not least in their everyday geography so they can participate as fully as possible both physically and socially in the communities they've chosen to live in. Had we been listening to them over the past three or more decades we would known this. Had we responded to their plea it would have been apparent that a rich trove of relevant research on aging and environment, some dating from the mid-1970s, was available to guide such efforts. Righting some of this neglect is a major goal of this book.

Pursuing that goal resulted in a lengthy and absorbing quest which, I appreciate now even more, couldn't have been completed without the help of many generous, caring people. For one, or two, Peter Milroy encouraged this project from the outset, as he had done for me more than once before, and Randy Schmidt shepherded it through two drafts and on to its present home. Two anonymous readers gave generously of their time and advice to help correct its course along the way. Then there were Bruce Rice who shared the experience of the City of Regina in its path-breaking seniors' planning efforts and Dr Norah Keating's gerontology team at the University of Alberta who kept me abreast of their pioneering work with rural seniors. Belatedly, I realize there were others who contributed like those at Statistics Canada and CMHC who responded to "urgent" emails, the librarians at the Vancouver Island Regional Library who facilitated my inter-library loans, as well as many others whose names I neglected to save, and to whom I also extend my thanks. Certainly, not least, I am especially appreciative of the five senior friends from various parts of Canada who took my challenge to set down a vignette from their everyday geography and help make this a book that is about older *people*: Dave Anderson, Norma Steven, M.A. Qadeer, Lloyd Ryan (for his mother, Stella), who are all now a bit older than when I asked, and R. Alex Sim who passed away at age 93 in 2005.

At this stage, producing a manuscript seems somewhat like the lesser task among the many associated with it becoming a book. This one took the confidence of Philip Cercone to publish it, of Joan McGilvray to guide it through all the needed steps, of Susan Glickman to apply a sure and sensitive eye to its editing, and of Joanne Ovitsland and Angeleah Hoeppner, two designers from my own community, to adeptly handle the computer graphics and complete the illustrations. And my dear friend Rudy Rogalsky was there early on when spreadsheets were needed. I am especially grateful to the following for allowing me to include illustrations from their publications: Dr Robert L. Rubinstein of the University of Maryland at Baltimore, Dr Marcia Finlayson of the University of Illinois at Chicago, and Ms Kerrie Strathy of the University of Regina's Seniors Education Centre.

Of course, producing a manuscript, much of which goes on in isolation, depends upon the forbearance and faith of the one who shares your life. My soon-to-be wife, Sharron Milstein, provided me the space, time, and encouragement I needed and for that I offer my deepest gratitude and love.

G. H.
Hornby Island BC
April 2008

Part One

Where Canada's Seniors Live

Chapter One

Perspectives for a Geography of Aging

INTRODUCTION: SPATIAL FACTORS IN POPULATION AGING

It is well known to most Canadians that the country's population is getting older, that senior citizens, meaning those aged 65 and older, comprise larger numbers and proportions among us, and that this trend will continue for several more decades. Much is said and written about the impact of these facts on our health care and pension systems. Much less is said, however, about what they mean to the people we call seniors, and to the communities in which their lives unfold. Yet we need this knowledge to better understand Canada's population aging. For it is in the neighbourhood, community, and regional milieux of Canada that population aging is experienced. It is here that the quality of life of our longest-lived citizens and that of their families, neighbours, and friends is determined. It is here that our national and provincial policies regarding the elderly and their increasing numbers are played out. Thus, responding more fully to population aging means going beyond mere counting of heads to deal with matters such as the housing seniors occupy, how they get around, the quality of their neighbourhood facilities, and the availability of supportive services. In other words, we need to deal with the implications of population aging in actual communities throughout the country, factors that are *spatial* or *geographical* in nature.

The late Lawton Powell, who contributed so much to our understanding of the spatial dimension in seniors' lives, once said: "older people are, on the whole, pretty much like the rest of us."[1] What he meant was that seniors reside in communities, utilize the services and facilities of those communities, and have the need to get around in them to conduct their daily activities. Seniors, almost without exception, say that their goal is to be independent. That is, to continue to function in their own homes, be safe in their neighbourhoods, and participate in their communities. Almost all seniors live in their own dwellings just about everywhere in this country – in metropolitan suburbs and small towns, in the countryside of southern Canada and frontier communities in the North. But what can they expect from these communities? Some valuable steps have been taken in pursuing such questions and achieving a deeper understanding of geographical factors affecting population aging.[2] Still, the information we have about the situation is disparate at best. One of the main aims of this volume is therefore to provide a coherent portrait of where Canada's seniors live and where and how they conduct their everyday activities.

There are two places one might begin in understanding this geographical side of population aging. The first is to start from the broad statistical outlines contained in the national census and then deal with progressively smaller geographical aggregates – going, for example, from nation to province to metropolitan area to other cities to rural communities – to see what picture emerges. The other is to start from the perspective of community-based seniors and their activity patterns and consider the general picture that emerges as such patterns accumulate. Both perspectives are needed for a comprehensive geography of aging. However, it is the second of these approaches, which deals with seniors' daily spatial patterns, that requires special attention, because there is a tendency for it to be overlooked.[3] To this end, three hypothetical vignettes are provided below that are typical of seniors' everyday situations.

1   Mr R is nearly 80 and Mrs R is 73. They live alone in a suburb in a large Eastern city in the same three-bedroom house they bought and moved into with their three children in 1971. As with most suburbs built at the time there were no sidewalks, so the Rs needed a car to obtain groceries and other local services at a plaza nearly two kilometres away. Their doctor's office was located in a shopping centre still farther way, and getting to

their church and their many friends meant a ten-minute drive on the freeway. Until last year, Mr R had done all the driving. He enjoyed it, but his eyesight began to fail and he had to give up his driver's license last year. Mrs R, who had driven very little in her life, is now apprehensive about driving everywhere, especially at night or on the freeway. They would consider moving to an apartment closer to services, especially if they could stay in their familiar neighbourhood, but no apartments were ever built in their uniformly single-family home suburb.

2   Ms G, 75 years old and never married, lives in a seniors' complex in a city in the Prairies. She gave up her job as a clerk in a local bakery six years ago after working there more than 40 years. For most of that time, she lived in a suite in a walk-up apartment building that was only a kilometre from the job to which she walked every day in good weather; other days she took the bus, which stopped right at her corner. Along the way to work she could shop for groceries and visit the drug store. Many of her friends from work also lived nearby and her doctor's office was just beyond the bakery. About six years ago the arthritis in her legs intensified, making it difficult for her to stand all day at work, and to walk to and from work, and even to get on and off the bus. Not least, the stairs to her apartment became increasingly difficult to manage. The only apartment she could afford with her limited income was in a seniors' subsidized housing project across the city, far from friends, familiar stores, and her doctor.

3   Mr and Mrs M live in a town of 1,500 people in a rural area on the West Coast. They are both 70 years old and moved to the town a year ago when they found they could no longer run their nearby farm or cope with all the driving that was necessary to get to stores, see friends, or visit the doctor (which was happening more frequently for both of them). The town has two grocery stores (one of which has a pharmacy), a doctor, restaurant, post office, and curling rink. The small bungalow they bought is located so they can walk to the shops and post office. Now that they have more time, they have become involved in

activities at the seniors' centre and with other groups in town. However, there is still too much driving: the closest bank is in a much larger town nearly forty kilometres away and specialized health care services and a hospital are a further hour's drive into the city. No bus service is available.

In each of these stories it can be seen that commonplace situations encountered by seniors every day have spatial implications regardless of the type of communities in which they live. These include where they shop, where their doctor is located, where friends live, and how they get to these various destinations. What is also revealed is that when seniors conduct such activities, their functional capabilities mediate the route they take, the mode of travel they use, and the time they prefer for carrying out the activity.[4] Most seniors experience reductions in their sensory capabilities that place limits on their everyday lives. The question of which capabilities, in which way, and to what degree they are reduced with increasing age is an individual matter. Still, within this diverse population of older people, the sum of their unique needs add up to a distinct array of challenges to the community environments in which they live.

Focusing the Discussion

The thrust of this opening discussion is the need to view the aging of Canada's population from a geographical, or spatial, perspective. Doing this requires us to examine both the *macro* and *micro* geographies of the country's seniors. That is, on the one hand, we need to know where the elderly live in Canada and, on the other hand, we need to know the spatial patterns of seniors' activities within their neighbourhoods and communities. The answer to the first question will enable us to determine the context of seniors' neighbourhoods, while the answer to the second will enable us to determine how well these neighbourhood environments work to promote and sustain the independence that seniors want.

The approach taken here is to establish a base of information for the year 2001, the date of the most recent comprehensive census, and to expand on it, where possible, using the 2006 census. This will ready us to consider what the future holds, for, as a population ages, not only will current senior cohorts age but new cohorts will join their ranks. The long-forecasted surge in seniors' numbers due to the aging of Canada's "Baby Boom" generation, those born between 1946 and 1965, is less than half a decade away. There can be little doubt that this will have an impact on both national and local spatial patterns of aging. Even today's seniors need communities that fit better with their everyday lives, and these needs are bound to expand over the next two or three decades.

This book seeks to fulfill the following basic objectives:

1 to describe the spatial distribution of Canada's seniors' population as of 2001, and where possible in 2006, including the trends which led to this (chapters 2 and 3);
2 to determine the parameters of the use seniors make of community space in a variety of urban and rural situations in Canada and abroad (chapters 4 and 5);
3 to provide a forecast of the spatial distribution of the population of Canada's seniors for 2021 (and 2031 and beyond, where appropriate) as a result of the aging of the Baby Boom cohorts, including selected characteristics of that population (chapter 6);
4 to estimate the impact on Canada in general and on its communities in particular of the aging of the Baby Boom cohorts (chapter 7);
5 to develop a perspective for planning communities so that they may better accommodate seniors now and in the future (chapter 8); and
6 to develop planning and design guidelines that assist communities to develop enabling – Senior-Smart – environments (chapter 9).

Before pursuing these objectives, it is important to establish first, how to portray the elderly and second, what are the spatial parameters that affect their well-being. These tasks comprise the remainder of this chapter. As we proceed, it is important to keep in mind this basic question:

In what ways do seniors interact with their community environments?

PORTRAYING THE ELDERLY

Who are the elderly? This is not the simplistic question it may appear to be, for the elderly must be seen both as individuals and as a population group. We also need to remember that they comprise a range of ages and differ in a host of other variables such as gender, income, health, ethnicity, and living arrangements. As well, it is important to be clear about the perspectives one uses to view seniors' residence and activity patterns.

Age, the Aged, and Aging

Gerontologists say that any study of older people must be clear about three aspects: *age, the aged, and aging.*[5] *Age* refers to a dimension, in years, relating to a person's life experience and/or social situation. *Aged* refers to membership in a group, the elderly or senior citizens as we call them here. *Aging* refers to a process of human development over a period of time. (The latter is also used in demographic terms to refer to an increase in a population's average age and/or its proportion of the elderly. The latter usage is described more fully in a later section.) All three terms are necessary in portraying the elderly and each has connections with the others.

AGE

The most prominent age in gerontological circles in North America is 65.[6] This is the threshold used in most studies for defining older adults as a group; the traditional age of retirement from regular employment and of societal entitlements such as public pensions. It is also considered a marker for an increased risk of health problems, not that the great majority of those who turn 65 aren't active and healthy, but because the likelihood of decline in future years cannot be discounted. Thus, age 65 is a proxy for the beginning of a number of social and physical transitions within a person's life course that can stretch, potentially, several dozen years more. Within this stage, another prominent age for the study of the elderly is 80. At this age, the probability that major health problems will occur increases sharply.[7]

It has been common to use age as a proxy for increased risk of health problems and, hence, for a negative impact on seniors' activities. However, age is not always a strong predictor because individual seniors vary immensely in their health experience. A senior's health is a mix of positive and negative aspects, each of which may be affected as much by the person's gender, income, and ethnicity as by age alone. Besides the age diversity among older adults, recent changes in retirement patterns,[8] earlier access to public pensions,[9] and the abolition of mandatory retirement at age 65 by several provinces have led to inconsistencies with the old-age threshold of 65. As well, increases in life expectancy are challenging the expectation of frailty at age 80. It should also be noted that the ages 65 or 80 used to describe Canadian seniors might not reflect the reality of old age in some of our cultural groups. Aboriginal elders, for example, are counted by Statistics Canada starting at age 55. The age of 60 is used in other countries as the senior threshold. Thus age in numerical terms is less a predictor of experience and more an indicator of a context in which one can expect life experiences to be different from those of younger adults.

THE AGED

Persons 65 years and older are defined by most studies as the *aged*. Notwithstanding the cautions about age 65 expressed above, this convention is followed here in order to present the results of other accumulated studies. We call the aged *older adults, senior citizens,* or just *seniors,* and I use these terms interchangeably throughout this text. It might help to think of the aged as comprising men and women in the latter one-third of life. Some, at 65, have barely entered this period while others, at 95, have seen one-third of a century go by since becoming seniors. The 65-year-old today was born when World War II was underway while the 95-year-old was born just before World War I began. They are each part of what demographers call a different *age cohort*. Gerontologists usually array these cohorts in 10-year increments: those aged 65–74 are called the "old," the 75–84 cohort is called the "old-old," and those aged 85 years and older the "very old." The cohort aged 55–64 is sometimes called the "young-old."[10] The latter group, incidentally, contains the increasing numbers of early retirees and early Canada Pension Plan recipients. It is reasonable to surmise that each such cohort will have had different experiences earlier in life and now have different expectations of life as a senior.[11]

Not only do older adults carry with them a diversity of experiences into later life, these experiences have also been accumulated within a matrix of other dimensions, both personal and social.[12] The characteristics of the aged have been formed by the social forces, economic structures, and political institutions they have experienced. Moreover, each senior's response to these encounters has been conditioned by her/his gender, economic class, and ethnicity. Gerontologists call these factors the *social location* of a senior and such factors inevitably carry over into old age. They continue to affect the needs and responses of seniors both to their physical surroundings and to policies and programs that might seek to shape them. In short, the experience of seniors is multi-faceted.

AGING

When studying the elderly, we must consider two sides to the aging process. *Individual aging* refers to the biological, psychological, and social aspects of growing old.[13] *Population aging* refers to the process whereby a total population experiences increasing proportions of the aged, as has happened with the Canadian population over the past several decades. Each of these plays a role when exploring the geography of aging.

Individual aging is associated with the course of events and experience in a senior's life, or the *life course* as it is called. The life course of each person is unique but, at the same time, is impacted by social forces, the stratification of society, and the social location of the person. These lead, in turn, to some common transitions and life stages among the elderly, including reduced work, retirement, frailty, and death. Encompassing all is the stage of simply being a senior citizen and experiencing how one is regarded within society. These aspects of human aging, as complex and diverse as they are, underlie all our considerations of seniors' geography, from their general population distribution to their personal neighbourhood activity patterns.[14]

The most common measure of population aging is the proportion of the total population that is aged 65 and older. In Canada, for example, the census of 2001 showed the proportion of elderly was 12.6 percent. The census of a decade earlier, in 1991, showed it was 11.5 percent. Such a change signifies to demographers that the Canadian population is aging. The numbers of seniors also increased in the same decade by about 600,000, or nearly 19 percent. However, it is not the total numbers of seniors or their rate of growth that signifies population aging, just the change in their proportion of the total population. This is also the case when one is considering the degree of aging in a province, city, or town. When population aging occurs, the proportion of all those less than 65 years of age declines, and this is what happened in Canada in this illustrative period. Increased life expectancy for the aged at one end of the scale and declining birth rates at the other were two factors that contributed most to the increase in the proportion of seniors from 1991–2001 even as the total population grew. A population can also age in a stable population: the numbers of people aged less than 65 may decline, say, through out-migration, thereby reducing their proportion, as occurs frequently in small towns. Of course, the degree of aging can decline if the opposite tendency is present, as when young adults move into a resource community.

The study of population aging starts with the baseline proportion of all persons 65 and older but can go much beyond that. For example, one may want to compare the degree to which the number of older, more frail seniors (say 85 and older) varies from place to place, or in specified population groups like First Nations or recent immigrants. Further, it may be useful to know the gender proportions of the entire elderly population or any group within it, given the longer life expectancy for women. In addition, population aging is concerned with age groups below as well as above the threshold of 65. Gerontologists have a particular concern with the cohorts who precede those who are 65. The 55–64 age cohorts today will all be seniors within ten years and the oldest ones will already be near their mid-70s. The most noteworthy cohort being watched by gerontologists and demographers is that of the Baby Boom generation, born between 1946–65, as it approaches and begins to move past the age 65 threshold. Not only is this cohort abnormally large, it is also likely to bring new sets of values, attitudes, and capabilities to the seniors' realm.[15] These changes will be discussed in chapters 6 and 7.

Aging and Health

Remaining healthy is one cornerstone of independence for seniors, and the majority of them are in good health. By their own assessment, nearly 74 percent of those 65 and older reported in Statistics Canada's Canadian Community Health Survey (CCHS) for 2003, that their health was good, very good, or excellent.[16] Even among those aged 85 and older, 63 percent report good-to-excellent health. This does not mean that the elderly do not suffer health problems; rather it shows their confidence in managing their own affairs. Indeed, two-thirds of all seniors reported at least one chronic condition, according to the same survey. These conditions cover a range of problems, including arthritis and rheumatism, high blood pressure, back problems, heart disease, and vision and hearing problems. The prevalence of such problems becomes more evident the older the senior, and women seniors report more chronic conditions than men of the same age.

The health problems noted above can impose limitations on the spatial extent of one or more of a senior's everyday activities, such as walking to the store, climbing steps, reading signs, driving at night, etc. In the above-mentioned survey, of seniors aged 65–74 living at home, 12 percent reported limitations to their "activities of daily living" (often called ADL by gerontologists) such as meal preparation, shopping, everyday housework, personal care, and moving about the home. For those aged 85 and older, the proportion suffering ADL limitations increased to 59 percent. An earlier survey, the 1991 Health and Activity Limitation Survey (HALS) of Statistics Canada, confirms that physical impairments restrict an older person's activities by limiting his/her mobility, agility, hearing, seeing, and/or speaking.[17] To take a simple example, the four most common problems urban seniors encounter in using public transit are: (1) getting up and down the steps, (2) standing in the vehicle while it is moving, (3) walking to the transit stop, and (4) waiting at the stop.[18] While physical impairment among the elderly is widespread, for most it is generally not severe enough to require daily help. This is less so, of course, among the oldest; one-quarter of those 85 and older require support with at least one activity like shopping, using public transit, and getting to the doctor or the seniors' centre. These are called "instrumental activities of daily living" (IADL). It should be noted that the health of seniors is not associated only with age. Numerous observers have pointed out other factors that influence seniors' health such as economic status, gender, and living arrangements.[19]

Gender, Income, Culture, and Living Arrangements

Much of the foregoing discussion focuses on ways in which old age causes problems with regard to losses of functional capabilities. As important as this is for many (but not all) seniors, later life is also differentiated by social attributes. Gender, income, culture, and living arrangements are four such factors that separately and in combination can affect activity patterns. These are factors that affect one's *social location*, that is to say, where one "fits" in society. To understand their importance, appropriate questions might be: What's it like to be an elderly woman? What's it like to be an older person of colour? What's it like to live alone in old age? What's it like to be poor in old age? Or one might pose questions that combine two or more of these dimensions of social location such as: What's it like being a poor female living alone in old age? There are three general areas of a senior's life in which answers to such questions as these are manifest and relevant for our purposes: (1) personal health; (2) social contact and social support; and (3) housing or shelter.

1   The *personal health* limitations seniors experience due to illness and impairment have strong correlations with three of these factors: income, gender, and living arrangements. Seniors with high incomes are more likely to enjoy better health than those with low incomes; older women are more likely to have poorer health than older men, and seniors who live alone tend to have poorer health than those who live in family situations.[20] Older women, in particular, are often found to be disadvantaged in several ways regarding their health:[21] (1) their incomes are consistently

lower than those of elderly men (nearly 40 percent lower in 2001) which means that fewer resources are available to them to reduce the impact of health problems; (2) their greater longevity compared to elderly men (they comprised almost 70 percent of seniors aged 85 and older in 2001) makes them more prone to the impairments experienced by the very old. And (3) the likelihood of their living alone (more than twice as high in 2001 as for elderly men) leaves them to cope alone with the impact of illness and possible disability.[22] Each of these situations can have an effect on the kind and location of activities they can participate in.

2   *Social contact and social support* is important to the independence and wellbeing of seniors but it is not equally accessible to all seniors. Those who are poor may be limited to public transportation to shop or conduct social activities, while those who live alone often have to depend on others to be able to make such contacts. One Canadian study showed that older women restricted their community mobility to avoid travel at night or in bad weather, and to avoid unsafe situations and/or those where confrontation could occur.[23] Such limitations as these may be magnified for seniors belonging to a cultural or ethnic minority where the opportunities for contact with kin or likeminded individuals may be small to begin with. Further, differences in dress, language, manners, and rituals from other community members may reduce access to public activities and facilities and programs. In an analogous way, older Native people in Canada, who live mostly in isolated settlements and who are often poor, tend to have limited access to support other than that provided by family members.[24] Another factor to be considered is the informal support that seniors themselves provide to other family members (such as siblings) and to friends, many of whom often are also seniors; this is especially so in the case of older women. The ability and the cost of getting around when providing such support plays a crucial role in sustaining caregiving activities by seniors, as well as in their obtaining support.

3   *Housing security* means being able to remain in one's home, another cornerstone of a senior's independence.[25] Housing secu-

rity is dependent on a senior having the financial means to meet her/his housing costs. Seniors' incomes tend to be one-third less than those of younger adults,[26] and meeting housing costs may be especially difficult for older women, who tend to have even smaller average incomes than older men. Affordability of housing may also dictate where a senior can live, and the social support, public facilities, and transportation to which he/she has access. It is not difficult to imagine how such constraints on housing may be compounded for seniors from ethnic and cultural minorities who often seek to live near kin or in close proximity to their cultural peers. Thus, patterns of senior residence are the product of a variety of factors both personal and social.

In sum, the elderly are a diverse population group with varying experiences of aging. A senior's life also unfolds within a context that includes her/his own social location, the social institutions and social trends that structure the world she/he lives in now and has lived in formerly, and the exigencies of physical aging. In addition to these external factors, there is also the characteristic human tendency to adapt to the environment. Like everybody else, seniors try to sustain their independence and autonomy.

The Data Mosaic

In order to portray the broad geography of Canada's seniors' population, especially in its diversity, it is necessary to use a variety of sources. Initially, their residence patterns can be sketched from the Canada Census. Census data provide the most consistent and continuing picture of the elderly population both by age and gender composition and permit a view of past trends in the aging, especially those from 1981 to the end of the century. Yet some limitations exist in these data: for example, living arrangements are provided only for the total of the 65+ population, and not for other seniors' age groups. This is also the case for seniors' incomes. The situation with regard to ethnic and cultural composition is generalized for all those aged 65 and older except for Native people, among whom elders are often counted as starting at age 60 or even 55 and few data are available. Several Statistics Canada surveys, notably the Canadian Community Health Survey referred to above and the

General Social Survey, fill in considerable background on health conditions and impairments of seniors by age and gender. However, these surveys tend to follow different time frames than the census and frequently do not provide the same detailed geographical coverage for the country.

To construct a more intimate picture of seniors' activity patterns requires that one draw upon a variety of studies. Some of these, from Canada and abroad, have a countrywide perspective, while others are focused on one or several communities. Limitations one can expect to find include differences in age cohorts, in scope of subject matter, and in the relatively small numbers of seniors sampled. Further, most of these studies were conducted as many as thirty years ago and may appear to be dated (including several done by the present author). At that time there was a surge of interest in the interaction of seniors with their housing and community environments but, unfortunately, there has been little interest since.[27] Nonetheless, these studies are rich micro-level portraits of the geography of seniors' everyday life. Moreover, recent interest in aging and environment studies, as they are called, indicates that many parameters have changed little.[28]

Whether using either the macro- or micro-level spatial perspectives, the data do not permit a uniform tableau. The best renderings of Canada's elderly available to us are, of necessity, *mosaics*. They may seem at times like mosaics in which some pieces don't fit exactly and others are missing. Nonetheless, these images, whether statistical, verbal, or visual, can still provide a substantial and reliable picture of the country's aging population.

SENIORS' SPATIAL PARAMETERS

The overall geography of aging we are striving for comprises macro and micro perspectives. Each has its own distinctive, though related, parameters, as discussed below.

Parameters of Residence Patterns

The common standard for population aging is to compare the proportion of persons aged 65 and older in the total population of the same locality at two successive points in time. In this way, changes can readily be compared between provinces or other spatial units such as cities, towns, and countries. Changes in the share of any elderly cohort can also be determined in this way. By the same token, the share of older adults in the population (or any of its cohorts) at a single point in time is often a useful indicator. For example, according to the United Nations, a country is said to have begun to age when more than seven percent of its population is 65 or older.[29] (Canada's seniors in 2001, as mentioned already, accounted for over 12 percent of the total population.) This single measure allows us to make ready comparisons about aspects of aging between different provinces, cities, rural areas, central cities, suburbs, and so on (see chapters 2 and 3). We call this the "concentration" of the elderly in the population of the particular place.

The *concentration* of the entire elderly cohort, of any of its component cohorts, or of changes in such concentrations over time is the basic parameter used in examining residential patterns of seniors. As well as the age of the elderly, other aspects of the composition of the aged population may be of interest such as gender, ethnicity, marital status, living arrangements, education, and income. These variables are usually measured as the degree of concentration within the total population aged 65 and older. As useful as measures of concentration are however, they say nothing about the *numbers* of elderly persons living in the place under study, either in absolute or relative terms. In other words, one may need to know exactly *how many seniors* may need housing or transportation in a community or region and whether those numbers are increasing to see if available resources are sufficient. Thus, actual numbers as well as percentage shares should comprise the minimum picture of elderly residence patterns.

Another variable that can lead to changes in residence patterns is migration of elderly people into and within the country. Although seniors have less propensity to move than younger adults, their movements can still have significant effects on the degree of aging of a community.[30] On the one hand, there is international migration, which can directly diversify the cultural and language composition of the elderly population of a place. Canada has an aggressive immigration policy and while the number of international immigrants to Canada aged 65 and older is relatively small, the number in the 45–64 range and in younger cohorts is considerably larger. The results of this migration are already noticeable in Canada's largest cities with the emergence of ethnic neighbourhoods.[31] On the other hand, there is migration of seniors within Canada, which can also affect the numbers and composition of seniors in a locality. There are three such flows: seniors moving from one province to another, seniors moving from one community to another within the same province, and seniors moving from one dwelling to another within the same community.

Then, of course, there are the majority of seniors who don't move from their dwellings (within a census period), which we term *aging in place*. Whether people move or not, their presence has ramifications, especially at the community level, for residence and activity patterns. Lastly, it should be kept in mind that migration of seniors (as with all groups) is destination-specific. Moves are made in order to be nearer to family members, to be close to natural amenities, to obtain more appropriate housing, or for financial and health reasons.[32] Such moves affect both the places people leave and those they move to. In the latter case, the accumulation of seniors in particular centres or regions may result in above-average concentrations, as with parts of coastal British Columbia, the Niagara Peninsula, and Prince Edward Island. (See chapter 2 for a detailed discussion of migration and aging in place.)

Parameters of Daily Activity Patterns

Activity patterns are the result of what people do, where they do it, and when they do it. The spatial dimensions of a person's daily living are often called the person's *life space*. As people become older, the probability increases that their activities will become increasingly constrained for health and other reasons.[33] An extensive literature developed around this subject three decades ago, in the 1970s and 1980s, including valuable theoretical formulations aimed at determining the impact of mobility limitations on seniors' well-being and independence.[34] It spawned a field known as environmental gerontology, which, lamentably, went into decline until recent years.[35] Nonetheless, many of the concepts and insights gained at that time are still valid today in understanding the physical parameters of seniors' activities and the factors that shape them. These concepts will be drawn upon here and in later chapters.

THE ECOLOGICAL THEORY OF AGING

One of the most important and durable theoretical concepts in environmental gerontology is the Ecological Theory of Aging, which was developed in 1973.[36] Lucille Nahemow, one of its originators, explained that it "explores the interplay between [older] individuals and their environments."[37] Two terms in her statement deserve further elaboration: *environments* and *interplay*. Lawton and Nahemow identified five environments that a senior encounters in her/his activities: the personal environment, the group environment, the suprapersonal environment, the social environment and, of most concern to us, the physical environment. A physical environment includes both the natural and the built environment. "Interplay" refers to the process of *adaptation* that occurs as a senior responds to various stimuli in the physical or other environments. Consider, briefly, two examples: (1) seeing icy sidewalks leading to the bus stop and deciding whether to walk or stay at home; (2) facing steep stairs to a public building and deciding whether to climb them alone or ask for assistance. Each of these mundane situations demands that the senior decide whether he/she can cope with this environment or not.

These examples also contain the essential elements the theory addresses. First, each environment makes a behavioural demand on the senior that is called *environmental press*. Some environments make great demands (i.e. have strong environmental press) and others do not (i.e. the environmental press is weak). Second, the senior's behaviour depends upon his/her *competence*, that is, upon his/her physical health, sensory and motor capabilities, cognitive skills, and personality. And, third, the outcome represents the *adaptation level* between the environmental press of the situation and a person's ability to respond. Adaptation to an environment's press, moreover, occurs across a range of individual circumstances that may change with the passage of time. For the individual senior this might mean the difference between the challenge posed by the environment in the initial contact and the greater comfort or familiarity with it after repeated contact. Differences in adaptation might also include the response that a senior might make over time because of her/his decreased (or increased) competence (a representation of this model is provided in Figure 4.1).

HOME AS THE FULCRUM FOR SENIORS' INDEPENDENCE

Canada's National Advisory Council on Aging defines seniors' independence as follows: "To be able to carry out life's activities within a normal community setting, to be able to make choices about these activities and to have a degree of control over one's life."[38] What are the factors that make independence possible for seniors? A task force set up by the British Columbia government in 1989 to study this question consulted seniors across the province and found that three *generic* factors encompass seniors' independence (SI) in the eyes of seniors:

1   Security of health;
2   Security of income; and
3   Security of housing.[39]

Such a triad of concerns is not surprising and other studies, including a recent Canadian project, have confirmed them.[40] However, what has not been sufficiently recognized by the various studies is the interdependence of this set of factors. Any change in a senior's level of security in one factor will affect the other two as well. For example, declining health may require one to move to another dwelling with possible consequences for one's financial resources. (These interconnections are shown by double-headed arrows in Figure 1.1.)

Nor have previous studies clearly emphasized the crucial role that housing security plays to SI. Most gerontologists, along with seniors and their families, agree that the well-being of an elderly person is best sustained when she/he can remain living in her/his own home or apartment. Indeed, most such studies start with the notion that seniors who live in their own homes are independent and thereby make a flawed assumption. Just having somewhere to live is not

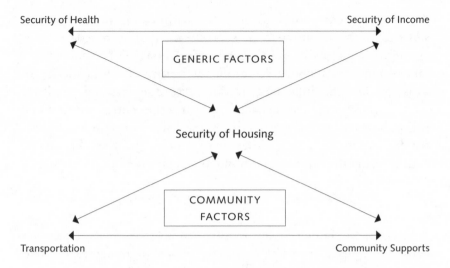

Figure 1.1   Factors Involved in Assuring Seniors' Independence

sufficient. "Older community-dwelling adults," as seniors who continue to live in their own homes are often called, often depend upon support from their communities to maintain their independence. Community support consists of both informal support (that obtained from family, friends, and neighbours) and formal support (such as public home support, meals-on wheels, and respite care). Moreover, transportation is also required for housing security. Transportation refers to everything that would make it possible for seniors to get around, and includes roads and sidewalks, public transit, access to automobiles (their own or others), buses for the disabled, etc. Its importance is caught in the title of a publication for seniors: *Transportation – The Key to It All.*[41] An *enabling environment* that allows seniors to enjoy independent living comprises all three factors: housing, community support, and transportation.

Seniors' independence, thus, consists of both sets of factors described above and shown in Figure 1.1. On the one hand, there are the three *generic* factors: health, income, and housing security. They are necessary for SI – without them independence is severely jeopardized – but they are not sufficient. On the other hand, for seniors "to be able to carry out life's activities within a normal community setting," as the definition for SI sets out, we need to embed the three *community* factors in the SI perspective: housing, transportation, and community support. A significant feature of this rendering of SI is how housing links the generic aspects of seniors' independence with its community aspects. This indicates the central position and role of housing, or more properly "home," in securing seniors' independence. One long-time observer of seniors and their life spaces calls housing the *fulcrum* of an independent senior's life.[42]

ACTIVITY SPACES AND LIFE SPACES

Activity Spaces. Home is the starting point for each older person's activities; indeed, the same is true for people of all ages. Consider, for example, the youngster walking to school, or the teenager taking the bus to the mall, or the adult commuting to work, or the early-retiree traveling across the country to visit kin, or the 80-year-old walking to a local store. In these instances of human activities we can see both how they are bound in with home and also how their geographical extent changes with the age of the person. The spatial extent of a young child's activities is usually limited to a small area outside the home; it gradually increases with the growing competence of adolescence and adulthood. The reverse tendency begins in late-adulthood as the spatial extent of activity declines for most older people.

Figure 1.2 shows that most people can expect to have three phases in their activity levels. First, there is a period from birth to early adulthood in which the number of activities and their activity space increases. More sophisticated activities are added as a child grows up, involving travel over greater distances until, by early adulthood, national and even international travel have expanded activity spaces almost to their maximum. Second, there is the period of adulthood when one's range of activities covers all spatial realms; expanded work and leisure travel using a wide array of transportation options as well as continuing local travel mean a maximum extension of a person's activity space. And third, in the period beginning in late adulthood and early old age one finds the number and spatial extent of activities decreasing until death. Declines in physical, cogni-

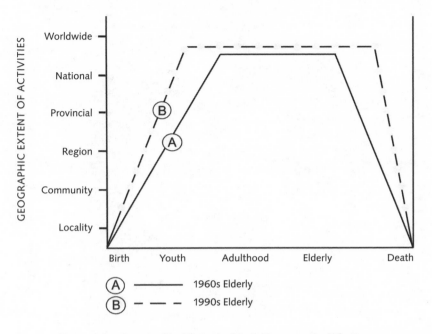

Figure 1.2   Geographical Extent of Activities over the Life Course

tive, and/or emotional levels of competence in later years reduce a senior's ability to cope with high levels of environmental press often found in sophisticated environments. Home, its immediate surroundings, and its neighbourhood become especially meaningful to most people in this third period.[43]

This chart also depicts people's activity levels and spaces for two periods, the 1960s and the 1990s. Curve A, depicting the situation for people say in the 1960s, shows a long period from childhood to the full spatial extent of possible activities, a short period available to partake of these activities, and a long period over which decline occurs. Curve B depicts a more contemporary situation, say in the 1990s, where young people reach the full spatial extent of activities more quickly, adults (including many seniors) enjoy a much longer period to partake of most activities, and old people, when decline comes, experience it over a much shorter period than for earlier cohorts of seniors. This more recent tendency is sometimes referred

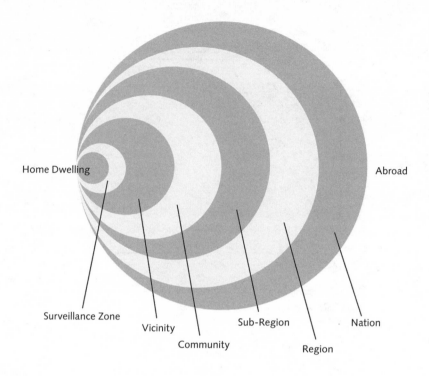

Home Dwelling

Abroad

Surveillance Zone

Vicinity

Community

Sub-Region

Region

Nation

Figure 1.3   Life Spaces of Seniors

to as "squaring" the lifespan curve. For the elderly, this longer period of active well-being is due to a number of factors: better health and greater longevity, higher incomes, improved means of travel, and a social climate favouring active lifestyles.

Life Spaces. Each activity a senior undertakes unfolds within its own geographic space, which we call a *life space*. There exist for the elderly person a series of life spaces each focused on the person's home and each progressively larger. Geographer Graham Rowles has posited a set of seven life spaces for the elderly, which he calls "support" spaces.[44] To these we have added an eighth zone and some clarification of his terms. They are illustrated in Figure 1.3.

1   Home [Dwelling]

2 Surveillance Zone [A visual field from home or yard]
3 Vicinity [Neighbourhood]
4 Community [City, Town, Rural Area]
5 Sub-Region [Metropolitan Area or other locale]
6 Region [All or part of a Province]
7 Nation
8 Abroad

The life space zones shown in Figure 1.3 form a nested hierarchy of spaces. That is, each successive zone encompasses the activities undertaken in the previous zone(s) and adds activities that can only be accomplished in this larger zone. The activities undertaken in a particular life space depend upon the mobility required for a senior to access the activity. For example, a senior without an automobile who wishes to shop at a department store may have to depend upon friends and relatives for a ride or use public transit; in either case, mobility will be constrained for this person. How much of a constraint will depend upon the personal preferences and predispositions of the individual. Thus, the life space zones express the spatial reality of an array of activities – where specific activities are possible – not whether these opportunities can or will be taken up by this or that senior (see also chapter 5).

CHALLENGES IN COMMUNITY ENVIRONMENTS

Physical environments in communities are pivotal in achieving the goal of seniors' independence. In many ways, they determine the extent to which the individual can enjoy autonomy in his/her daily life and activities. The form, content, and functioning of a community environment can either enable the older person to meet her/his daily needs or exert such a strong environmental press that many of these needs go unfulfilled and the senior is, effectively, *dis*-abled. Unfortunately, as the National Advisory Council on Aging has been saying since 1989, most communities tend not to have "enabling" environments.[45] Many seniors encounter obstacles in the areas of housing, transportation, and community services, as well as negative attitudes about the elderly that reinforce these physical barriers.

They also encounter difficulty accessing information. For the sake of today's four million seniors, and the eight million we anticipate by 2031, we need to address these challenges now. [46]

HOUSING CHALLENGES

Although housing and its accompanying street system comprise the largest portion of every community's land use, this does not mean residential areas are always appropriate for the needs of an elderly population, especially one that is growing in numbers and diversity and, possibly, becoming more frail. Crucial challenges in making adequate and appropriate housing available for seniors revolve around three basic factors:

1   DESIGN: A senior's dwelling should be free of barriers that limit normal activities; it should be safe and secure; it should be adaptable to changing needs and circumstances; it should permit easy access to the out-of-doors and neighbourhood.

2   CHOICE: Seniors are a diverse population with a wide array of needs and preferences and require a range of housing choices to reflect this; options should be available for seniors to choose between *types* of housing, kinds of *tenure*, various *living arrangements*, the *location* of the dwelling, and, not least, its *affordability*.

3   LOCATION: A senior's home is part of a community and functions effectively when its location allows easy and ready access to community facilities, transportation services, and the social, cultural and commercial life of the rest of the community.

TRANSPORTATION CHALLENGES

Transportation means access to health, recreation, and social services. It ensures that older people can continue to participate in and contribute to the community as well as enhance their own quality of life. Transportation is, thus, a vital factor in linking seniors to community life and activities and to perform this role effectively invokes challenges in two of its aspects:

1   AVAILABILITY: Transportation must be present in a variety of forms to meet the diverse needs of seniors: roads need to be built and maintained for those who drive and public transit needs to be available for those who don't drive, those who choose not to drive, and those who can't afford to drive; special transit must be offered for those with impairments, including both commercial and volunteer options. Pedestrians need proper sidewalks with adequate lighting, signage, and signals.

2   ACCESSIBILITY: Once transportation is available, seniors must be able to access it easily and safely. Transit stops should be situated with regard for seniors' walking capabilities, surfaces should be free of impediments that might cause falls; ramps and other assistive devices for the wheelchair-bound or otherwise impaired seniors should also be available.

SUPPORT SERVICES CHALLENGES

Support in the community is needed to ensure an enabling environment for seniors. That provided by family and friends – who provide the bulk of support to seniors – is referred to as *informal,* and that provided by public and non-profit agencies and groups as *formal support.* The challenges in this area revolve around:

1   ARRAY OF SUPPORT: Support should provide for a continuum of care to meet the differing levels of needs of seniors in the community and for the changing care needs of individual seniors (see chapter 7).

2   ACCESS: Support should be provided within easy reach of seniors (and their families) and its existence should be readily apparent to all providers. Where distance to support is a problem, transportation should be available.

3   COORDINATION: To make a continuum of support effective requires explicit communication among providers. This should include acknowledgement and reinforcement of the majority support provided by family members.

CHALLENGES OF SENIORS' DIVERSITY

The seniors' population is almost as diverse as the population of the nation as a whole. Its primary variants are age, gender, health, income, ethnicity, culture, and place of residence. Seniors' lives unfold with regard to one, and often several, of these variables as they individually seek independence and autonomy. Once we acknowledge this diversity, we must face the challenges it presents. Public programs for the aged need to be flexible and avoid stereotypes of seniors and their needs.

PERSPECTIVE AND RESOURCES OF THE BOOK

This book is divided into four parts describing, first, where Canadian seniors live, second, where their activities take place, third, the implications of Baby Boom aging for communities, and fourth, the preparations communities will need to make in order to create enabling environments for seniors.

PART ONE: WHERE CANADA'S SENIORS LIVE

The remaining chapters of Part One explore the residential geography of Canada's seniors now and in the recent past. A picture is derived in chapter 2, mainly from census population data, of the numbers of elderly and their concentrations in the populations of the nation and the provinces/territories for 2001 and 2006, as well as the changes that have occurred since 1981. Besides their numbers, changes in age structure, gender, cultural makeup, and living arrangements are examined. Chapter 3 continues this exploration at the level of the communities in which seniors live whether urban, rural, central city, suburban, or First Nations'. The role of migration is reviewed, and how it determines numbers, concentration, and composition of seniors within communities. In both of these chapters, implications for national and provincial policy toward the senior population are drawn.

PART TWO: HOW SENIORS USE COMMUNITY SPACE

When considering the activity patterns of seniors, we must not overlook the substantial literature dealing with the nexus of *aging* and *environment*, person-milieu, or environmental gerontology, as it is variously called. Rich in its implications for a geography of aging, especially seniors' everyday geography, this literature is reviewed in chapter 4. Parameters of seniors' everyday geography are developed and applied in chapter 5. Empirical examples are provided of how seniors' lives unfold from the home, to the neighbourhood, community, and wider region beyond. In turn, consideration is given to how this may be affected by the nature and location of the community and the characteristics of the elderly user. The experience gained from empirical studies helps to identify the barriers and limitations to seniors' accessibility that exist within communities.

PART THREE: FUTURE SENIORS AND THEIR COMMUNITIES

Less than half a decade away, in 2011, the seniors' population in Canada will begin a dramatic shift that will see numbers of the elderly double over the following twenty years due to the spike in the number of births between 1946 and 1965 – the Baby Boom. Chapter 6 follows the projected trends to 2031 and beyond. It examines several important strands, including the fast growing sectors of Aboriginal seniors and visible minority seniors, and notes several significant refinements that will occur in the overall geography of aging in Canada. The picture of seniors' residence patterns through to 2031 is given in chapter 7 for the country as a whole, as well as for each of the provinces and territories. The impact of the aging Baby Boom generation at the community level is also examined in terms of activity patterns, housing, and community support needs with examples of how communities can respond.

PART FOUR: PREPARING COMMUNITIES
FOR THE SENIORS' SURGE

The final part of the book addresses the question: How should communities prepare themselves for the coming surge in seniors? The answer provided in the concluding two chapters is for them to plan and develop enabling environments that are Senior-Smart. Chapter 8 reiterates the parameters of seniors' interactions with their environments and points out how environmental press may be modified within a community planning perspective that respects seniors' needs. Chapter 9 provides a planning framework for the design of barrier-free, enabling environments for seniors, including guidelines to assist communities in becoming Senior-Smart.

LEARNING RESOURCES

In addition to the main text, supplementary resources are provided to expand the scope of learning about the elderly and their environments.

Guiding Questions. Two leading questions are posed in each chapter. The first, at the outset of the chapter, emphasizes the thrust of the chapter, while the second reflects on the preceding discussion and points toward the material to come in succeeding chapters.

Seniors' Realities. Canadian seniors from various parts of the country and different community environments have provided reflections on their lives and daily activities. These vignettes, which are distributed throughout the book, give a better sense of the reality of the world in which older people live than can be achieved though numbers and data alone.

Internet Resources. The Internet is rich in resources that can be used for further study of seniors and their environments. A consolidated list is provided in the appendix, "Internet Resources on Aging and Community Environments." Web addresses are current as of the year of publication.

Senior-Smart Community Planning Tools. Chapter 9 presents several tools that can be used for appraising existing community environments and for planning and designing Senior-Smart Communities.

Lastly, this question should be frequently considered in the following chapters:

> *What characteristics of seniors do you expect to be most cogent when examining where seniors live in Canada?*

The Art of Aging

R. ALEX SIM

I am sitting at my desk a few weeks before my ninety-second birthday. My perspective on aging has been gained through a long process, for I became a senior officially 27 years ago on the day of my sixty-fifth birthday. People get old, at least those who survive do, and there is an enormous literature on aging. Perusing that material informs us of the various definitions of old age and the many ways of treating old people.

All of this entitles me to comment on aging as a personal experience and to see the process of coping with old age as an art. For instance, on May 20, 1976 I was informed that I was old, but lest that word would give offence in a culture that valued youth and beauty I became a "senior". Since I did not feel old and apparently did not look old, I was given a card to prove my old age. I soon found, after receiving my card, that I had to display it in order to claim senior's discounts. It was only when that demand was no longer made that I realized that I looked old.

In the last year or two I have become aware of a steady deterioration of my physical condition. I still wish to walk every day but the risk of falling is ever-present. I never go out without my cane. I try to stretch it to a half-hour, after which I need a short nap. I shrink from making contact for my profound deafness renders contact uninviting. There are countless explanations for my longevity, some of which I can recall. I often give the reason as a wise choice of grandparents, most of whom lived into their 80s. But it goes without saying my survival to this grand old age could not have been reached without the constant vigilance and care of my wife Barbara regarding my affairs, the telephone, driving the car, banking, and my timetable and appointments. Further, she is dedicated to exacting strict nutritional values with meals that are at the same time delicious. All of this and more than I can enumerate has enabled me to maintain a vivid sense of being alive and enjoying involvement in the world.

Getting old has been a long trip but not an unpleasant one. Looking back, I perceive a creative experience which justifies my ambitious claim that survival is an art. Yet I do claim this at the same time as acknowledging the contribution of wife, ancestors, and the medical teams I have relied on, in fact all the people I have depended upon over the years.

R. ALEX SIM, who died in 2005 at the age of 93, maintained a lifelong commitment to rural Canada. Trained in rural sociology and adult education at the University of Toronto and Columbia, this gentle advocate for the rural community reminds us of the important values found there through his book *Land and Community* (1988), his initiatives for a Rural Canada Bibliography, and the Rural Ministry Fund at Queen's University. He lived with his wife, Barbara, in Guelph, Ontario.

Chapter Two

Where Seniors Live in Canada

The starting point for our geographical exploration of Canada's seniors is the entire country. Because the national milieu comprises the seniors' population in all its diversity, it is the best place to ask the question: who are the seniors who live in Canada? Next we can ask: has Canada's seniors' population been changing and if so, how? And then: where do seniors live within Canada and has this been changing as well? Throughout this chapter, a further question to consider is:

> *Which characteristics of seniors would you expect to differ when comparing the aging population for the whole country to that of individual provinces?*

CANADA'S SENIORS IN 2001: A PROFILE

At the millennium, Canada's seniors numbered nearly 3.9 million and constituted almost 13% of the country's population. By 2006, seniors numbered more than 4.3 million. Knowing these facts and many more from the decennial census undertaken in 2001, we can develop a broad statistical profile of the country's seniors, as in Table 2.1. However, the nature of Canada's current seniors' population is best grasped through the findings of the 2001 Census, presented next. The more recent quinquennial census of 2006, though a less detailed rendering of the country's population, allows several characteristics of seniors to be up-dated. These are added to the table that follows.

HIGHLIGHTS OF CANADA'S SENIORS, 2001

· Of the three broad age groups that comprise Canada's seniors, over half are aged 65–74 (the old), one-third are aged 75–84 (the old-old), and one-tenth are aged 85 and older (the very old).

· Women are in the majority among Canada's seniors at 57 percent; among the very old, women constitute 70 percent. In both instances this is due to their greater longevity compared to men.

· Canada's seniors are culturally diverse: 27 percent have immigrated from abroad and seven percent are visible minorities.

· Of persons of Aboriginal ancestry, four percent are aged 65 and older.

· 93 percent of Canada's seniors live in their own homes: just over 70 percent live in a family setting, mostly with a spouse or partner, while nearly 30 percent live alone; of those living alone three-quarters are women. Of the seven percent who live in institutions, most are aged 85 and older.

· The majority of Canada's seniors, 71 percent, are home-owners; the remainder rent their dwellings.

· The predominant level of educational attainment among Canada's seniors is high school graduation or less while just over seven percent have a university degree.

· Average individual income levels among Canada's seniors are modest (and gender-biased): in 2000 they were $30,775 for men and $19,461 for women

OVERVIEW AND IMPLICATIONS

Canada's national aggregate of seniors, as portrayed in these data, are still relatively young, have modest incomes and education levels, live in their own homes, and, as we saw in the last chapter, are generally healthy.[1] Altogether, this suggests that most of today's seniors, probably 70 percent, possess sufficient functional capability to conduct their daily activities without much assistance for the next several years. Concomitantly, close to 30 percent of today's seniors (not including those needing institutional care) require

Table 2.1   Characteristics of Canada's Seniors' Population,
2001 and 2006 (partial)

	2001	2006
TOTAL SENIORS' POPULATION (65+)	3,888,550	4,335,255
% Canada Total Population	12.96%	13.71%
Total Aged 65–74	2,142,835	2,288,360
% 65+ Population	55.10%	52.78%
Total Aged 75–84	1,329.810	1,526,280
% 65+ Population	34.20%	35.20%
Total Aged 85+	415,905	520,605
% 65+ Population	10.70%	12.02%
GENDER COMPOSITION OF 65+ POPULATION		
Total Female	2,225,900	2,448,155
% 65+ Population	57.24%	56.47%
Total Male	1,274,160	1,887,100
% 65+ Population	42.76%	43.53%
ETHNOCULTURAL COMPOSITION OF 65+ POPULATION		*
Total Aboriginal 65+ Population	39,680	
% Aboriginal Population	4.06%	
% 65+ Population	1.09%	
Total Visible Minority 65+ Population	266,340	
% 65+ Population	6.85%	
LIVING ARRANGEMENTS OF 65+ POPULATION		*
Total in Family Households	2.472, 890	
% 65+ Population	71.14%	
Total Living Alone	1,040,020	
% 65+ Population	28.86%	
% Female of 65+ Living Alone	74.34%	
HOUSING TENURE OF 65+ POPULATION		*
% Owners	71.17%	
% Renters	28.83%	
EDUCATIONAL ATTAINMENT OF 65+ POPULATION		*
% Less than High School	57.29%	
% High School	11.15%	
INCOME LEVELS OF 65+ POPULATION		*
Avg. 2000 Individual Income for Males 65+	$30,775	
Avg. 2000 Individual Income for Females 65+	$19,461	

* Not available at time of compilation.   *Source: Census of Canada, 2001, 2006.*

varying degrees of support in their daily activities. The latter, more vulnerable group, tend to be 80 years of age or older.

Further, within these broad groupings of seniors there are a number of characteristics, notably age, gender, income, housing tenure, and ethnicity, that can have significant implications for senior independence and thus, also for public policy. For example, income levels among seniors vary such that, in 2003, 35% needed to top off their basic public pensions with national and provincial supplements.[2] Income disparities, in turn, may affect seniors' choices of housing, transportation, and so forth. When it comes to housing, nearly one-third of seniors are renters and therefore do not have the security of home ownership, and 44 percent spend more than 30 percent of their income on shelter.[3] Moreover, visible minority seniors are more likely to experience crowding in their housing, as well as above-average housing costs compared to Canadian-born and non-visible minority seniors.[4]

Woven throughout these situations and others regarding seniors' well-being are two over-arching characteristics: age and gender. The older the senior, the more likely he/she is to live alone, pay proportionately more for housing, not drive, be poor, and be frail. And the negative attributes are magnified for women, especially the oldest. Thus, of the approximately one-third of older Canadian seniors who require support, being female and/or having a low income are significant markers of need.

This profile is a picture of the current seniors' population, but it is also wise to remember that seniors are continually aging. Current seniors in all age groups will continue to get older, which means that more of them will be restricted in their daily activities and in their life spaces. And, of course, their ranks will be augmented by others whose advancing age has brought them to senior status. To illustrate these points further, we need to examine past trends.

GROWTH AND CHANGE AMONG CANADIAN SENIORS, 1981–2001 AND 2006

Most of those aged 85 and older in 2001 had barely become seniors 20 years earlier, in 1981, and those aged 65–74 were still ten years from becoming seniors at that time. Looking at population aging

Table 2.2   Growth and Change of Canadian Seniors, 1981–2001 and 2006

	1981	1991	2001	2006
NUMBERS AND GROWTH:				
Total Elderly (65+)	2,360,975	3,169,970	3,888,550	4,335,255
% Total Population	9.70%	13.61%	12.96%	13.71%
Increase in 65+ over previous census	616,565	809,995	718,580	446,705
% Increase	35.36%	34.26%	22.67%	8.71%
COMPOSITION:				
Total 65–74	1,477,745	1,895,070	2,142,835	2,288,360
% 65+	62.42%	59.78%	55.10%	52.78%
Total 75–84	689,445	991,565	1,329,180	1,526,280
% 65+	29.20%	31.28%	34.20%	35.20%
Total 85+	197,785	283,335	415,905	520,605
%65+	8.38%	8.94%	10.70%	12.02%

Source: Census of Canada 1981, 1991, 2001, 2006.

this way helps us to remember that it is about *people* growing older. With that in mind, the conventional method for gauging population aging (the percent of the population aged 65 and older) provides a standard that allows different areas (nation, province, region, etc.) to be consistently measured and, if needed, to be compared with other areas. Table 2.2 and Figure 2.1 show the evolution of the Canadian seniors' population since 1981.

Trends in Population Aging

1981–2001. In formal demographic terms, the data in this table show that Canada's population has been aging: the proportion of the seniors in the total population grew from just under 10 percent in 1981 to almost 13 percent in 2001. As others have pointed out, [5] this is due to a confluence of two trends in the population: significant declines in birth rates and death rates that have led, on the one hand, to larger numbers of people living past age 64 and,

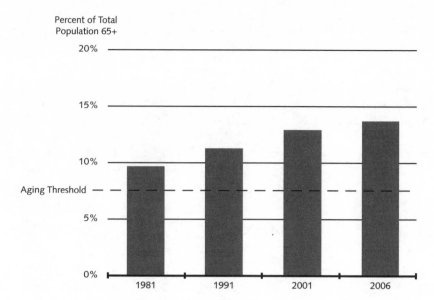

Figure 2.1   Population Aging in Canada, 1981–2006 (Source: Canada Census)

on the other, to fewer children being born to those younger than 65. The decline in death rates has been occurring for about a century whereas birth rates, while tending downwards over this same period, have fluctuated.

The surge in the seniors' population seen in these data began in the 1950s with the aging of the children of those who immigrated to Canada before and after World War I (see also Table 2.6). That was a period of high birthrates and large families, with the prospect for greater longevity. It can also be seen that, although their numbers continued to grow, the *rate of increase* in the number of seniors declined significantly after 1991. The latter is a reflection of lower fertility rates from 1931–45, during the Great Depression and World War II. However, despite this slowdown, population aging continued to increase.

2001–6. The trends of the past continued into the present century. Numbers of seniors and their concentration in the total population both increased from 2001–6. The dampened growth rate of the number of older Canadians continued to 2006, and can be expected to continue until 2011. At that time it will begin to shift upwards, slightly at first and then dramatically, due to the substantial increases in birth rates that occurred during the Baby Boom, from 1946–65.[6] Another result of these demographic dynamics is the changing age composition of the seniors' population. As the population has aged, the proportion of those aged 65–74, the "young old," has progressively declined while the proportions of older age groups have increased, as we shall see in the next section.

The Evolving Composition of Canada's Seniors

Not only has the general Canadian population been growing older in the past several decades, the seniors' population itself has also been growing older. As we see from Table 2.2, the old-old and the very old, those 75–84 and 85+, have been increasing both in number and in their share of all seniors, especially since 1991. Indeed, these two older cohorts have been growing faster than the overall elderly population, largely due to increases in life expectancy. The net result is that, compared to two decades ago, there are a greater number of seniors who are significantly more vulnerable to activity limitations due to health problems and who are also affected more substantially by changes in living arrangements and lower incomes. The 85-and-older age group, for example, more than doubled in size in the 1981–2006 period, adding more than 320,000 to their numbers. Probing these data further reveals that while the gender composition of the overall seniors' population remained fairly constant over the period (57% female, 43% male), the female/male ratio shifted significantly among older cohorts (nearly 70 percent of seniors aged 85+ are women).[7] Extrapolating these tendencies indicates a future seniors' population in which half are over 75 years of age, two-thirds are women and, of the latter, three-quarters live alone on lower-than-average incomes.

INCREASING ETHNIC DIVERSITY

Since 1971, the flow of immigrants into Canada has been changing both in size and composition. First, from 1971 through 2001, the number of immigrants nearly doubled from about 1 million per decade to 1.8 million in the 1990s.[8] The second major change is in the "face" of the immigrant population. Prior to 1971, the majority of immigrants (75%) were from Europe and the U.S. But in the 1991–2001 period, only one-fifth came from Europe and the U.S. while two-thirds came from Asia, Africa, South America, and the Caribbean. Currently close to 70 percent of Canada's immigrants comprise "visible minorities." Statistics Canada defines visible minorities as "persons, other than Aboriginal peoples, who are non-Caucasian in race or non-white in colour."[9] Because these newest immigrants have also been aging since their arrival as much as 30 years ago, 7.2 percent of seniors, in 2001, were from visible minorities. (A very small proportion comprise immigrants who came to Canada before 1931 from countries such as China, Japan, and India, and from the Caribbean and Latin America, or their progeny.)

Moreover, elders from visible minorities are increasing in number at a very fast rate. Projections by Statistics Canada indicate that this group could double in size in the first decade of this century, and account for nearly 10 percent of all seniors by 2011.[10] They constitute a bulge within Canada's aging population that is growing even faster than the Baby Boomers. Their presence will be most noticed within metropolitan areas, particularly the three largest: Toronto, Vancouver, and Montreal.[11] The implications for these seniors' use of community environments is discussed extensively in chapter 6.

The International Context of Aging

Canada is not alone among developed countries in having a high level of population aging. Indeed, many other countries have even higher levels. Table 2.3 presents population-aging levels for a selection of countries for the year 2004, as gathered by the United Nations.[12] In this table, the UN's Population Division provides a uniform data array using 60+ years as the threshold of aging in order to standardize databases by country. Thus, these data are not directly comparable to the Canadian data presented in Tables 2.1 and 2.2. However, when the Canadian data are adjusted, Canada's population aging tendencies are much the same as other nations.

The selected countries are arrayed according to their degree of population aging. Japan tops the list of almost 200 countries with

Table 2.3   Selected International Levels of
Population Aging and Median Age, 2004

	% Population 60+	Median Age (years)
Japan	26.3	42.9
Italy	25.6	42.3
Sweden	22.3	39.6
United Kingdom	21.2	39.0
France	21.1	39.3
Hungary	20.8	38.8
CANADA	17.9	38.6
Australia	17.3	36.5
Russian Federation	17.1	37.3
United States	16.7	36.1
India	7.9	24.3
Columbia	7.5	25.4
Kenya	4.1	17.9

Source: United Nations, 2005.

more than one-quarter of its population aged 60 and over; Italy and Sweden follow closely. Canada, at nearly 18 percent,[13] is a relatively "young" country, largely because of its continued stream of young immigrant families. Australia and the United States are in a similar situation with their growing numbers of seniors also offset somewhat by continued immigration. Three Third World countries included here show the effects of high birth rates coupled with low life expectancy on population aging levels. Among them, India and Columbia are now considered by the UN to have an aging population (i.e. seven percent and over).

Median age levels at the turn of the century are also given for all countries in the list. These figures show the middle age in the entire array of population ages: that is, 50 percent of the people in a country are older than this age and 50 percent are younger. In the case of Japan, this means that in 2004 half of its population was aged 43 or older. There is, of course, a high degree of association between a country's median age and its degree of population aging, which reflects the increasing share of the older age groups, especially when life expectancy is also high or growing.

RESIDENCE OF SENIORS WITHIN CANADA, 2001 AND 2006

One may wish to know if the same aging tendencies that prevail in Canada as a whole occur in the country's major regions – the provinces and territories. Table 2.4 provides some answers.

Patterns of Residence in Provinces/Territories

2001. It can be seen from Table 2.4 that the levels of senior concentration (age 65+) in the 2001 populations of nine of the ten provinces exceeded 12 percent, while seven provinces exceeded the 2001 national level of nearly 13 percent. Alberta was the exception, with a level just over 10 percent despite being bordered east and west by provinces with significantly higher concentrations of seniors, especially Saskatchewan, which exceeded 15 percent. In other words, the southern part of Canada had substantial concentrations of seniors in all its major regions. In sharp contrast, the northern territories had concentrations of seniors of less than one-half or lower than the national average. In northern regions, few among the predominantly Aboriginal population had, until recently, aged into the seniors' category because of their high mortality rates and few non-Aboriginal people continued to live there beyond age 65.

The net result of these aging differences between the northern territories and the southern provinces is that Canada currently has a "dual" geography of aging – *North* and *South.*[14] (See Figure 2.2.) This duality persists even in the portions of the eight provinces that bound the northern territories. It is, moreover, a duality that has its parallels in other social, economic and environmental realities in this country.

The 2001 concentration of seniors in the populations of the provinces and territories of Canada are arrayed in Table 2.4. Across the southern part of the country a fairly uniform spatial pattern is indicated with the average concentration of seniors among the provinces being 13.27 percent. However, when looked at in terms of the numbers of seniors represented, these percentages reflect a different perspective. Three provinces – Ontario, Quebec, and British

Table 2.4   Provincial/Territorial Concentrations of the Elderly, 2001 and 2006

Province/Territory	2001		2006	
	Percent Population 65+	Total 65+ Population	Percent Population 65+	Total 65+ Population
SOUTHERN CANADA:				
Saskatchewan	15.07	147,565	15.42	149,305
Manitoba	13.97	156,400	14.10	161,890
Nova Scotia	13.94	126,565	15.13	138,210
Prince Edward Island	13.73	18,570	14.86	20,185
British Columbia	13.64	533,085	14.58	599,810
New Brunswick	13.56	98,935	14.74	107,435
Québec	13.27	960,310	14.32	1,080,285
CANADA	12.96	3,888,550	13.71	4,335,255
Ontario	12.90	1,472,175	13.56	1,649,180
Newfoundland/Labrador	12.29	63,060	13.90	70,265
Alberta	10.37	308,395	10.74	353,410
NORTHERN CANADA:				
Yukon	6.03	1,730	7.54	2,290
Northwest Territories	4.38	1,640	4.76	1,975
Nunavut	2.22	595	2.75	810

Source: Census of Canada, 2001, 2006.

Columbia – between them had 2.1 million seniors, or nearly 76 percent of all Canada's seniors as of 2001. If Alberta is added, almost 84 percent of all seniors reside in the four most populous and prosperous provinces. The remaining provinces also had substantial numbers of seniors and several had concentrations well above average, including Saskatchewan, Manitoba, and the three Maritime Provinces. Again, only the North was significantly different.

2006. The census data from 2006 show that the number of seniors continued to increase in each province and territory. However, some noticeable shifts occurred cross-country between 2001 and 2006. While Saskatchewan remained the "oldest" province, both its number of seniors and their concentration changed very little. Nova Scotia replaced Manitoba as the second oldest province and

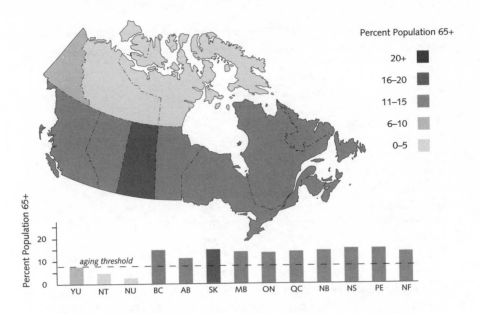

Fig. 2.2   Geography of Aging in Canada, 2006 (Source: Canada Census)

the three other Atlantic provinces also aged significantly. There was, in short, a noticeable convergence of aging levels across the southern part of the country; the average concentration of seniors (among provinces) increased to 14.13 percent. Indeed, only Alberta had a level of aging below that of the nation; the continued in-migration of younger people to that province kept the level down even though its senior population grew by 14 percent. In the North, Yukon moved over the threshold of seven percent and the other two territories experienced substantial seniors' population growth.

CHARACTERISTICS OF PROVINCIAL/TERRITORIAL SENIORS

This brings us to a further question: *how do the characteristics of the elderly in the provinces and territories compare with the national profile?* Using the Canada-wide profile for 2001 provided in Table 2.1 as a basis of comparison, we can examine the same variables for the elderly in the provinces and territories. Rather than provide localized data for each variable, general provincial tendencies will be presented, along with highlights and anomalies, some of which can also be seen in Figure 2.3.

ELDERLY AGE STRUCTURE

CANADA 2001: % 65+   aged 65–74   55.10
                               aged 75–84   34.20
                               aged 85+   10.70

PROVINCES: The general tendency among Canadian provinces is that those with the highest concentration of seniors also have the oldest age structures among the elderly. Thus, Saskatchewan and Manitoba have much smaller concentrations of the "old" (65–74) and much higher concentrations of the "old-old" (aged 75–84) and "very old" (aged 85+). Indeed, only 49 percent of Saskatchewan's seniors were aged 65–74 in 2001 while over 14 percent were 85+. Similar tendencies also exist among the Prince Edward Island, Nova Scotia, and New Brunswick elderly. The remaining provinces have similar age structures to the nation as a whole.

The converse tendency of low levels of population aging combined with a younger age structure among seniors is very noticeable in the northern territories. The most vivid example in 2001 was Nunavut, where 72 percent of seniors were aged 65–74 and only five percent were 85+. The other two territories paralleled these levels which reflect, on the one hand, the tendency for older non-Aboriginal seniors to leave and, on the other hand, the lower life expectancy among Aboriginal people.

GENDER COMPOSITION OF SENIORS

CANADA 2001: % 65+   female   57.24
                               male   42.76

PROVINCES: Quebec is the only province with a higher-than-average female concentration among its elderly (59%); British Columbia, Alberta, and Newfoundland have noticeably lower concentrations (55–6%). These variations also show up in the proportion of women 85 and older, with Quebec having an above-average share of women among the very old and British Columbia and Alberta having correspondingly lower than average levels. The northern territories, again, are significantly different: concentrations of women seniors among the elderly are lower still, and range from 39 percent in Nunavut to 48 percent in the Northwest Territories.

ABORIGINAL SENIORS/ELDERS

CANADA 2001: % 65+ Aboriginal   1.09
PROVINCES: Most provinces have relatively few Aboriginal seniors (or elders as they are traditionally called); their proportions are noticeably higher than the Canadian average in the western provinces: Manitoba (3.80), Saskatchewan (3.08), Alberta (1.80), and British Columbia (1.43). The three northern territories, by contrast, have seniors' concentrations that range from 20 percent in the Yukon to 65 percent in the Northwest Territories and nearly 90 percent in Nunavut. The latter levels, of course, represent relatively small numbers of Aboriginal elders (from a few hundred in the Yukon to just over 1,000 in the Northwest Territories). Despite their small numbers, they are widely distributed; most live in small settlements spread over an area equal to half of Canada's land mass.

VISIBLE MINORITY SENIORS

CANADA 2001: % 65+ Visible Minorities   7.20
PROVINCES: Concentrations of visible minority seniors are well below average in all but three provinces. British Columbia with 13.42 percent has the highest concentration, followed by Ontario (9.71) and Alberta (7.96). These three are the most urbanized provinces in the country, and their cities also serve as "gateways" for immigrants from abroad. Quebec, though also highly urbanized, does not show the same tendency to attract visible minorities except in the city of Montreal.

SENIORS' LIVING ARRANGEMENTS

CANADA 2001: % 65+ Living Alone   28.86
          % Female 65+ Living Alone   74.34
PROVINCES: Seniors are most likely to be living alone in the Yukon (37.38), Saskatchewan (35.03), Manitoba (34.28), and Quebec (31.12) and least likely in Newfoundland and Labrador (24.00) and

Nunavut (17.52). The remaining provinces and territories have levels near the national average. Among seniors living alone, women constitute about three-quarters of the total in all the southern provinces. Men represent a much larger proportion of those seniors living alone in the three northern territories. In the Northwest Territories and Nunavut, over half the seniors living alone are male.

SENIORS' EDUCATIONAL ATTAINMENT

CANADA 2001: % 65+ Less than High School   57.29%
High School   11.15
PROVINCES: The best-educated seniors in Canada reside in British Columbia, Ontario, Alberta, and the Yukon; in turn, each has the lowest levels of seniors with less than high school education. Concomitantly, higher proportions of their seniors also have some form of post-secondary education including university degrees. The Atlantic Provinces, Saskatchewan and Manitoba, and the northern territories – containing the most rural parts of Canada – have the least educated seniors, with about 70 percent of their seniors having only a high school diploma or less.

SENIORS' INCOMES

CANADA 2000: Avg. Individual Income for Males 65+ $30,775
Females 65+ $19,461
PROVINCES: Geographically, income levels among seniors in the provinces and territories are almost a mirror image of those for educational attainment. In 2000, both male and female seniors in British Columbia, Alberta, and Ontario had average incomes at or above their corresponding national levels. All the other provinces and the territories had senior income levels between $2,000 and $5,000 lower than those for the nation.

FACTORS AFFECTING CANADA'S GEOGRAPHY OF AGING

From the various data describing provincial seniors, a broad picture of Canada's aging population has begun to emerge. Some observations, such as north-south differences, have been alluded to above. In the sections that follow, such general geographic tendencies are amplified and some of the major reasons for their occurrence are posited.

Basic Geographic Patterns (Figure 2.2)

The essential geographical patterns of Canada's population aging evident since 2001, and reinforced by 2006 census data, are presented below in verbal and visual images.

· Two broad bands of population aging exist in Canada: one across the breadth of southern Canada where population aging is high, and the other across northern regions where population aging is substantially lower.
· Two general groupings of provinces exist regarding the distribution of the country's seniors: one, comprising the four largest provinces (Ontario, Quebec, British Columbia, and Alberta), contains 84 percent of all seniors; the other six provinces, two in the Prairies and four in Atlantic Canada, contain just 16 percent of seniors.
· Northern Canada has concentrations of Aboriginal elders that are several times that of southern Canada.
· Three provinces – Ontario, Alberta, and British Columbia – have (1) high concentrations of seniors from visible minorities; (2) the best-educated seniors; and (3) seniors with the highest individual incomes compared to the rest of the country (see Figure 2.3).

These patterns provide only a broad sketch of the geography of Canadian seniors. However, they are valuable for two reasons: first, they highlight the differences among Canada's elderly in various regions of the country and second, they begin to reveal the diverse combinations of factors associated with population aging among regions, as we see in Figure 2.3. Aside from the concentrations of the elderly in their populations, the provinces and territories differ in the age composition, living arrangements, and education and individual income levels of their seniors. This leads, in turn, to

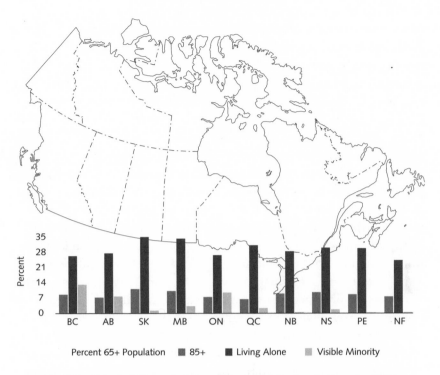

Fig. 2.3   Selected Characteristics of Provincial Seniors in Canada, 2001
(Source: Canada Census)

an important question: how did these differences arise? The short answer is: through *increasing life expectancy, natural increase* and *migration;* processes that are, in turn, associated with the economy of each province. These distinctive processes are discussed below.

Aging Patterns, Life Expectancy, and Immigration History

The broad patterns we see in the seniors' population above are the product of several decades of population aging. Most of today's seniors were 25–40-year-olds in the 1950s and 60s; they were born in the 1920s and 30s. And those seniors currently in their 80s and 90s were born even earlier, in the 1910s and 1920s. They have lived into old age largely because of dramatically increased life expectancy that occurred during their lifetimes. At birth, most of them could not have expected to live much past age 60. If they reached age 65, they could expect to live a further 10–13 years. But today, a 65-year-old has an estimated 18–20 years remaining.[15] Such factors as medical advances, better public health measures, healthier lifestyles, and less-hazardous occupations have contributed to this trend. Declines in mortality are most noticeable among young seniors and women.

To understand more fully the surging *number* of seniors in the last several decades – the seniors' population has more than tripled since 1961 – it is necessary to turn to an historical perspective. Two major waves of international immigration are relevant to our study. Many of our seniors are the offspring of first and second-generation immigrants who came to Canada during the great period of immigration and settlement between 1880 and 1930. Seniors in the four western provinces are most likely to be children of first-generation immigrants, while in Ontario, Quebec, and the Atlantic provinces, they are most likely to be the grandchildren (or even great-grandchildren) of earlier immigrants. The second influx was that of young and middle-aged people after World War II, from 1946–61 in particular. Both of these immigration streams were predominantly from Europe, and both were from eras when families were considerably larger and birth rates higher. As Statistics Canada notes: "The size of the population at a given age depends essentially on the size of the birth groups."[16] It could be added that the influence of increased life expectancy for each particular cohort is also important. Thus, for example, the relatively large group born in the 1920s nearly doubled seniors' numbers between 1991 and 2001, and are now in their 70s. Table 2.5, adapted from the latter report, provides a perspective on such changes.

The foregoing paragraphs refer to the effects of international immigration on the total seniors' population, but such immigration influxes may also have effects on population aging levels within Canada as much as two or three generations later. The current high concentration of the elderly in Saskatchewan and Manitoba, for example, result from the aging in place of the early settlers of the Prairie Provinces and their offspring. British Columbia received a substantial migration stream from Asian countries before and just

Table 2.5   Historical Parameters for Canadian Birth Cohorts

Age in 2001	Year of Birth	Historic Birth Cohort	Average Number of Births Per Year
88+	Before 1914	Pre-World War I	201,000
82–87	1914–19	World War I	244,000
72–81	1920–29	1920s	249,000
62–71	1930–39	Great Depression	236,000
56–61	1940–45	World War II	280,000
36–55	1946–65	Baby Boom	426,000
22–35	1966–79	Baby Bust	362,000
6–21	1980–95	Children of Baby Boomers	382,000
0–5	1996–2001	Children of Baby Bust	344,000

Source: Statistics Canada, Cat. No. 96F0030XIE2001002.

after 1900. This is evident today in British Columbia's higher-than-average proportion of visible minority seniors. More recent immigration of non-European populations to Canada will have an impact on both numbers and composition of the elderly in the future. More imminent is the surge in the seniors' population expected from the Baby Boom of 1946–66. In short, what we experience as population aging in any given period is mainly the result of demographic tendencies that occurred several decades earlier.

Aging in Place and Seniors' Migration

The geographical distribution of the elderly in Canada seems to suggest some commonality in the national process of population aging. For example, all ten provinces have relatively high levels of population aging and all have experienced substantial growth in the numbers of seniors. Yet why should provinces as diverse as Ontario and Newfoundland have similar concentrations of seniors? Analogously, why are Prince Edward Island and British Columbia in the same category? The reality is that the confluence in population aging levels among provinces is simply a coincidence! Each province has been affected in its own way by the interaction of two spatial components of population aging: *aging in place* and *net migration.*[17] It is the distinctive interaction of these components in each province that has led to the concentration of seniors there.

There are three basic spatial processes leading to the concentration of seniors in a community.[18] They are a) accumulation, b) recomposition, and c) congregation; they are illustrated in Figure 2.4 (a, b, c) and described below. Each of these processes, as we shall see, involves shifts between two groups of residents of a place – seniors and non-seniors – regarding whether they stay, enter and/or leave.

ACCUMULATION (FIGURE 2.4A)

When seniors remain living in their community at the same time as younger residents are migrating to another area, the result is an *accumulation* of seniors. Put another way, the proportion of seniors in the community increases as the proportion of non-seniors decreases. Called "aging in place" this process is dominant in two provinces – Saskatchewan and Prince Edward Island – as well as many small communities in rural regions.

RECOMPOSITION (FIGURE 2.4B)

When seniors are attracted to an area, joining those who have decided to stay on, and younger residents migrate to another area, the result is both a growth in seniors' numbers and a *recomposition* of its age structure (depending upon the relative age of the elderly in-migrants). In this process both "aging in place" and "net migration" affect population aging. Recomposition is often at work within rural areas such as Eastern Ontario and the Bay of Fundy region of New Brunswick, where younger seniors seek non-urban settings to retire. Such recomposition may be sufficiently large to increase the overall concentration of seniors in the province.

CONGREGATION (FIGURE 2.4C)

When an area attracts both young and old migrants, but seniors arrive at a faster pace than younger people, there results a *congregation* of seniors that is numerically and proportionately larger than

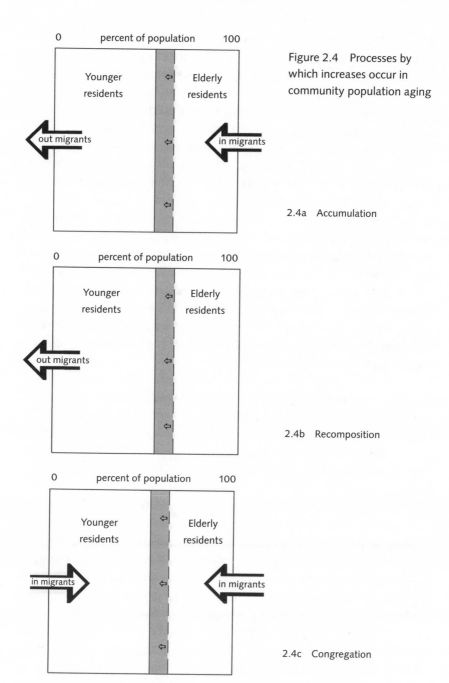

Figure 2.4 Processes by which increases occur in community population aging

2.4a Accumulation

2.4b Recomposition

2.4c Congregation

before. Parts of British Columbia, such as the Okanagan Valley and Eastern Vancouver Island, fit this model in which the seniors' "net in-migration" component is dominant in affecting population aging.

The three models of population aging described above are broad generalizations, and areas seldom conform strictly to any one model. The reasons for this are that young and old residents alike *both* stay and leave areas where they live. Thus, in all communities there is some degree of both "aging in place" and "net migration" taking place, which affect population-aging outcomes. Indeed, Canadian geographers Moore and Rosenberg posit nine scenarios for describing spatial patterns of aging.[19] Each is the result of the interaction of the rates of natural increase (i.e. births minus deaths) and the rates of net migration (i.e. in-migration minus out-migration) of both elderly and younger residents. Some of the young may leave to seek education while others may enter to seek jobs and some seniors may enter, seeking natural amenities, while others leave to be near their children. For both population groups, their reasons for staying vary as much as their reasons for leaving.

PERSPECTIVES ON SENIORS' MOBILITY

The movement of seniors, or its lack, can have significant effects on the distribution of the elderly between provinces within Canada and, especially, between regions and communities within them.

Movement between Provinces, 1996–2001

The movement of seniors from one province to another, known as inter-provincial migration, is a key factor in determining the geographical distribution of the elderly in Canada. The province from which seniors depart may see both their number of seniors decrease, and the age composition and other characteristics of the remaining seniors' population change. The same may be true for the province to which seniors are destined. Opposite results, or no change, may also occur because seniors move in *and* out of each of the provinces to various degrees. Moreover, the age and/or gender composition of the flows of seniors in and out may also vary. Migration, therefore, is a complex factor in population aging. It is made more complex by the fact that each senior's decision to move from his/her present dwelling, or to move to another province, is bound up with numerous personal considerations. Factors underlying migration decisions are discussed later in this chapter.

It is also important to recognize at the outset that seniors migrate between provinces much less frequently than do younger groups. For example, in the period between 1996–2001, the census recorded that almost 45,000 seniors moved from one province to another. This amounts to 1.2 percent of the 1996 seniors' population. During the same period 5.2 percent of young adults aged 15–29 moved between provinces.[20] Furthermore, mobility continues to decline after age 65, with those aged 65–9 moving slightly more frequently between provinces (1.4%) than older seniors (1.1% for those 75+). There are noticeable, though small, gender differences in that period as well, with senior men moving provincially slightly more frequently than senior women.

The actual inter-provincial migration flows of seniors for the five years prior to the 2001 census are shown in Table 2.6. Several aspects of these flows are noteworthy:

· Every province experienced both inflows and outflows of seniors.
· The largest flows, in and out, were associated with the four most populous provinces: Ontario, Quebec, British Columbia, and Alberta.
· The provinces that attracted the most seniors were, in order, Ontario, British Columbia, and Alberta. But even they experienced large outflows of seniors to other provinces.
· The provinces with the largest net gains of seniors were, in order, Alberta (3,690), British Columbia (2,900), and Ontario (1,290).
· Quebec had the largest net loss of seniors – nearly 5,400.

Probing these data further shows that the largest flows of seniors were those from Quebec to Ontario; they were reciprocated by Ontario seniors only to a small degree. On the other hand, large

Table 2.6   Flows of Seniors Moving between Provinces, 1996–2001

Province	Out-Migrants (-)	In-Migrants (+)	Net Migrants
Newfoundland and Labrador	-760	575	-185
Prince Edward Island	-270	525	255
Nova Scotia	-1,640	2,440	800
New Brunswick	-1,330	1,445	115
Québec	-7,970	2,615	-5,355
Ontario	-10,550	11,840	1,290
Manitoba	-3,430	1,925	-1,505
Saskatchewan	-3,915	2,050	-1,865
Alberta	-5,830	9,520	3,690
British Columbia	-8,560	11,460	2,900

Source: Census of Canada, 2001.

flows of seniors occurred both ways between British Columbia and Alberta. Further, seniors were drawn to Ontario, Alberta, and British Columbia from all the other provinces and these provinces, in turn, saw their seniors flow across the country. Other provinces tended to have dominant flows with one or a few, often neighbouring, provinces. Flows to and from the northern territories are omitted here because the numbers are small and statistically unreliable, but suffice it to say that the net flows were all negative.

A final question before leaving this topic: *are some provinces more prone to losing seniors to others?* In all cases the proportion of seniors migrating outside provincial boundaries is small, ranging between 0.9 and 3.1 percent of the total provincial seniors' population. There are, however, some differences: Quebec and Ontario have the lowest levels of seniors' out-migration, followed closely by Newfoundland and Nova Scotia. And Saskatchewan and Manitoba have the highest rates of seniors leaving for other provinces, 3.1 and 2.3 percent respectively. Alberta and British Columbia have high rates of outflow as well, but also have high rates of seniors flowing in.

Table 2.7   Mobility of Canadian Seniors by Type, 1996–2001

Type of Mobility	Numbers 65+	Percent 65+
Non-movers	2,930,265	80.8
Movers	694,550	19.2
Non-migrants	387,365	10.7
Migrants	310,185	8.5
Internal migrants	278,175	7.7
Intra-provincial migrants	233,595	6.4
Inter-provincial migrants	44,580	1.2
External migrants	32,010	0.9
TOTAL	3,624,815*	100.0

* Differs from total in Table 2.1 because of incomplete census responses to this topic.
Source: Census of Canada, 2001.

Mobility Tendencies of Seniors, 1996–2001

The migration of seniors between provinces is only one aspect of the *mobility* of the elderly population. Other aspects of mobility involve them moving from one dwelling to another in the same community or to another community in the same province, as well as not moving at all. It turns out for Canadian seniors that the most dominant mobility tendency is *not to move* from their present dwellings. Table 2.7 shows the several mobility tendencies of seniors for the five years preceding the 2001 census.

One can readily see that the overwhelming proportion (nearly 81%) of seniors remained in their dwellings over this five-year period. Moreover, of those who moved, over half (almost 11%) simply changed dwellings within their own communities, i.e. were non-migrants. Thus, over 91 percent of seniors *aged in place*, in their own communities if not in their own homes. Although these numbers are for one short period, 1996–2001, their strength indicates that this tendency is probably not short-lived. Prior data, such as those for the 1986–91 period examined by Moore and Rosenberg, showed the same strong tendency. What they concluded a decade ago remains true: "aging in place is now the dominant process" in population aging in Canada.[21]

Parameters of Migration

Despite the tendency to stay put, over one-quarter of a million seniors did move away from their home communities between 1996 and 2001. Most of them (84%) relocated from one census subdivision (e.g. municipality) to another within the same province (see intra-provincial migrants in Table 2.7 above). This could mean seniors simply moving from a core city to a suburb within a metropolitan area, or to another metropolitan area, or from a countryside location to a nearby small town or city, among a variety of possible options. Given its scale, this kind of flow represents a redistribution of seniors within a province. Furthermore, if one constructed a table of seniors' movements for each of the provinces like that of Table 2.7, it would show that each experienced similar shifts in their seniors' population.

There has been little investigation of either the types or scale of intra-provincial movements of Canadian seniors. The work of Moore and Rosenberg, using 1986–91 migration data, revealed some tendencies for seniors to migrate to growing urban areas, to regions with higher mean temperatures in January, and to those where the annual number of hours of sunshine is high.[22] Movements of seniors from the northern to southern parts of many provinces, from rural to urban areas, and from other provinces to British Columbia may be inferred from these findings; more recent work by the principal author, using 1991–2001 data, has confirmed that changes in rates of population aging are a function of economic conditions that affect an area's (or city's) growth.[23] Places with strong, growing economies attract persons of labour-force age seeking employment while tending to deter senior migrants and thereby decrease population aging. In places with less vibrant or stagnant economies, younger migrants are deterred from coming in and/or younger residents may leave, with the result that population aging increases. In short, economic factors that affect the movement of *younger people* into or out of a community are often central to both the level and changes in population aging.

In the studies described above, the emphasis was on what affects those younger than age 65 to migrate in or out, and thereby increase or decrease the seniors' proportion of the population. What is missing is any understanding of seniors' *own* tendencies to move. This requires knowledge derived from seniors themselves. Fortunately, we can establish some basic parameters in this regard from American studies.

TYPES OF SENIORS' MIGRATION

Concerted study of long-distance migration of the elderly in the United States began in the late-1970s when large numbers of seniors were leaving some states, especially in the north, and moving to others, especially those comprising the southern "Sunbelt" from Florida on the east to California on the west. Research showed that the seniors who moved from one state to another were younger, wealthier, better educated and more likely to be married, than those who didn't move.[24] Their apparent motivation to move was to seek climatic and recreation amenities. Three types of long-distance migration were subsequently identified:

· amenity
· assistance
· return[25]

Amenity migrants are those seniors who seek to change their lifestyle and/or environment; *assistance* migrants are motivated by an actual or perceived need for assistance or personal support that they believe can be achieved by being near to kin, especially children. *Return* migrants are those seniors who move back to familiar surroundings usually in the "state of their birth" (in U.S. census terms), for reasons that may include both amenity and assistance migration.

The phenomenon of return migration revealed that some senior migration was "cyclical." Two additional streams of cyclical migration were then identified – *counterstream* and *seasonal* – thus further refining *return* migration. Counterstream migrants are those seniors who, after a living elsewhere for a considerable time, return to their home state (or province). They may be leaving an amenity destination to which they migrated as younger seniors or be returning from a different province (or state) to which they moved during their working years. Counterstream migration is a subset of return migration. The motivations for this kind of return tend to be (1) to recover "satisfying memories of the past" in their "home town" and/or (2) to be near family and friends because of increased frailty and/or loss of a partner.[26] Seniors returning for the second reason tend to be "negatively selective," that is to be older, more frail, and without a partner.

Seniors who migrate seasonally are generally motivated to seek lifestyle changes and/or environmental amenities just as are longer-term amenity migrants, but they move for only a portion of a year. Those from the western provinces who migrate annually to Arizona, California, or Mexico, and those from eastern provinces, who go to Florida and other parts of the U.S. southeast, are familiarly referred to as "Snowbirds."[27] These seniors counter the conventional notion of migration as a one-way, permanent (or at least multi-year) move of residence. Instead, seasonal migrants practice a recurrent cycle of journeys over many years, with a home at each end – a "circle of migration."[28] Like long-term amenity migrants, seasonal migrants are highly likely to have known their destination from vacations or family visits in the years before retirement. The total yearly number of older seasonal migrants from Canada to Florida alone totaled over 250,000 as early as 1991 and is undoubtedly much higher now.[29] Canadian seniors have a strong motivation to migrate seasonally to a destination outside the country, rather than permanently, because they lose their health care benefits if they are abroad for more than six months each year. Seasonal senior migrants, both Canadian and American, tend to be younger, healthier, more affluent, and be couples; they are what observers call "positively selective."

MODELING SENIORS' MIGRATION

The types of seniors' migration described above are based only on general motivations such as seeking amenities or returning for support. They leave unasked such questions as: "Why move at this time? What was involved in making the decision to migrate? Why

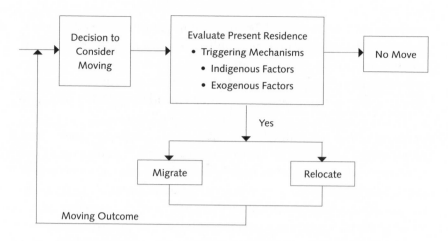

Figure 2.5   Factors Entering into a Senior's Decision to Move
(After Wiseman 1980)

choose this destination? Who are the seniors that migrate?" Or even, "why move at all?" Four broad conceptual models have developed in response to these types of questions: (1) the migration decision model, (2) the life course model, (3) the housing disequilibrium model, and (4) the place identity model.[30] These models do not so much compete with one another as fill out complementary aspects of the multi-faceted process seniors' migration is known to be.

Migration Decision Model: This model was one of the first to be developed (in 1980) and posits a sequence of steps that go into the decision-making of the elderly person (or household) about whether to move and where.[31] Figure 2.5 shows the five basic steps propounded by this model: first, the possibility of moving is contemplated; second, the elderly person evaluates her/his present residence and its situation; third, a decision is made to move or not, fourth; if the decision has been made to move, a choice is made between relocating in the same community or to a different one; fifth, the housing outcome resulting from the move will be evaluated for its degree of success. The second step is the crucial one. Embedded in it is the notion that the move by a senior is "triggered" by both *push* and *pull* factors and mediated by *indigenous* and *exogenous* factors. For example, seniors may feel pulled toward another part of the country or province by climate and/or recreational opportunities and pushed out of their current dwelling by neighbourhood deterioration and/or housing costs. And when considering such pushes and pulls, other factors enter into the picture, indigenous factors such as personal resources available for a move and exogenous factors such as the state of the local housing market if a sale is undertaken.

In this model, migration is only considered after the decision to move has been taken. This has been criticized and various refinements offered. Some have contended that most seniors who choose to migrate already have selected the destination from previous acquaintance with it and this helps to trigger the possibility of a move.[32] Others contend that information sources about different destinations, including the presence of friends, affect migration decisions.[33] These and various other elaborations have been made to this model leaving it stronger and thereby reaffirming the importance of personal decision-making processes in assessing elderly migration outcomes.

Life Course Model: This model focuses on events occurring within the course of one's life that invoke, or trigger, the possibility of moving from one's current dwelling; such events as one's first job, first child, divorce, or retirement. These are called "life course transitions" of which the three identified for seniors are (1) retirement, (2) bereavement or income collapse, and (3) frailty or chronic illness.[34] Two points made by proponents of this model are first, that not all seniors may follow the same sequence of these stages (e.g. frailty may come before retirement for some and others may not retire at all) and second, that each senior's life course is closely correlated with his/her demographic cohort. Thus retirement is a time when seniors consider moving to an amenity destination, while in the face of bereavement or frailty seniors may become return migrants.[35] Other observers suggest there are just three basic moves during old age. The first move, often away from kin, is at retirement while health and personal resources are still strong. The second, back toward kin, occurs at the onset of moderate disability or widowhood. The third is the move to a care facility, when a senior's health problems become too difficult for family members to care for.

Of course, age is prominent as a retirement factor and also in association with health problems. But just as important as age itself are the tendencies of comparable cohorts of the elderly. For example, the past example of several decades of amenity migration, of both a permanent and seasonal nature, has made this a more common venture for today's seniors. With the cohort of the Baby Boom soon to enter seniors' ranks, forecasting their geographical patterns will require us to observe whether their migration tendencies continue or deviate from those of earlier cohorts.

Housing Disequilibrium Model: This model focuses on differences between a senior's current residence and one in other locations.[36] The essential feature of the model is that the older person will be motivated to move when there are economic advantages to be gained regarding their investment in housing. This is not unreasonable given that the cost of new housing is likely to be the single largest cost incurred in relocating. Not infrequently, seniors at this stage of life have accumulated considerable equity in their home and this may facilitate a move to a more affordable housing market.

Place Identity Model: The newest migration model is largely attributable to humanist geographers, notably Graham Rowles. His work identified the importance of home and community to seniors and, hence, the stresses involved in breaking such ties when a move is contemplated.[37] Seniors, like everyone else, identify with their "place." This can include ties to one's personal possessions, dwelling, family, and friendship networks, so moving means breaking both physical and emotional ties.[38] The attachment to place varies among seniors: those with strong ties may not consider migration as an option, while those with weaker ties move readily. Here the attachment is to what Lawton refers to as the personal and suprapersonal environments of a senior, and the ease, or lack of it, with which she/he feels able to leave, is a reflection of the press of those environments.[39] There are, of course, many variations of this "place identity model"; for example, if seniors don't attain a strong connection with their new destination, it could lead to return migration. Importantly, this model emphasizes a significant point: *the decision to migrate cannot be separated from that of deciding to age-in-place.* Whichever decision a senior makes has its complementary result. Nor can either of these decisions be separated from the human tendency to have aspirations and expectations of the future. In other words, place attachment is continually reevaluated as one ages.[40]

GEOGRAPHIC IMPACTS OF SENIORS' MIGRATION

The impacts of seniors' migration are both selective and asymmetrical in their geographic effects. Migration impacts are selective in the types of seniors who choose to migrate and also of the communities they leave and those they move into. These impacts are asymmetrical in the regional flows from origin to destination and also in the community composition of seniors at both origin and destination. We know that the seniors who migrate comprise two broad types of seniors. Seniors who seek amenities and lifestyle changes tend to be healthier, better educated, more affluent, younger, and married. Those who undertake return migrations tend to be older, less healthy, less affluent, and are frequently widowed. Both types of senior migrant can have geographical impacts on regions and communities.

REGIONAL IMPACTS

When seniors migrate in search of more amenable living conditions they move from a *wide* spectrum of individual communities. However, their flows typically conclude within a *narrow* spectrum of destinations. Most pronounced are the flows of Canadian seniors to locations in the southern U.S. For example, Anglophone Snowbirds (mostly from Ontario) tend to concentrate on the west coast of Florida near St Petersburg, while Francophone seniors settle on the east coast, north of Miami.[41] Snowbirds from British Columbia and the Prairie Provinces are known to converge on a few destinations in Arizona, California, and Hawaii.[42] Although data on seniors' migration within Canada are sparse, distinct flows of seniors from the Prairie Provinces and Ontario to British Columbia have been identified since the 1980s.[43] They too can be considered amenity migrants and, like snowbirds, they originate from a host of different communities but select only a small number of destinations.

Although these flows are primarily ephemeral at the regional level, at the destination end a region of retirement communities may be created, of which more will be said below.

Those seniors involved in a return migration to their home community, either for assistance or for nostalgic reasons, create the opposite kind of geographic pattern to that of amenity migrants. That is, they originate from a *narrow* spectrum of communities and diverge to a *wide* spectrum of communities. Seniors returning from seasonal migrations have the same divergent pattern back to their many communities. Indeed, these cyclical migrants are part of both types of flows in a single season.

COMMUNITY IMPACTS

When seniors migrate there are impacts both on the communities they leave and on those to which they move. The main reason for this is that those who migrate tend to be cohort-specific by both age and other characteristics. Thus, amenity-seeking seniors constitute a loss of younger, healthier, wealthier, better-educated seniors from the elderly population in the community they leave. Concomitantly, they represent a gain of seniors with these characteristics at their destination community, which in all likelihood already has a majority of similar seniors. The origin community, meanwhile, sees an increase in the proportion of older, less healthy, and less affluent seniors unless this is offset by seniors moving in. The destination community fits the Congregation mode of population aging, and the community of origin fits the Accumulation mode with seniors aging in place (see Figure 2.4a above). Return migrants seeking assistance have the opposite impacts on communities. They represent a reduction in the share of older, frailer, poorer seniors in the communities they leave, and an addition of such seniors in those they return to. One general implication is that communities experiencing an increase in older, less healthy seniors could require additional support services while those communities in which younger, healthier seniors congregate may need a different array of services.

The effects of seniors' migration on a community become cumulative when continued over a long period of time. As we noted, amenity-seeking seniors gravitate to a relatively small number of places, which then come to be known as attractive retirement communities. These often occur in proximate clusters such as those on the eastern coast of Vancouver Island, in the Lower Fraser Valley, East Kootenay region, and the Okanagan Valley of British Columbia.[44] As early as 1981, it was found that over half of the senior interprovincial migrants destined for places in British Columbia outside metropolitan areas settled in just eleven towns and cities in the latter regions. Similar retirement clusters have occurred in Ontario, along the eastern shore of Lake Ontario and around Georgian Bay, in Quebec in the Laurentians and Eastern Townships, and in the Maritimes, along the Bay of Fundy.

Over time, places that become destinations for retirees, whether from other provinces or from within their own province, become stable. But communities not sought out by senior migrants may also achieve a stable role for those who desire to age in place. This suggests the existence of two broad types of retirement communities.[45] On the one hand are Indigenous Retirement Communities, places in which seniors have a high propensity to remain living. Other studies have referred to such places as Naturally Occurring Retirement Communities.[46] The latter make up the bulk of all communities in any province or territory. On the other hand are a much smaller number of Itinerant Retirement Communities, places that attract seniors from other regions and provinces.

When Canadian Seniors Move

A detailed study of senior Canadians who changed dwellings from 1999–2001 throws more light on their characteristics, the life events associated with their moves, and the types of housing into which they moved.[47] Among the approximately 240,000 seniors who had moved, the survey found three-quarters travelled no further than 50 kilometres from their previous dwelling. The primary reason given for their move was their wish to live in a smaller home. Other reasons included building or purchasing a new home, wanting to be close to family, declining health, and locating in a better neighbourhood. These reasons, all borne out in previous studies, were now confirmed for Canadian seniors. And, as in other studies, senior movers usually had more than one reason for moving.

In general, those seniors who moved were married (49%), homeowners (62%), and women (60%). Since these categories are not mutually exclusive, a senior mover might fit one or all three. More pointedly, seniors who were widowed were almost twice as likely to move than those who were married or in common-law relationships. And senior renters were almost twice as prone to move as owners, as was also the case with seniors living in apartments compared to those living in houses. Among all seniors who moved in this period, 43 percent moved into a smaller dwelling (downsized) and of these nearly three-quarters became renters of either an apartment or smaller house. At the same time, close to one-fifth moved into a larger house or apartment. Comparative data for people aged 55–64 showed very similar tendencies.

REFLECTIONS

To consider the geography of aging for a nation, as we have been doing for Canada, requires examination of its several spatial contexts. Indeed, these spatial contexts take the form of a nested set. First there is the *global* geography by means of which we can compare Canada's stage of aging with that of other nations. Globally, Canada stands about midway among developed nations in terms of age concentration. Second is the *national* context, within which age concentrations can be examined in different parts of the country. Are all parts aging to the same extent, for example? The Canadian situation shows that the answer to that question is no; moreover, it is likely one would find regional differences among other nations like the clear north-south division in Canada. Third is the *provincial and territorial* context within which the reasons lie for such spatial differences. Each province and territory has experienced distinctive birth rates, death rates, and migration and these processes have, over long periods, combined to produce the present composition of each of their elderly populations.

It is the present composition of their elderly populations with which the provinces and territories have to be concerned, for it not only makes clear the support seniors need today but also portends the possible new needs of tomorrow's seniors. To understand what is needed, we must get to know who the elderly are as persons, rather than seeing them as numbers. It means thinking of the elderly as women and men who are not simply aged 65 and older, and who do not all have the same incomes, education, ethnicity, and so on. We need to recognize that seniors live by choice and circumstance in different communities, provinces, or territories. The ultimate impacts of these choices are felt, and must be examined, in the fourth spatial context of aging – the *community* spatial context – to which we turn in the next chapter.

Each of the spatial contexts described above is a valid perspective from which to view our elderly population and their needs. Each is a self-contained whole and simultaneously exists as part of some larger dimension. That is, the community exists within the province, which is part of the nation, just as a letter is part of a word that is itself part of a sentence. Such whole/part combinations have been called "holons," and the set of spatial contexts described above is a set of holons.[48] A comprehensive geography of aging, thus, comprises holons of successive spatial contexts. The value of this concept is that it forces one to acknowledge the interrelationships between contexts. For example, if one were to examine seniors' housing conditions at the provincial level, one would be obliged to recognize as well that this housing exists within smaller geographical communities and the nation as a whole. One would then ensure that consistent measures be employed to describe the housing within each spatial context.

There is a close parallel between the spatial contexts invoked here and the nested set of "life spaces" posited in chapter 1 (see Figure 1.3). The latter comprises a set of eight geographic holons that allow for a progressively more intimate view of the everyday geography of seniors by including *vicinity, neighbourhood, surveillance zone,* and *home.* These life spaces will be a central part of the discussion in the next and succeeding chapters bringing the following question to the forefront:

How do different spatial contexts of seniors' lives affect the way we describe and measure them?

Chapter Three

Community Contexts of Seniors

As the last chapter noted, Canadian seniors live, simultaneously, within several spatial contexts. They live in Canada, in one of the provinces or territories, and at the same time in a community. Each of these settings has its own parameters in regard to an aging population. In the national setting, seniors are often considered as undifferentiated aggregates whose aging impinges on general resources such as health care and housing. In the provincial and territorial setting, the seniors' population, although still an aggregate, has to be considered in terms of the allocation of specific resources. In the community setting, seniors are seen more often as individual community members whose housing is a real dwelling in a particular neighbourhood, and whose health care needs must be met in specific facilities. Each of these spatial settings, thus, provides a different *context* for both observing and serving seniors.

The community, importantly, provides a setting for the lives of seniors; it is the context for their everyday geography.[1] Consider the differences between how a senior's activities may unfold within a large city as against those of someone living in a small rural community – the first with a multiplicity of facilities and transportation modes and the other with few. Each type of community plays a distinctive role in selecting activities and fashioning patterns of everyday life for its senior population. Thus, when considering the settlement patterns of Canada's seniors, a question worth keeping in mind is:

> *In what ways may a community influence the choice and type of activities in which seniors participate?*

COMMUNITIES OF THE ELDERLY

The communities in which Canadian seniors live are many in number and diverse in size and type. Seniors live in our biggest and our smallest cities, in small towns, tiny villages, the countryside, and in all of the variants of these locales. The "vantage points" available to consider these communities are the standard statistical categories of population size, urban or rural location, and metropolitan and non-metropolitan place of residence. While these data provide useful perspectives, much of what distinguishes communities from one another necessarily remains implicit in them.

Large Communities and Small

Seniors mostly live in cities and, notably, in large ones. In 2001, almost half lived in cities of at least 50,000 while less than five percent lived in places with less than 1,000, as seen in Table 3.1. "Community" is defined here by using data derived from the smallest nationwide collection unit used in the census, the Census Subdivision.[2]

Although the largest communities, those with populations over 100,000, house the greatest number of seniors, the concentration of the elderly is lowest in these places. The main reason for this is that large cities have a strong attraction for younger people as inmigrants, which lowers their level of population aging. Conversely, smaller places tend to lose younger people to the city, resulting in high concentrations of seniors, who have a strong tendency to remain living in their home communities – to age-in-place. A few examples of the concentration of seniors in small communities are given below along with their 2001 populations in brackets:

Greenpond, NF (385)	15.58%	Emerson, MB (655)	28.24%
Mahone Bay, NS (990)	29.29%	Greenwood, BC (665)	27.82%
Beauceville, PQ (6,260)	14.30%	Gananoque, ON (5,165)	21.97%

Not only is there considerable variation in the aging level among small communities, but so too among cities, as we see below:

Table 3.1   Seniors' Communities by Population Size, Canada, 2001

Community Population	Population 65+	% Seniors' Population	% Seniors' Concentration
Over 100,000	1,696,135	43.65	12.40
50,000–99,999	482,205	12.40	13.37
10,000–49,999	801,520	20.62	13.33
1,000–9,999	746,850	19.21	13.48
500–999	101,560	2.61	13.85
Under 500	58,960	1.51	13.89
CANADA	3,888,550*	100.00	12.96

* Individual categories may not add to total due to data rounding.
Source: Census of Canada, 2001.

Quebec City, PQ (169,075)	16.78%	Halifax, NS (359,110)	11.01%
Guelph, ON (106,170)	12.34%	Brandon, MB (39,175)	15.91%
Red Deer, AB (67,705)	9.72%	Kelowna, BC (96,290)	19.17%

If one looks across the age spectrum as well, there are higher concentrations of the young-old (65–74) and the old (75–84) in smaller places than in larger places. A notable exception is that seniors aged 85 and older are less likely than younger seniors to be found in the smallest centres, those having less than 500 inhabitants. Large towns and small cities have higher concentrations of the very old. This is understandable, since such places are more likely to offer the supports – housing, health care and transportation – that the oldest seniors frequently need.

The pattern described above is not uniform among Canada's ten southern provinces and three northern territories. The four largest provinces – Ontario, Quebec, British Columbia, and Alberta – have a similar distribution of seniors among the various community sizes as the nation as a whole. This is due in large part to the weight of their numbers. Nonetheless, most of these province's seniors live in the largest cities: in Ontario, 61 percent of seniors live in places with populations of over 100,000; the comparable figure for

Table 3.2   Seniors' Communities by Urban and Rural Setting, Canada, 2001

Place of Residence	Population 65+	Percent Concentration of Seniors			
		65–74	75–84	85+	65+
Urban Area (Communities 10,000 and up)	2,979,180 (76.66%)	6.99	4.41	1.38	12.78
Rural Area (Communities 9,999 and under)	907,370 (23.34%)	7.75	4.50	1.40	13.55
CANADA	3,888,550	7.14	4.43	1.38	12.96

Source: Census of Canada, 2001.

Alberta is 52 percent. However the converse is true for the smallest provinces. In 2001, while barely four percent of Canada's seniors lived in centres with less than 1,000 people, in several individual provinces that figure was far higher: in Newfoundland, 25 percent of seniors called the smaller centres home, in Saskatchewan it was 29 percent, and in Prince Edward Island, 32 percent. In the three northern territories similarly high proportions of seniors lived in the smallest places.

Urban and Rural Communities

Beyond community size, to what extent do seniors live in urban or rural surroundings? To make this distinction, the data in Table 3.1 above may be divided between those places with populations of 10,000 and over, which can be considered *urban* settings, and those with populations below 10,000, which can be considered *rural* settings.[3] When this is done, it can be seen that nearly three million seniors were urban dwellers and not quite one million were rural dwellers in 2001. At the same time, rural concentrations were not only higher than those for urban areas, but also higher than those for all of Canada's seniors (Table 3.2).

Table 3.3   Provincial Levels of Seniors' Urbanization, Canada, 2001

Province	Seniors' Place of Residence	
	URBAN %	RURAL %
Ontario	89.64	10.36
British Columbia	79.53	20.47
Alberta	73.60	26.40
Québec	71.90	29.10
Manitoba	63.59	36.41
Nova Scotia	63.81	36.19
Yukon Territory	62.35	37.65
Saskatchewan	46.35	53.65
New Brunswick	41.34	58.66
Prince Edward Island	40.66	59.34
Newfoundland	33.88	66.12
Northwest Territories	24.45	74.55
Nunavut	–	100.00
CANADA	76.67	23.33

Source: Census of Canada, 2001.

The Pattern of Seniors' Urbanization

Although the data above make it clear Canada's seniors are dominantly city-dwellers, their degree of urbanization varies markedly, from zero in Nunavut to almost 90 percent in Ontario. Table 3.3 shows the degree to which seniors live in urban and rural surroundings. It can be seen that there is little geographic regularity in the distribution of urban seniors. The four provinces with the largest populations all have well over 70 percent of seniors living in urban places, but two are located in the east and two in the west. And while three provinces in the Atlantic Region are among those with the lowest proportions of urban seniors, the fourth is not. The northern territories are all very rural, but nearly two-thirds of the Yukon's seniors are urban, by virtue of the presence of one small city, Whitehorse. This anomaly provides a clue to the situation in other provinces: the proportion of urban seniors is greatest in those

Table 3.4   Seniors' Numbers and Age Structure in Metropolitan and
Non-Metropolitan Communities, Canada, 2001

Place of Residence	Population 65+	Percent Concentration of Seniors			
		65–74	75–84	85+	65+
Metropolitan area	2,350,405 (60.4%)	6.72	4.17	1.29	12.18
Non-metropolitan area	1,538,145 (39.6%)	7.89	4.91	1.55	14.35
CANADA	3,888,550	7.14	4.43	1.38	12.96

Source: Census of Canada, 2001.

provinces that have one or more large and medium-size cities. Saskatchewan and New Brunswick are the exceptions, with over half of their seniors living in rural communities even though each has two large urban areas.

Metropolitan and Non-Metropolitan Communities

Given that most seniors live in urban communities, are these in metropolitan or non-metropolitan settings? "Metropolitan settings" refer to the 27 Census Metropolitan Areas (CMAs) in Canada each of which is based on an urban core of at least 100,000 inhabitants along with adjacent subdivisions of various sizes (usually municipalities) that are considered to be economically and socially integrated with the core city. "Non-metropolitan settings" refer to all other census subdivisions (CSDs), both urban and rural communities, not falling within a metropolitan area. Using this classification allows us to better see the role played by large urban complexes as communities for the elderly, as distinct from the broad community groupings discussed above (see Table 3.4).

It is clear from Table 3.4 that most seniors prefer to live in the largest metropolitan areas. Indeed, metropolitan areas housed 60 percent of all seniors in 2001. However, major differences do occur in the concentrations of seniors in these two types of communities. Seniors of all age groups are significantly more prominent in non-metropolitan settings, with the net effect that their overall concentration is nearly 20 percent higher than in CMAs. As well, each senior age group's concentration in non-metropolitan communities is higher than 2001 national averages.

The strong tendency of seniors to age-in-place may be seen in both metropolitan and non-metropolitan areas. Older people residing in non-metropolitan communities have for the most part continued to do so even as young people left for the metropolis, the result being that seniors have come to assume a larger share of the remaining population. On the other hand, the concentration of seniors in metropolitan areas is due to the in-migration of the young in previous decades, because those who arrived have grown older and opted to remain.[4]

Of course, there is considerable variation among communities in each of these situations. For example, among non-metropolitan cities Charlottetown's (PEI) concentration of seniors is over 16 percent while Timmins (ON) is under 12 percent and Grande Prairie (AB) is less than seven percent, even though these three places are similar in population size. Metropolitan areas also vary in their levels of aging: Victoria (BC) is the "oldest" (as it has been for several decades) at nearly 18 percent seniors and Calgary (AB) is the "youngest" at just over nine percent. In between is St John's (NF) at nearly 11 percent and Trois-Rivières (PQ) at over 15 percent. In the following section we look in detail at metropolitan areas that are now the dominant type of seniors' community.

METROPOLITANIZATION OF THE ELDERLY

The extent to which seniors now call metropolitan communities home represents a significant shift in Canada's geography of aging. As recently as 1971, the number of seniors in metropolitan areas only slightly outnumbered those living in non-metropolitan areas. Nowadays, there are nearly one million more metropolitan than non-metropolitan seniors.

The Shift to the Metropolis

The growth in the number of seniors living in Canadian metropolitan areas over the past several decades has been dramatic. Between 1971 and 2001, those aged 65+ in CMAs increased from less than

Table 3.5   Changing Distribution and Concentration of Seniors in
Metropolitan and Non-Metropolitan Areas, Canada, 1971–2001

Place of Residence	1971	1981	1991	2001
NUMBER OF SENIORS (65+):	000s	000s	000s	000s
Metropolitan Area	914.8	1,272.1	1,825.4	2,350.4
Non-Metropolitan Area	829.6	1,088.8	1,344.6	1,538.2
Canada	1,744.4	2,360.9	3,170.0	3,888.6
CONCENTRATION OF SENIORS:	PERCENT OF POPULATION 65+			
Metropolitan Area	7.71	9.32	10.95	12.18
Non-Metropolitan Area	8.55	10.18	12.66	14.35
Canada	8.09	9.70	11.61	12.96

Source: Census of Canada 1971, 1981, 1991, 2001.

1,000,000 to nearly 2,500,000, a rate of increase of 160 percent! Moreover, in this same period, the senior population grew faster than the non-senior population in metropolitan areas. The result, as Table 3.5 shows, is a significant increase in the proportion of seniors among metropolitan residents.

To speak about a "shift" of seniors to the metropolis is not to talk about their physical migration but rather to focus on the rapid growth of their numbers in our largest urban units. The basis of this shift, as mentioned above, lies in the large-scale migration of young populations that occurred, especially, in the 1950s, '60s and '70s from rural and other non-metropolitan areas to the largest cities. Most of these younger in-migrants, who might have aged else-where, simply remained living in the metropolitan areas to which they moved right into old age. This is the most dominant factor in the increasing numbers of the metropolitan elderly in Canada and it parallels the experience in the United States in roughly the same period.[5] What occurred in both countries was a *demographic aging* of metropolitan populations, not a physical shift of seniors.

It should be noted that part of the shift in the numbers of met-ropolitan seniors was attributable to the elevation of five previously non-metropolitan urban areas to CMA status between 1971 and

2001. They are Oshawa (1976), Trois-Rivières (1981), Sherbrooke (1986), Abbotsford (2001), and Kingston (2001). Seniors from these new CMAs contributed about 10 percent to the metropolitan shift and, conversely, a loss of 20 percent in seniors from non-metropolitan totals. Also, the expansion of metropolitan boundaries during this period to encompass previously non-metropolitan municipalities and districts on the fringe of metropolitan areas also added a small number of seniors to CMA ranks in the range of perhaps two to four percent. Not withstanding these changes, over 85 percent of the shift is attributable to the demographic aging of existing metropolitan populations.

THE AGING OF METROPOLITAN CANADA

Accompanying the extensive growth in number of metropolitan seniors has been the progressive aging of CMA populations. This can be seen in Table 3.5 in the growing concentration levels of seniors – from 7.71 to 12.18 percent – from 1971 to 2001. These trends and tendencies in metropolitan Canada are similar to those that occurred in the United States. The pace of elderly metropolitanization has been faster in the U.S. than in Canada however, with the result that close to three-quarters of American seniors currently live in metropolitan areas compared to 60 percent in Canada.[6]

The progressive aging of metropolitan populations is further borne out by examining seniors' concentrations in individual CMAs as shown in Table 3.6. Here we see that every CMA increased its concentration of persons 65+ between 1991 and 2001. Further, in 2001, nearly half (13) of the 27 metropolitan areas had concentrations that exceeded the national level of 12.96 percent. Noteworthy, too, every CMA increased the number of its seniors in this period as it had in the two decades previous to 1991. Looking more closely, the five metropolitan areas with the highest degree of aging – the "oldest" CMAs – in 2001 are:

Victoria, BC	17.79%
St Catharines-Niagara Falls, ON	17.41%
Trois-Rivières, PQ	15.34%
Thunder Bay, ON	15.07%
Hamilton, ON	14.27%

Table 3.6   Concentration of Seniors in Canadian
Metropolitan Areas, 1991 and 2001

	Total CMA Population	% Population 65+	
	2001	2001	1991
Abbotsford	147,370	13.11	*
Calgary	951,395	9.02	7.79
Chicoutimi-Jonquière	154,935	12.85	8.80
Edmonton	937,840	10.57	8.49
Greater Sudbury	155,600	13.83	10.44
Halifax	359,185	11.01	8.23
Hamilton	662,400	14.27	12.83
Kingston	146,840	14.18	*
Kitchener-Waterloo	414,285	11.21	10.23
London	432,450	13.17	12.11
Montreal	3,426,350	12.92	10.42
Oshawa	296,300	10.44	9.01
Ottawa-Hull	1,063,665	10.81	9.52
Quebec City	682,755	13.08	10.69
Regina	192,800	12.55	10.90
Saint John	122,680	13.20	12.41
Saskatoon	225,930	11.81	10.34
Sherbrooke	153,810	13.22	11.50
St Catharines-Niagara Falls	377,010	17.41	14.98
St John's	172,915	10.67	9.32
Thunder Bay	121,985	15.07	13.35
Toronto	4,682,900	11.29	10.33
Trois-Rivières	137,505	15.34	11.78
Vancouver	1,986,965	12.20	12.16
Victoria	311,905	17.79	18.81
Windsor	307,875	12.57	12.75
Winnipeg	671,275	13.73	12.84

* CMA added after 1991 Census.

Source: Census of Canada 1991, 2001.

By contrast, the five "youngest" CMAs are:

Calgary, AB	9.02%
Oshawa, ON	10.44%
Edmonton, AB	10.57%
St John's, NF	10.67%
Halifax, NS	11.01%

In these examples, metropolitan aging shows no regular geographic pattern either by size or location. Very large concentrations of seniors are found in CMAs with both large and small populations and the same is true for those with very low concentrations. These variations are also seen when one applies an east-west dimension to the CMA data. The differences in CMA aging appear more closely linked to the historical circumstances of individual metropolitan areas. Victoria, for example, has been a destination for migrating seniors for many decades while St Catharines-Niagara Falls has begun to play that role more recently. Trois-Rivières and Thunder Bay have seen their traditional industrial roles contract and their older labour force has aged in place as compared to CMAs with low concentrations of seniors that have experienced more recent economic growth and, in turn, attracted younger populations.[7]

SUBURBANIZATION OF THE ELDERLY

The aggregate trends described above provide only a partial picture of aging in Canadian CMAs. Metropolitan areas are neither monolithic nor homogenous but are an accumulation of numerous communities. They have, by accretion around a core city, coalesced into the large urban entities we see today. Among the various theories advanced to explain metropolitan area development, the essential feature is that it proceeds in stages with new communities being formed with new functions and new populations while remaining linked to existing communities. We call these new communities *suburbs* of the *urban* core city.[8] Suburban development, generally, proceeds in concentric rings outward, but many variations occur due to such factors as topography, transportation, other existing centres, rapidity of growth, cultural influences, degree of affluence, etc.[9] For our purposes, it is important to note that each new stage of suburban development becomes home to a new, and usually younger, population.

The Shift to the Suburbs

The elderly typically have been found in greatest numbers and concentration in core cities, largely because these were the oldest parts of metropolitan areas and the suburbs were designed to appeal to much younger people.[10] This precept guided most thinking about the metropolitan elderly until 1990. Then suddenly, or so it appeared, two studies revealed that the number of seniors living in the suburbs of metropolitan areas of both Canada and the United States exceeded the number living in core cities. Census data for the U.S. indicated that those 65 and older living in metropolitan areas were evenly split between core cities and suburbs as early as 1977 while in Canada, 1991 census data revealed that just over half of the seniors in metropolitan areas now lived in the suburbs.[11]

In core cities the absolute number of seniors continued to grow even as the share of the metropolitan elderly decreased. What was happening was that (1) people in core cities continued to age and (2) generations who had moved to the suburbs between 1950–70 stayed and aged-in-place.[12] Moreover, since the core cities had not been growing as fast as their suburbs, the number of older adults in the suburbs who were about to become seniors was much larger. Again, as with the shift of elderly to the metropolis, the suburban shift was primarily demographic in nature in that it was the aging in place of a particular historical cohort of very large size.

Determining the extent of seniors' presence in the suburbs depends upon differentiating the urban core from the rest of the metropolitan area, and this in turn relies on the stability of core city boundaries. Typically, one would identify the core city as that which gave its name to the CMA, such as the City of Toronto or the City of Victoria. The remaining communities would constitute the suburbs of the CMA. Such a distinction was possible with few exceptions prior to the 2001 census. However, during the 1990s, substantial changes with boundaries between core cities and their suburbs in six large CMAs. In both Ontario and Nova Scotia, there occurred extensive amalgamations of core cities with adjacent municipalities that were previously suburbs.[13] These changes make impractical comparisons with earlier core/suburban data for these six metropolitan areas. Moreover, the seniors in these CMAs account for over one-third of all metropolitan seniors. Thus, one must view the dynamics of the suburban shift of seniors in recent decades from two perspectives: first, for the period of 1971–91 and then, separately, for the situation in 2001, as set out below.

SUBURBAN SHIFTS 1971–91[14]

Vast and unprecedented population growth occurred in Canadian metropolitan areas during the 1950s and 1960s. This growth, which mostly happened outside of core cities, constituted families headed by 35–45 year olds that, within a few decades, became households headed by seniors or near-seniors. In the decade from 1971–81, the number of seniors living in metropolitan suburbs grew by more than two-thirds and a decade later, in 1991, had increased again by over 70 percent. Growth rates of suburban seniors far outstripped those in the core cities as well as that of the total population in the 25 CMAs existing at the time. These outcomes can be seen in Table 3.7.

The trend towards the suburbanization of seniors described above is widely distributed among metropolitan areas. Every CMA increased its numbers of seniors between 1971–91. Moreover, the numbers of seniors grew in all core cities (except for Toronto) and in the suburbs of all CMAs. Core cities, however, "aged" faster than their suburbs and consistently had senior concentrations that exceeded those of the suburbs in all the CMAs. In 18 of the 25 CMAs, core city senior concentrations also exceeded those of the nation as a whole. Of those metropolitan areas with "younger" core cities, four were in Alberta and Saskatchewan and two in Ontario.

This suburban shift was evident among the different age groups of seniors as well as in their overall numbers. The number of the elderly aged 65–74 was actually higher in the metropolitan suburbs (51.8%) than in core cities (48.2%) in 1991. And those aged 75 and over in the suburbs nearly equaled the same age group in core cities at that time.[15] Only fifteen years previously, in 1976, both suburban

Table 3.7   Changing Distribution and Concentration of Seniors
within Metropolitan Areas, Canada, 1971–91

Place of Residence	1971		1981		1991	
DISTRIBUTION OF SENIORS:	000S	%	000S	%	000S	%
Core Cities	573.7	62.7	742.0	58.3	912.3	50.0
Suburbs	341.1	37.3	530.1	41.7	913.1	50.0
All CMAs	914.8	100.0	1,272.1	100.0	1,825.4	100.0
CONCENTRATION OF SENIORS:	PERCENT OF POPULATION 65+					
Core Cities	9.14		11.11		12.54	
Suburbs	6.10		7.60		9.72	
All CMAs	7.71		9.32		10.95	

Source: Census of Canada 1971, 1981, 1991.

groups had constituted only about 40 percent of their respective cohorts.

SENIORS WITHIN SUBURBAN ZONES, 1971–91

By distinguishing successive "rings" of suburban development and their populations, one can track the aging of the population throughout different suburbs. The inner suburbs, those closest to the core city, develop first and then, progressively, the outer suburbs and suburban fringe communities. Whether all these "rings" exist depends upon the longevity of the metropolitan area.[16] Older metropolises such as Toronto, Quebec City, and Saint John comprise all three suburban stages; newer CMAs such as Regina, Thunder Bay, and Calgary tend to have fewer suburban accretions. This geographic construct – core city, inner suburbs, outer suburbs, and suburban fringe – was used to examine the shift of seniors to the suburbs of Canadian CMAs during the 1971–91 period.

Aging in Suburban Zones: From 1971–91, the number of seniors grew in each suburban zone beyond the core city. Seniors more than doubled in the inner suburbs and more than tripled in the two far-

Table 3.8   Changing Distribution and Concentration of Seniors within
Suburban Zones of Metropolitan Areas, Canada, 1971–91

Place of Residence	1971		1981		1991	
DISTRIBUTION OF SENIORS:	000S	%	000S	%	000S	%
Core Cities	573.7	62.7	742.0	58.3	912.3	50.0
Inner Suburbs	225.0	24.6	340.7	26.8	536.2	29.4
Outer Suburbs	86.0	9.4	144.9	11.4	278.1	15.2
Suburban Fringe	30.1	3.3	44.5	3.5	98.8	5.4
All CMAs	914.8	100.0	1,272.1	100.0	1,825.4	100.0
CONCENTRATION OF SENIORS:		PERCENT OF POPULATION 65+				
Core Cities	9.14		11.11		12.54	
Inner Suburbs	6.35		8.62		11.27	
Outer Suburbs	5.44		6.05		7.93	
Suburban Fringe	6.51		7.21		8.73	
All CMAs	7.71		9.32		10.95	

Source: Census of Canada 1971, 1981, 1991.

thest zones, the outer suburbs and suburban fringe (see Table 3.8).
Not only were their numbers growing but so, too, were the concentrations of seniors in each of the three suburban zones. Indeed,
each zone kept pace with the aging of core cities, the oldest parts
of CMAs. The most dramatic aging occurred in the inner suburbs
where the concentration of seniors doubled and, by 1991, had come
to nearly equal national levels. More and more, the inner suburbs
became home to old and very old seniors. Both the outer suburbs
and the suburban fringe communities, the "younger" parts of
metropolitan areas, also experienced a progressive aging of their
populations in this period. Their increases in senior concentration were, however, less dramatic due in large part to their overall younger populations and the continued influx of young families
(see Figure 3.1).

Core City Aging: In all 25 CMAs, core cities had the highest concentrations of seniors of the four metropolitan zones from 1971 through

Percent Population 65+	Suburban Fringe	Outer Suburbs	Inner Suburbs	Core Cities
1971	6.5%	5.4%	6.3%	9.1%
1981	7.2%	6.1%	8.6%	11.1%
1991	8.7%	7.9%	11.3%	12.5%
2001	◄──────── All Suburbs 10.9% ────────►			13.2%

Figure 3.1   Population Aging in Metropolitan Canada: 1971–2001

to 1991. Moreover, by 1991, 17 CMAs had concentrations that exceeded the national level of 11.61 percent, with Victoria having more than twice the national level. Other core cities with very high concentrations of 65+ were Trois-Rivières, Saint John, and Quebec City. The eight CMA core cities with lower-than-national levels included Edmonton, Saskatoon, Oshawa, and Kitchener-Waterloo. Core city aging also included high proportions of older seniors, those 75 and over. Even core cities with lower senior concentrations had levels for those 75+ that were higher than for the rest of the metropolitan zones. In other words, aging in core cities had a firm foothold and persisted for two or more decades up to 1991.

Inner Suburb Aging: Inner suburbs like Burnaby in the Vancouver CMA, East York in Toronto, and Westmount in Montreal represent the first wave of metropolitan expansion and, as one would expect, their populations are somewhat younger than those of core cities. In 1991, although inner suburbs had lower concentrations of seniors than their core cities in all CMAs, five had seniors' shares (as well as those 75+) that were higher than the national average led again by Victoria but also including Toronto, Vancouver, and Montreal. Differences between CMAs in regard to the degree of aging in inner suburbs appears to be related to the period at which suburbanization took place. The latter CMAs, Canada's largest, expanded early in the twentieth century and older cities like London, Hamilton, Victoria, and Quebec City not long after.

Outer Suburb Aging: The outer suburbs represent a more recent zone of metropolitan development and, therefore, are peopled by younger age cohorts compared to adjacent inner suburbs. This is true for one-third of Canadian metropolitan areas where one finds that outer suburbs have lower concentrations of 65+ than inner suburbs and that these concentrations increased from 1971–91. However, the outer suburbs of two-thirds of CMAs follow a different pattern; they actually have higher concentration of seniors than inner suburbs. This difference occurs in ten CMAs in which the outer suburbs are the farthest extent of metropolitan development and also in a further half dozen where there is suburban fringe development as well. This seemingly disparate situation occurs as one nears the outer limits of metropolitan areas. Here the expanding metropolis frequently overtakes older, settled rural areas and small communities. These types of communities probably already had substantial seniors' populations, which then manifested themselves in elevated concentrations in the new suburbs.

Aging in the Suburban Fringe: Seniors in the suburban fringe zone increased in number faster than those in the other two suburban zones from 1971–91. This was due in large part to the continued aging of an already-older population in rural areas and small communities encompassed by metropolitan expansion. As Table 3.7 shows, the suburban fringe had a concentration of seniors higher than that of inner suburbs as early as 1971. Later in-migration of younger age groups and their subsequent aging-in-place added to these levels over the following two decades. Most CMAs showed a distinctive upswing in the aging tendency of the suburban fringe (or in the outer suburbs if there were no fringe communities). In a few instances, the concentration of seniors in the suburban fringe rivaled those of close-in suburbs. In three CMAs – Edmonton, Saint John, and Victoria – they reached more than 11 percent in 1991, more than the level for all seniors in CMAs at the time.

Core City and Suburban Elderly in 2001

In 2001, a decade after the situation just described, over one-half million additional seniors were living in Canada's metropolitan

Table 3.9   Distribution and Age Structure of Core City and
Suburban Seniors in Metropolitan Areas, Canada, 2001

| | Metropolitan Place of Residence | |
	Core Cities	Suburbs
SENIORS' POPULATION:		
Numbers	1,415,505	934,900
Distribution %	55.70	44.30
AGE STRUCTURE:	PERCENT TOTAL POPULATION	
65–74	7.05	6.32
75–84	4.63	3.58
85+	1.48	1.05
65+	13.16	10.94

Source: Census of Canada, 2001.

areas. This was due in part to the addition of two new CMAs to the previous total of 27. However, more substantial changes came with shifts in metropolitan boundaries in six CMAs (including the largest, Toronto) between 1991 and 2001. These changes altered the boundaries between core cities and suburbs, which, in turn, prevent any easy comparison with earlier censuses. In several instances, the boundaries of core cities were expanded to include much of what were previously inner and outer suburbs.[17] Thus, 2001 census figures that are generally available are only able to show two broad spatial contexts: core cities and suburbs as indicated in Figure 3.1.[18] These data present not so much a new picture of metropolitan seniors as a new benchmark for considering the suburbanization of seniors (compare Tables 3.8 and 3.9).

CORE/SUBURBS CHARACTERISTICS, 2001

The suburbanization of Canada's metropolitan elderly is still very evident in 2001, although proportions have shifted since the 1991 census (see Table 3.9). Of the nearly 2.4 million seniors living in CMAs at the millennium just over one-half lived in the core cities and a little less than half in the suburbs. Both CMA core cities and

suburbs added to their seniors' populations under the new definitions. Further, both increased their concentrations of seniors over
that of 1991.

In terms of age structure, seniors' concentrations in all age
groups were higher in core cities than in metropolitan suburbs. As
well, core cities tended to be home to older seniors and suburbs to
younger seniors.

Several metropolitan areas had core cities with very high concentrations of seniors in 2001. The most notable are listed below:

Victoria	19.93%
Trois-Rivières	19.83%
Sherbrooke	18.08%
St Catharines	17.64%
Quebec City-Lévis	16.59%

In these five core cities, in 2001, seniors constitute close to one-
fifth of the population. Further, these concentrations are well above
core city averages for seniors' levels as well as being far and above
CMA and Canadian levels. And when the separate age groups of the
elderly are examined, these core cities have much higher-than-average levels of all ages of seniors. Thus, core cities with high levels of
aging have high concentrations right across the age spectrum. The
converse is true for metropolitan areas whose core cities have generally lower concentrations of seniors, such as Calgary and St John's.

The same relationship does not hold between core cities and
their suburbs, however. High concentrations of seniors in a CMA's
core city tend not to be reflected in the CMA's suburbs. In only two
of the above five metropolitan areas (Victoria and St Catharines-
Niagara) were there comparably high concentrations of seniors in
the suburbs. The norm is that suburban concentrations are about
30–40 percent lower than those for core cities for the entire 65 and
older group as well as for each age cohort. In both cases, the factors
at work in the aging of populations have been mostly *demographic*
in nature: the populations in both situations aged-in-place but core
city populations were older to start with. In effect, core cities had
a "head start" on aging. This suggests that the suburbs will catch
up in the future in all CMAs. The future aging of CMAs and other

types of communities in which seniors live is the subject of later chapters, especially chapter 7.

SENIORS IN SMALL TOWNS AND RURAL COMMUNITIES

Although its seniors are mostly city dwellers, Canada still has an extensive seniors' population living in small towns and rural communities. Indeed, slightly fewer than one million seniors call rural regions home in 2001. And their numbers continue to grow: over 100,000 seniors were added from 1981–2001!

The Diverse Milieux of Rural Seniors

While the number of rural seniors is substantial, it is important to see them in their geographical context. They live in the 96 percent of the nation's total area that is essentially rural, an area of over 9,000,000 square kilometres. Within that space there are several thousand settlements that are diverse in nature and size.[19] (This compares with fewer than 150 metropolitan areas and census urban areas.) Rural communities range from good-size towns such as Prévost, PQ and Lacombe, AB, down through small towns such as Clark's Harbour, NS and Rainy River, ON, to even smaller villages and hamlets such as Waskala, MB and Zeballos, BC. To these need to be added numerous crossroads clusters, several hundred outports, and close to 3,000 Indian Reserves, as well as countryside and farm locales in every province and territory. Three broad features characterize rural seniors' communities:

· They are low in residential density;
· They have large distances between them; and
· They are mostly small in size, e.g. 77% have fewer than 500 residents.[20]

In addition, rural communities may be influenced by the presence of metropolitan areas and other cities depending upon the latter's proximity and accessibility. In the sections that follow we consider rural seniors from several perspectives.

Table 3.10   Population and Age Structure in
Rural Seniors' Communities, Canada, 2001

| Community | Population | Percent Concentration of Seniors | | | |
Size	65+	65–74	75–84	85+	65+
1,000–9,999	746,850	7.59	4.47	1.41	13.48
500–999	101,560	7.86	4.60	1.39	13.85
Under 500	58,960	7.99	4.64	1.26	13.89
RURAL CANADA	907,370	7.75	4.50	1.40	13.55

Source: Census of Canada, 2001.

COMMUNITY SIZE AND AGE STRUCTURE

Consider, first, the size of rural community seniors live in, and whether seniors of all ages reside there. Table 3.10 shows that the bulk of rural seniors – four-fifths of them – live in communities between 1,000 and 10,000 in population while only six percent live in places of less than 500. In all sizes of community the concentration of seniors exceeds that of urban Canada and of the nation's seniors as a whole.

There are few noticeable differences in the shares of the various senior age groups in the different size communities. One exception is that the old-old (85+) show less inclination to live in smallest centres and a greater tendency to live in larger towns. This is likely due to facilities such as nursing homes and seniors' housing only being available in larger centres. Still, many seniors continue to live in the small places with few services for them.[21] And, as is discussed below, their concentration may be very high.

RURAL SENIORS IN THE PROVINCES AND TERRITORIES

Now, consider where rural seniors live across the country. Nearly half of them live in Quebec and Ontario, the most urbanized provinces. In 2001, Quebec had the largest number, almost 270,000, or nearly 30 percent of all rural seniors. Alberta and British Columbia, also highly urbanized, were home to a further 20 percent. Although these four provinces had large numbers of rural seniors, city-dwelling seniors far outnumbered them. On the other hand, in four provinces and two northern territories – Saskatchewan, New Brunswick, Prince Edward Island, Newfoundland, Northwest Territories, and Nunavut – *more than half* of the seniors lived in rural settings in 2001 (see Table 3.3).

Just as noteworthy is that this second group is home to remarkably high proportions of seniors of all ages who live in communities of less than 1,000 inhabitants. In Prince Edward Island 32 percent of seniors live in such places; in Saskatchewan it is 30 percent, in Newfoundland, 25 percent, and in the Northwest Territories, 39 percent. Furthermore, in the three Prairie Provinces and New Brunswick, in communities having populations of *less than 500,* the concentrations of seniors are well above national and provincial averages. In Saskatchewan, seniors constitute over 17 percent of the population in these places; in three other provinces seniors' concentrations reach close to 15 percent in similar communities. These average concentrations do not, however, convey the reality of the seniors' population in scores of small centres in these provinces and others where the levels may often be twice as high. A few examples, along with 2001 populations, will point this up:

Holden, AB (385)	29.33%	Beechy, SK (295)	35.59%
Port Elgin, NB (435)	29.89%	Cartwright, MB (305)	34.43%
Invermay, SK (285)	38.60%	Empress, AB (170)	35.29%
Harvey, NB (350)	27.14%	Benito, MB (415)	38.55%

In these small places and others like them it may fairly be said that "every third person one meets on Main Street will be 65 or older." Researchers studying this same tendency toward high age concentrations among U.S. small towns named them "rural naturally occurring retirement communities," or NORCs.[22] To be more specific, these are rural communities that have undergone (or are undergoing) any of the three processes of population aging described in chapter 2 (see Figure 2.4). They are not, by contrast, purpose-built retirement communities, which are often found in rural areas. NORCs also occur in urban and suburban neighbourhoods. The usual measure of their existence in urban and rural communities is that at least one senior resides in 30 percent or more of the households.[23]

Moreover, one also finds above-average concentrations of very old seniors (85+) in these very small centres in Saskatchewan, Manitoba, and New Brunswick. Other studies have also found that sex ratios among small town and rural seniors (i.e., males 65+/females 65+ x 100) are higher than they are among even the oldest age group (85+) in cities and even in the smallest communities.[24] This tendency for there to be greater numbers of older men than older women was especially noticeable in small communities in the Prairie Provinces.

In the northern territories, the levels of aging are well below national levels and the numbers of seniors relatively small. Nonetheless, a high proportion of northern seniors live in the fewer than one hundred, very small communities that dot the four million square kilometres comprising the three territories. This means that less one percent of rural seniors live on 40 percent of the nation's land area. And nearly one-quarter live in communities of less than 500 inhabitants, including many who are aged 85 and older. Lastly, rural seniors in the territories are mostly of Aboriginal (North American Indian, Metis, Inuit) origin. These geographic, demographic and cultural factors combine to produce distinctive community contexts for northern seniors with concomitant effects on daily needs and activities.

RURAL SENIORS AS SEEN FROM THE METROPOLIS

Rural areas and their populations, including seniors, do not stand apart from the rest of Canada. Canada is an urban country, so rural areas are linked with the urban areas in their regions through the location of services such as high-level health care facilities. The strength of the relation between rural and urban areas depends, of course, upon their proximity and accessibility to one another. With the 2001 census, Statistics Canada introduced a means whereby rural locales could be viewed according to the degree to which they were under the "influence" of urban entities.[25] A series of four zones were established which generally reflected increasing

Table 3.11   Population and Age Structure of Rural Seniors Living in Urban and Metropolitan Zones of Influence (MIZs), Canada, 2001

Urban and Metropolitan Influence Zones	Population 65+ No.	Concentration of Seniors			
		65–74 %	75–84 %	85+ %	65+ %
Strong MIZ	192,855	7.56	3.98	1.11	12.65
Moderate MIZ	361,105	8.83	5.29	1.68	15.80
Weak MIZ	283,470	7.64	5.02	1.74	14.40
No MIZ	27,555	7.24	4.65	1.50	13.39
ALL RURAL MIZs	864,985	8.06	4.85	1.55	14.45

Source: Census of Canada, 2001.

distance and/or accessibility of areas that surround metropolitan areas (CMA) and urban agglomerations (CAs). They are called "metropolitan and urban zones of influence" or MIZs. These zones provide another perspective on rural seniors.

The four MIZ zones in total are similar but not identical to the rural areas referred to above, but they do not include the northern territories.[26] All rural/non-urban CSDs are subdivided by the degree of influence on them of cities and metropolitan areas in their region. The four zones of influence – Strong, Moderate, Weak, and No Influence – are defined by the extent of job commuting from the rural area to the CMA and/or CA. Much commuting takes place in the Strong zone and none in the No Influence zone. In effect, these zones reflect increasing distance from the urban centre. Estimates by Statistics Canada indicate that the Strong MIZ extends 20–40 kilometres outward from a city or urban cluster, the Moderate MIZ extends 40–80, the Weak MIZ 80–150, and the No Influence MIZ is considered to be those areas over 150 kilometres from the urban centre.[27] This allows one to examine the distribution and concentration of rural seniors at varying distances from large urban centres.

Table 3.11 reveals that most rural seniors are apt to be found in communities located at some distance away from metropolitan

ANALYTICAL NOTE ON DEFINING RURAL: It is important to recognize that the size, growth, and distribution of the rural seniors' population given in the sections above is always, of necessity, an estimate. It depends, first of all, upon which definition of "rural" is used when analyzing census data, and there are several.[28] The main definition used here closely follows the "Census Rural Area" approach wherein the "population living in places of 1,000 people or less" is considered rural. For our purposes, the populations of all small towns between 1,000 and 9,999 have also been included. The latter are considered part of the fabric of rural Canada and therefore necessary to provide a more complete picture.[29] This definition also ensures that the focus is kept on the community level.

A different issue is whether data remains constant from one census to the next. Rural areas and their populations are the *residual* of the total for Canada *after* urban areas and their populations have been subtracted. Thus, when urban areas expand into adjacent rural areas (physically and/or by economic influence), there is a shift from the rural to the urban totals. This enduring problem persists regardless of the definition of rural that is used.

and/or urban areas. The Moderate and Weak MIZs, in the 40–150 kilometre range, are home to three-quarters of rural seniors. Just under one-quarter live in communities adjacent to urban and metropolitan areas. Few seniors reside in communities located more than 150 kilometres from a metropolitan area, essentially the northern fringes of the larger provinces.

Overall, rural seniors in the MIZs have higher concentrations in all age groups than the Canadian averages for 2001, although there are noticeable differences between the zones. The highest concentrations of rural seniors are found in communities within the Moderate and Weak MIZ zones; both are well above the Canadian average in all senior age groups. There are lower concentrations in all senior age groups in the zone in closest proximity to urban and metropolitan areas, which reflects the presence of generally younger population also living there who find it possible to commute to work in the city.

ASSESSING COMMUNITY CONTEXTS

Canadian seniors live in communities that range from metropolitan areas of several million people to hamlets of a few dozen inhabitants, and each is unique in its geography and community composition. However, the distribution of seniors among the various types of communities is not uniform, as the data below from the 2001 census show:

- 77% of all Canada's seniors live in 400 urban centres while 23% live in more than 7,000 rural towns and villages.
- 79% of urban seniors live in 27 metropolitan areas while 21% live in 373 smaller cities and large towns.
- 82% of rural seniors live in 1,760 small and large towns while 18% live in more than 5,000 villages, hamlets, and the countryside.
- 23% of Canada's seniors live in rural regions that comprise 96% of the nation's land area while 77% live in urban areas that comprise the remaining four percent.

Portrayed here are two general contexts for Canada's seniors. One is centred on a few hundred urban places where most seniors live and which normally have a broad array of community supports. Against this is a context that is very spread out spatially and involves many thousands of small communities that usually have limited arrays of support. The North, which was singled out in the previous chapter, is the epitome of the second type of community context. It is not, however, the only part of Canada in which this community context is prevalent. The bulk of the area encompassed by the southern provinces, arguably 90 percent, falls within this category as well. Such a dichotomy of situations, and the variety within each, necessitates greater awareness of the kinds of local environments seniors contend with.

To be more sensitive in this regard, one needs to assess how well communities enable seniors to achieve independence. Two sets of factors can assist in this. The first is a set of *geographic* factors associated with a community's site, its situation relative to other centres, and its kind of physical development that establish basic parameters for the community context. The second is a set of *community* factors that provide the substantive basis for independent living. Each is discussed below within the perspective that seniors' independence is about being able "to carry out life's activities within a normal community setting."[30]

Geographic Contextual Factors

Four geographic characteristics of a community can impinge on the ability of seniors to realize independence in their daily lives: size of population, relative location to other places, site topography, and density of population. These four factors comprise a good deal of the "physical environment" which Lawton described in path-breaking work almost four decades ago.[31]

Size of Population: Obvious though it may seem, the size of population of a community accounts for the presence of facilities and services that make it possible for seniors to carry out their daily activities. As a general rule, the larger the population is, the greater the number and variety of facilities and services available. This covers commercial and social as well as public and private amenities. Having a large population means, for example, a greater number and variety of stores, housing, hospitals and parks; in addition, it means more modes of transportation to access them.

Relative Location: Although smaller communities have fewer attributes that contribute to seniors' independence, this lack may be overcome by utilizing services in larger places. This depends, of course, on whether better-equipped communities are accessible, not only being within reasonable distance but also having the means of transportation available to reach them. The matter of relative location may also be relevant in large communities. Facilities located in the core city of a metropolitan area may not be readily accessible to seniors who live in the farthest suburbs, for example, or even to those located nearby if they no longer drive.

Site Topography: Accessibility to the facilities and services which seniors desire may also be a matter of concern within communities whose sites are hilly. This is because many seniors prefer to conduct their daily activities by walking. It has been found, for example, that when walking routes exceed a five percent grade, far fewer seniors will walk to their destination.[32] This may be offset by the availability of other forms of transport. Winter conditions may further exacerbate problems of mobility for both senior walkers and drivers in communities with variegated topography.

Density of Population: The population density of a community may affect the number and location of facilities seniors need to access. In lower density situations, the tendency is to centralize facilities and services in fewer locations. This happens at both ends of the size spectrum: suburbs and rural regions. Low-density settlement, urban or rural, also means fewer people nearby to provide direct household support or even the informal assistance of neighbours. It also means longer distances to travel for mobile services such as home nursing and homemaker services.

Community Contextual Factors

In addition to geographical factors, which establish a physical framework for community functioning, there are three community factors necessary for seniors to realize and maintain independence: (1) Housing, (2) Transportation, and (3) Community Supports. These three factors were introduced in chapter 1 and portrayed in Figure 1.1; they are elaborated further in chapter 7.

Housing: Housing has been called the "most fundamental symbol of independence" for the elderly.[33] A senior's home is both a "base of operations" and a haven from the outside world; it provides security and autonomy. Given that an elder's housing needs may change as changes occur in her/his competence or through loss of a spouse, alternative homes may be needed in a community. The larger the community, the more likely there will be not only more housing but more housing options for seniors. Seniors in small communities faced with the need for alternative housing may have to move away to larger places.

Transportation: Nearly as important as housing to a senior's independence is transportation. In the words of the National Advisory Council on Aging, "transportation means access to health, recreation, and social services," to which should be added commercial facilities, family, and friends.[34] "Transportation" covers all the various vehicular means of movement as well as roads, sidewalks, and footpaths. There will be obviously be more varieties of transportation in larger communities. Topographical conditions may necessitate certain forms or levels of service, as may differing population densities. And transportation may be necessary to overcome distance in situations where communities have few available facilities and services.

Community Support: Although most seniors live in their own homes, this may often not be enough to assure their independence. Transportation is a necessary adjunct, and so are community-based services, including personal support (e.g. meals-on-wheels and homemakers), social support (e.g. home visiting and shopping assistance), health promotion (e.g. fitness programs), and information and referral services. Community supports may also include physical facilities such as a seniors' centre and specially equipped buses to provide door-to-door transportation for those who are frail and disabled.

Community Contexts and Seniors' Independence

The parameters of a community's geographical context – size, location, topography, and density – tend to be fixed, especially in the short- and medium-term. When they can be changed it is usually by broad market forces, government policy, and/or long-term migration tendencies. But community context factors are more malleable and may be deliberately modified to meet seniors' needs for independence. For example, an assisted living centre may be added to the seniors' housing stock in a city, or several units of seniors' housing may be added to the housing in a town. Taxis equipped to convey wheelchairs may be added to the fleet of an urban cab company, or a volunteer driver program may be organized in a rural area. Likewise, respite services to relieve caregiving burdens on family members may be added to the menu of public homemaker services, or a business may be started to provide home-maintenance and repair services to seniors.

The point to grasp here is that the type, level, and variety of supports that a community makes available for seniors should flow from the needs of the elderly who actually live in the community or those nearby. To determine which supports may be needed one must know the characteristics of the seniors to be served. In other words, a profile of each community's seniors is needed to guide such decisions. More will be said about constructing such a profile in chapter 8.

REFLECTIONS

Each one of the community contexts alluded to above is a physical and social environment that imposes a unique set of challenges and opportunities; each imposes its own environmental press. It may be thought that small communities, because of their limited array of resources, always impose a stronger environmental press upon their seniors than metropolitan communities with many resources. But each community's situation must be considered separately. A small town that is compact, level, provided with sidewalks, and has a full complement of commercial and social resources may be much more manageable for seniors than a low-density metropolitan suburb that is hilly and has few sidewalks, especially if its services are accessible only by automobile.

There are three broad implications of the immense variety of community contexts faced by Canadian seniors. First, each of these community situations is now, or will be in the near future, a place where facilitating seniors' independence is an issue. Arguably, every community in the country is, or will be, directly impacted by population aging. Second, every community must be considered as a combination of both its contextual factors and its local population of seniors with its particular attributes. Third, each community setting provides a special context for its senior residents, each of whom, in the conduct of his or her daily activities, reacts to that context in distinctive ways. For some, there will be features that constrain them and make it difficult to adapt; others will overcome these challenges. In short, seniors are not passive in their behaviour: like everyone else, they have a predisposition to interact with their environments and adapt where necessary. Indeed, according to one of the formulators of environmental press, the stimulus of adapting is taken by seniors as a sign of their independence.[35]

In the next two chapters, we shall see the efforts seniors make to conduct their everyday activities and to assert their independence by the choices *they* make.[36] It must also be remembered that neither the physical environments nor the seniors' population are static: they both age and change. Thus, seniors' daily activities and the ease with which the community allows them to be carried out may also change. As we examine the daily lives of seniors and their everyday geography, we should be guided by the following question:

What are the main influences on the patterns of seniors' daily lives?

Dealing With Idle Hands

DAVE J. ANDERSON

I grew up during The Great Depression in a small southern Saskatchewan town at the centre of the province's "dust bowl." Being poor in those disastrous times greatly influenced my later life with traits of resourcefulness, independence, initiative, curiosity, and unflinching optimism. At a 1986 pre-retirement seminar I was bemused over one participant's woeful plea: "I'll be a nobody when I retire." However, I had learned from my Mother that idle hands would get me into trouble, so my retired life has had rare moments of inactivity.

So, after retirement at age sixty, keeping my head busy became important, believing as I do that it contributes to my overall health. Early on, my wife and I committed ourselves to volunteer church work for several years until we found more Christianity outside organized religion than inside, so we busied ourselves elsewhere. In 1976, I had taught myself the craft of stained glass, and many lamps and windows grace our home and those of my children and step-children. With twenty-three grandchildren, the need for study lamps prolongs the hobby. Later, with the aid of trifocals, counted cross-stitch became an interest. Its detailed work is done in lieu of falling asleep watching television interlaced with countless minutes of advertisements, time that I put to better use.

I have had two post-retirement love affairs: the first flourished for seven years aboard our twenty-five foot sailboat "Idyll," cruising amongst the Gulf Islands. When my agility deteriorated so that sailing her single-handedly was no longer an option, I jilted her. The other more enduring and exciting liaison has been with my camera. Always a picture-taker, it was in 1988 that I learned how to make photographs. Nothing pleases me more than, at dawn's first light, to capture on film the wonders of nature. And, rather than store my images under a bushel basket in the basement, I felt they should be shared. So I produced a number of two-projector, slide-sound dissolve shows, and now show them to camera clubs, church and volunteer groups, service clubs, fraternal organizations and in retirement homes several times a month in Victoria and on BC's Lower Mainland. Since 1997, my audiences have totaled more than five thousand viewers. Currently, I am writing my memoirs, and the first of two volumes, "To Get the Lights," about my experiences helping to electrify rural Saskatchewan, is with my editor and, hopefully, will be published in 2005.

My physical being was compromised in 1988 with a pacemaker and since then arthritis, plus the usual aches and pains of an 80-year-old, make some days problematic. They are sobering mortality reminders the end may be close, but those thoughts are dismissed as I don't have the time for that right now. While there is a present need to rest more often, my days are jammed with jaunts to visit family and, with my hobbies, I wish on some days there were a couple more hours than the prescribed twenty-four.

DAVE ANDERSON, born in 1925, was raised and educated in Saskatchewan. He volunteered and served two years in Canada's navy, was 19 when WWII ended. He and Betty, his second wife, moved to Victoria, BC in 1986 after he retired from the Saskatchewan Power Corporation as its vice president, public affairs, a post he attained after rising through the ranks from a junior clerk. He is an accomplished photographer among many other retirement activities. His memoir was published in 2005.

Part Two

How Seniors Use Community Space

Chapter Four

Daily Life in Later Life[1]

Seniors frequently complain about being "too busy." Younger adults engaged in full-time work or education might tend to discount this claim. They believe seniors must have ample time since they no longer need to do paid work and their families have left home. Yet, as one Canadian study of seniors' daily lives concluded: "the elderly spend more time than the employed population in all activities, save paid work."[2] Seniors' lives are full for they, like their younger cohorts, have goals, needs, and aspirations they wish to attain and now they have time to pursue them. They can moderate the pace of their activities and perhaps also take on new activities involving recreation, hobbies or more extensive visiting. The conduct of these activities generates patterns in the use of space and time, the result of which is a geography of everyday lives.[3] In the case of seniors, this geography is linked to other dimensions of an older person's life: age, health, gender, background, experience, personal resources, marital status and so forth.

In this and the following chapter, the activity patterns and life spaces that comprise the geography of later life are described and assessed. This everyday realm of seniors' activities is complex, has garnered substantial literature, and continues to challenge gerontologists.[4] A grasp of this thinking and research is essential to our understanding of the geography of aging. The following question will prove central as this chapter proceeds:

What components, personal and physical, determine seniors' activities and life spaces?

AGING AND ENVIRONMENT

Despite an extensive literature on the interplay between seniors and their environments dating back more than four decades, a recent study decried "the astonishing paucity of research on the macroenvironments of neighbourhoods, regions, and urban-rural divides that are so significant in structuring experiences of aging."[5] How can we account for this gap? It exists because, while there is agreement on the multi-dimensionality of seniors' experience of the environment, and while much work has been done on the functional side of issues like time-use by seniors, types of activities they participate in, and the spatial mobility of seniors, the integration of these components into an explanatory model remains at the heuristic level. In the sections that follow, both theoretical and empirical approaches are discussed to throw as much light as possible on the daily life of seniors.

Theoretical Antecedents

The first social scientists to take an interest in the patterns of seniors' daily lives were psychologists working on life course studies in the 1950s and 1960s. Others took up issues of behaviour and aging, and the field of social gerontology was well established by the 1970s. The major achievement of this period was the formulation of the "Ecological Theory of Aging," which is described below. The 1980s saw more empirical work on aging and environments, some by the present author; it is described here and in chapter 5. However, the paucity of contemporary research in this field means one is often dependent upon older studies that may seem dated. Several recent attempts to correct this situation acknowledge the inherent validity of past work while calling for a revival of effort to confirm it and enlarge on it.[6] Every effort has been made here to use only those materials that reflect current conditions in seniors' lives, regardless of their date of publication,

THE LIFE COURSE PERSPECTIVE

In the 1960s, psychologists started focusing on behavioural changes occurring in the life course of older adults. Of special interest at the time were those changes that might arise with retirement from employment. Like the end of active parenting, which also came in for attention, retirement represents the discontinuation of important social roles and the activities that go with them, e.g. the daily trip to work or driving children to school. How seniors might respond behaviourally to these changes in previous daily activities drew forth several different formulations:

· Seniors gradually *withdraw* from various middle-age activities because of reduced competence,[7]
· Seniors *maintain* activities in order to preserve continuity,[8]
· Seniors *substitute* new activities for those foregone,[9] or
· Seniors *include* all the above means of adjustment in seeking a "successful" retirement.[10]

The latter view found the most favour because (1) seniors differ in their experience of and response to these life course changes, and (2) seniors often employ several strategies in adjusting to later life, for example withdrawing from some activities and adding new ones. Subsequent research concentrated on either the amount of time seniors spend on leisure activities or the type of activities comprising that time. Generally, it was found that while time spent in paid work ended upon retirement, the amount of time spent on other activities (e.g. volunteering, hobbies, shopping, watching TV, reading, and sleeping) increased. We return to the results of these studies later in the chapter.

THE ECOLOGICAL PERSPECTIVE

In the 1970s, an interest in environmental and cognitive psychology emerged. The focus initially was on seniors' responses to nursing homes and housing projects but it later included urban environments. The most notable work is that of Lawton and Nahemow, which was introduced in chapter 1. Their "Ecological Theory of Aging," presented in 1973, draws upon the notion that human beings and the physical environment in which they conduct their activities form an interdependent and interactive system.[11] Further, as in natural ecosystems, the components need to adapt to one another's presence so each can maintain its integrity and co-exist.

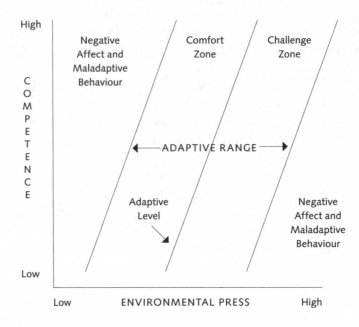

Figure 4.1   Ecological Model of Environmental Press
(After Nahmenow 2000)

In the senior-environment system we are addressing, it is the senior who is mostly called upon to adapt, since physical environments are difficult to change, at least in the short run.

Every environment, whether a room, dwelling, park, bus, or mall, makes a behavioural demand called *environmental press* to which one must respond. A senior may respond to an environment's press by adapting to it, but whether and to what degree that adaptation occurs depends upon the competence of that individual (see Figure 4.1). Moreover, a senior's competence goes beyond her/his physical capabilities such as strength, agility, endurance, or sight. Lawton viewed competence as comprising several factors including "biological health, sensorimotor functioning, cognitive functioning, and ego strength."[12] These factors relate to physical health, psychological outlook, and social norms.

Four points need to be made regarding person-environment relations:

1   The environment's press can be too high or too low for a
    senior, no matter how high his/her competence, thereby
    leading to either stressful or boring outcomes and a
    reduced sense of well-being (i.e. falling to the left or right
    of the Adaptive Range in the diagram).

2   Environments do not remain static: new buildings appear
    while others are modified, once-quiet streets become busy
    and so forth, thereby requiring new learning and a further
    period of adaptation (i.e. the Adaptive Ranges broadens or
    narrows).

3   The time dimension needs always to be considered in
    relation to this model. For example, people's competence
    changes not only with increasing age but also in response
    to changes in the environment and according to the time
    of day or the season of the year. Even social contexts such
    as attitudes toward the elderly may change, resulting in
    seniors encountering greater or less environmental press at
    different times.[13]

4   Competence derives from psychological and social attri-
    butes as well as physical functioning. Thus, a question
    faced by an elderly person in winter such as "is the trip
    necessary, given the icy conditions?" invokes a senior's
    perception of the environmental press as well as her/his
    personal needs and preferences and, not least, the impor-
    tant matter of her/his *choice* (i.e. level of competence is a
    product of several factors).

When a senior carries out a daily activity, it has both an objective
and a subjective dimension. The objective side includes measurable
qualities such as the senior's age, health, gender, education, marital status, and even the time available for the activity. The subjective side comprises relatively non-measurable aspects such as the
senior's needs and preferences and his or her perceptions both of the
activity's meaning and the satisfaction to be gained by participating in it. Furthermore, people bring personal experience and social
norms, gained through socialization and acculturation in their life
course, into the decision to carry out an activity, and this intro-
duces a further set of factors, a consensual set, into the assessment

of seniors' activities.[14] These aspects are the shared expectations or rules regarding activities by which others evaluate such activities. All three aspects – objective, subjective, and consensual – are necessary to measure and analyze seniors' daily activities. The interrelations of these various aspects, adapted from a model by Lawton, are illustrated in Figure 4.2 later in this chapter.[15]

ACTIVITY PATTERNS IN LATER LIFE

Knowing about the everyday activities of older people can be helpful in at least two important ways. First, the activities seniors choose to participate in represent a selection from a wide array of possible activities. In other words, these are the activities in which seniors wish to invest time and effort, activities that reflect their personal goals, priorities, and preferences.[16] These activity choices give shape to a senior's everyday geography by way of the spatial patterns generated in their pursuit – their life spaces. For example, the spatial patterns of shopping activities will likely differ from those involving outdoor leisure activities or visiting. Second, seniors' daily activities reflect the environments and the press they encounter in that environment as well as the personal resources they may need to call upon. In this way, the activities they are able to participate in and the time spent on them give structure to seniors' daily lives.[17]

Activity patterns are bound by two broad dimensions: *space* and *time*. Each of these dimensions may either limit the number and type of activities or afford more and different activities for a senior to participate in. Thus the number and type of activities in which a senior can participate will be affected by the length of time needed for each one and/or the distance to be traveled going to and from it. One can choose to spend time at an activity and/or getting to and from it. The three "universal principles" that govern activity patterns operate for seniors as they do for everyone else. That is to say:

· There are only 24 hours in a day
· No one can be in more than one place at a time
· No one can move simultaneously from one place to another.[18]

To understand how and where seniors spend their 24 hours requires a concern with (1) the nature of the activities being carried out, (2) the time spent in the various activities, and (3) the spatial reach involved.

TYPES OF ACTIVITIES

Seniors are busy, as we have said. Three primary types of everyday activities are usually included in studies of seniors and their activities. First are those activities that pertain to basic personal maintenance and survival, which gerontologists call Activities of Daily Living, or ADL. They include bathing, other personal care, and eating. Second are those activities needed to support daily lives, which are called Instrumental Activities of Daily Living, or IADL. They include shopping, household chores, obtaining health care, and walking or driving to these activities. Third are those activities involving personal need and preference that are frequently called Leisure Activities. This category, as one might imagine, can contain a wide variety of social, recreational, spiritual, and intellectual, activities both indoors and out. The rationale for inclusion in this category is that the activity be *discretionary,* as distinct from those *obligatory* activities in the first two categories. Social activities such as talking to and visiting people or helping them are often included in a separate, fourth category. Sometime resting during the day and sleeping during the night are considered yet two more types of activity. Finally, some studies make provision for engagement in paid or volunteer work.[19]

ACTIVITY DURATION

Every activity in which a senior participates consumes a portion of his/her available time. Since this time is finite, seniors make choices about how to spend it. By obtaining a record of the time seniors spend on various activities, one is provided with a sense of their priorities for "investing" or "budgeting" time. Appropriately named, "time-budgets" are the methodological tools used for this purpose. We know, for example, that the amount of time spent on paid work decreases dramatically after retirement and the amount of time spent on household, sleeping, and free time activities increases. But how does this reallocation of time show up in the lives of seniors of different ages, gender, living arrangements, and health status? On the objective level, health status is the most important determinant in an older person's life as to how much time is spent on which activities, especially among those who are physically or cognitively impaired.[20] On the subjective level, the key is whether the activity is liked or disliked, regardless of the amount of time spent on it. Here, the extent of choice among activities is important, with obligatory activities being less in favour than leisure activities. The central feature that has emerged in numerous studies is that seniors are able to have a *choice* not only of activities but also of how much time to spend on them. This signifies to seniors that *they have autonomy and independence*; that they can control their own lives.

SPATIAL REACH OF ACTIVITIES

Seniors' activities of daily living are centred on their dwellings and may extend progressively outward depending upon personal competence, personal needs, and environmental factors. Those activities associated with ADL (e.g. eating, personal care, bathing) almost all take place within a senior's dwelling and require a minimum of functional and cognitive competence and/or the help of another person. (Indeed, those not able to perform ADL usually are able to qualify for nursing home or other assistance and are not included in the observations made here.) IADL, Activities that are instrumental to daily living at home take place in and around the dwelling (e.g. cleaning, repairs, yard work) as well as in the neighbourhood, or even farther afield in the community (e.g. shopping, post office, banking, medical care). Free time, or leisure, activities may also have several spatial realms. For example, they may encompass one's dwelling and yard (e.g. watching TV, gardening, telephoning friends); neighbourhood (e.g. church, seniors' centre, park, coffee shop); community (e.g. visiting friends and family, participating in volunteer activities); and even the larger region (e.g. sporting and cultural events, paid work). Then there are those occasional long-distance trips to what have been called "beyond spaces," to visit family and friends and/or enjoy a vacation.[21]

It has been found that activities such as seeing family, relatives, close friends and neighbours, having fun, and spending free time are most likely to be carried out in areas close to home.[22] The spatial extent, or distance traversed, by a senior to conduct activities beyond his/her dwelling and immediate surroundings depends upon, first, personal competence and background, and second, environmental conditions. Broadly speaking, as people age their competence declines and their daily activities become increasingly confined to their dwellings and neighbourhoods. Nonetheless, this outcome depends upon what the physical and cognitive decrements are and when they occur for the older person, for there is considerable variability among individuals in this regard. The spatial sphere of some activities may have to be limited due to functional decline, but not necessarily *all* activities – or all at the same point in time. Declining ability to walk can be especially limiting to mobility, as can losses in sight and hearing; any or all of these can constrain one to the immediate residential environment.[23] Aspects of one's personal background such as living arrangements, gender, ability to drive, and so on may also enter into the spatial reach of activities.[24] For example, if a senior desires to attend a particular church located in a distant part of the community, her/his activity space will be enlarged; in the same way, a senior living alone whose family or friends do not live nearby may have to travel far to visit them.

A number of environmental conditions can enter into a senior's ability to access activity destinations she/he desires. The most common factors are time of day, weather, traffic, perceived risks to safety, available transportation, and needed facilities and services being available locally.[25] Among the ways that time of day, weather and traffic affect seniors who drive are the following: older drivers prefer not to drive at night, in peak traffic, or in bad weather.[26] Indeed, older people in general travel less at night whether driving themselves, taking public transit, or walking.[27] The availability of transportation is a key factor for seniors, and it is multi-faceted factor. For example, whether the senior is able to make the trip unaccompanied, whether walking or driving, involves personal competence. But these competencies also call forth the question of availability of other means of transportation. If one is unable to drive, is public transport available? Are bus stops within walking distance? Are there sidewalks? Does the terrain permit walking? And, if one is unable to walk long distances or is wheelchair bound, is transportation available by mini-bus or taxi?

Added to these factors affecting seniors' activity patterns is the nature of the local land use pattern. If needed services (e.g. grocery stores, doctor's office, pharmacy) are located in a senior's neighbourhood, he/she may be able to walk to them. This will be most true for seniors who live in densely built up cities and other compact communities. It will be less true for seniors living in metropolitan suburbs where almost all services must be accessed by automobile.[28] As well, there are often no sidewalks in new suburbs. Such services are often absent in small towns, and access to them means driving to a larger centre. Seniors living in the countryside almost always require a ride to obtain needed services, and northern seniors often do not have even this option.

SENIORS' LIFE SPACES

Everyone has a life space: it is the spatial realm in which one habitually lives. One's life space is a complex of familiar objects, people, and places spatially distributed according a set of functions considered meaningful to the person.[29] Further, both the physical dimensions and the content of a person's life space are a concomitant of one's stage in the life course. An individual's life space expands with age and personal development and remains fairly stable into old age when, due to reductions in health, sensory acuity, energy etc., it begins to contract. (Figure 1.2 depicts aspects of this process.)

Modeling Life Spaces

The size and shape of a senior's life space is influenced by his/her level of competence, personal background, personality, individual needs, perceptions of activities, and the physical and social environments the person inhabits. These components of life space are shown in Figure 4.2 in the form of a model adapted from Lawton.[30] The essential point of this model is that the activities in which a senior actually participates are arrived at through a decision-making process. They are mediated and evaluated by various objective [see

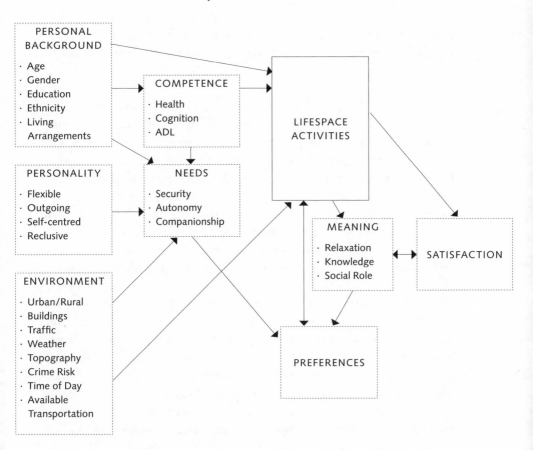

Figure 4.2   Components of Seniors' Life Spaces (After Lawton, 1983)

Personal Background and Environment boxes] and subjective [Personality, Needs, and Preference boxes] factors. This happens in an ongoing, iterative process the senior employs both consciously and unconsciously. Habits are generated and preferences determined for types of activities, their location, the routes taken to carry them out, and the time spent in carrying them out. The resultant life space of a senior may, then, persist for a considerable period until modified by further changes in his/her competence, the environment, her/his needs, or any combination of these factors.

This process of deciding upon which activities to undertake and the resultant life spaces may be grasped more readily by casting

them in terms of the daily lives of seniors. Brief vignettes, portraying daily activities for two anonymous seniors, are provided below
to assist in this:

Vignette No. 1: Ms A is a 79-year-old widow who lives alone in the
home she has lived in for 21 years, which is located in an inner
suburb of a large metropolitan area. Although in relatively good
health, she no longer drives because of vision problems. She still
likes to walk, prepares her own meals, and loves to garden. She
once lived in a nearby suburb and several close friends still live
there. Early on a typical day in the summer, she will walk in her
yard and decide which garden chores need to be done; she would
prefer not to get help with the garden because she enjoys the relax-
ation and sense of accomplishment the chores provide her. In mid-
morning, she walks to the nearby store for groceries and although it
is on a busy street, the traffic is not heavy at that time. She knows,
too, that she is likely to meet other members of her neighbourhood
quilting group also out shopping at that time and can, perhaps,
have coffee with them. After an early afternoon nap, she decides
to visit her close friends who are homebound with various frailties.
She would like to walk there, despite the long distance, in order to
have the physical exercise. However, rain has started and she walks,
instead, to the bus stop, noting also the transfer points she'll need
to use and whether they'll be safe if she can't get home before dark.
Next-door neighbours have invited her to play bridge that evening
but she decides the day has been arduous; so she stays home, telephones her children in a nearby city, and then watches TV.

Vignette No. 2: Mr B is an active 76-year-old who lives in a small
house with his frail wife, aged 75, in a town of 1,000 people in a
rural region. Mr B farmed full-time until six years ago when they
moved to town; he loves curling and still participates, and he is able
to drive. There are only a few stores and service establishments in
their town. The nearest good-sized centre is 58 kilometres away.
On a typical spring day, he rises early; after eating, he helps his wife
with household chores and then checks the progress of the garden.
At 10 AM, he walks to the local café to have coffee with lifelong
buddies, a ritual they have had for many years. Mr B tries not to

Table 4.1   Average Time Spent per Day on Various
Activities by Seniors, Canada, 2005

| | MEN | | WOMEN | |
Activity Group	65–74	75+	65–74	75+
		Hours per day*		
1. Sleeping (night)	8.7	9.1	8.9	9.3
2. Eating	1.4	1.5	1.4	1.3
3. Domestic Chores/Maint.	2.5	2.0	2.5	2.3
4. Shopping	0.9	1.0	0.9	0.7
5. Other Unpaid Work	0.5	0.4	0.7	0.3
6. Leisure Activities				
a) Watching TV	3.6	3.8	3.0	3.4
b) Reading etc.	1.1	1.1	1.1	1.2
c) Physical Leisure	0.7	0.6	0.4	0.3
d) Other Leisure	2.4	2.3	2.6	2.9
7. Paid Work	1.0	–	–	–

* Averaged over a 7-day week.

Source: Statistics Canada, Cat. No.89-622-XIE, no.2.

miss this daily outing both for the companionship and the continued sense of community it imparts to him. After lunch, he drives
his wife to a doctor in the small nearby city; they follow the route
along the river rather than drive on the busy highway. Later, they
meet up with old friends, have an early supper with them, and drive
home before dark. Mr B walks to the local curling rink to watch a
tournament for a couple of hours while his wife reads a novel the
town librarian recommended.

Activities over an Average Day

Time budgets provide an analytical means for determining the
array of activities that comprise a senior's day. A major study of
how Canadians of various ages use their time in an average day
was conducted in 2005 as part of Statistics Canada's General Social
Survey.[31] Data from this study are presented in Table 4.1; they dis-

tinguish time use by gender and then by age groups 65-74 and 75 and older.

An average senior's day comprises three broad segments: sleeping, domestic activities, and leisure activities. Sleeping takes up about 37 percent of daily time, domestic activities about 20 percent, and leisure activities about 32 percent. These shares of daily time use are similar for both women and men in both age groups. There are differences, however, between the two age groups. Older seniors devote more time to sleeping and slightly less time to domestic and leisure activities than those younger than 75. With increasing age, there is also a noticeable shift from active leisure activities to passive ones (e.g. watching TV). As expected, seniors tend not to be engaged in paid work except some men in the 65–74 age range. Seniors of both age groups engage in various forms of unpaid work e.g. grandparenting, volunteering, and support to other seniors, though this to decreases with age.

These are, of course, average time expenditures for seniors and, as we always need to remind ourselves, there is considerable diversity among individuals. Hence, a wide distribution of actual time expenditures is to be expected, especially among leisure activities. For example, some seniors continue to perform paid work such as managing their family businesses or developing home-based businesses. Others are very active in community activities while still others, who are frailer, may need to spend considerable time resting. The available time use data for seniors, unfortunately, do not allow one to know whether there are strong variations among regions, income groups, and/or ethnic groups.[32]

The data that are available have several implications for the shape and extent of seniors' life spaces:

- About 80 percent of a senior's waking hours (i.e. excluding nighttime sleeping) are spent on activities in and around the home. This involves 12 hours daily, on average, and includes personal care, eating, watching TV, reading, and other passive leisure.
- About 20 percent of a senior's waking hours, about three to four hours on an average day, are spent on activities that extend into the proximate neighbourhood and community. This includes shopping, civic and volunteer work, active

recreation, visiting friends and family, providing support to other seniors, and physical activities.

· Senior men spend more time in discretionary activities, such as sports like curling and bowling, than senior women and thereby have the opportunity to establish more extensive life spaces.

· With increasing age, the activities that take a senior out of the home decline and passive leisure increases.

One might expect seniors' activities to decline with increasing age. This would be true for the number of free-time activities, but not in the time spent on them, according to another Canadian study.[33] In other words, older seniors spend more time on fewer leisure activities, especially physically active ones, compared to younger seniors. With increasing age, people do not withdraw from daily activities so much as they "restructure" their behaviour, with trade-offs and substitutions among activities. As a consequence, the extent of seniors' daily life spaces, their geographic reach, is constrained. This does not preclude continuing to travel long distances for family visits and vacations well into their final years. In the end, the extent of a senior's life space depends upon his/her propensity to go far afield as well as the ability to do so.

PARAMETERS OF SENIORS' EVERYDAY GEOGRAPHY

Most seniors are active, mobile people; they are out and about in their communities and regions right into late life. And as a recent report on Canadian seniors says, "There is more to community mobility than simply getting from one place to another."[34] The mobility of seniors, as they trace their everyday geography, will be explored in this section in regard to both "getting from one place to another" and the non-spatial aspects that are associated with it.

THE WALKING OPTION

In our automobile-oriented society, walking is often overlooked. But it is a major means of pursuing activities, especially for the very young and the very old, out of necessity for the former but out of choice for a majority of seniors. This is because walking is valued both for the healthful exercise it provides and the sense of accomplishment it represents. Earlier studies estimated that 50–70 percent of mobile seniors walked to neighbourhood stores and facilities two or three times per week.[35] Furthermore, the maximum distance they preferred to walk (one-way) was four to six blocks, or the equivalent of 400–600 metres.[36] These numbers are appropriate for seniors today as well.

There are several factors that can modify seniors' walking patterns. One of these is the *destination*. Generally, the shortest trips are to grocery stores, drug stores, parks, and coffee shops, because these places are frequented most often. Walking trips to banks, churches, seniors' centres, and doctors' offices, which are less frequent, may be longer. Destinations that exceed the normal walking distance may be supplemented by taking the return trip by bus or taxi, or getting a ride back.

Another factor that may influence whether someone chooses to walk or not is the *attractiveness* of the destination and of the neighbourhood that must be traversed. In other words, if the destination is worth walking to and the route is pleasant and familiar, seniors will choose to walk to it, even if it is far away.[37] The *gradient* of the route (steepness, slope) is also important in determining whether seniors will want to walk (see Figure 4.3). A grade of five percent (i.e. a gain of five metres in elevation in every 100 metres) is usually too steep for most seniors, but this will also depend on the length of the walk, and how much of it is on the level.[38] The matter of gradient also comes up in considering whether to walk to a transit stop to make a longer journey, and therefore needs to be considered when locating transit routes and stops.

Finally, *conditions* such as the time of day, prevailing weather, surfaces of roads and sidewalks, and traffic intensity are other factors seniors take into account when considering whether to walk. Sidewalks and roadways in poor condition may increase the risk of falls, especially for people with physical impairments. Closely related to these considerations are *fears for personal safety*. Fears of falling or of injuries from traffic, dog bites, and so on keep many seniors close to home.[39] Often, too, it is the perception of such risks in areas with deteriorated buildings, litter, graffiti, homeless people, or other features like bushes, low lighting, and tunnels that

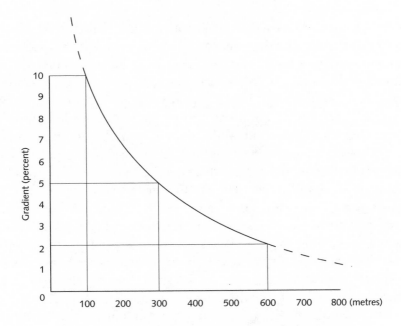

Figure 4.3   Effect of Gradient on Seniors' Walking Distance
(Source: Wilson 1980)

deter walking.[40] While these concerns may seem to apply mainly to seniors in urban situations, they are also applicable to seniors who live in small towns.

SENIORS' FALLS AND PEDESTRIAN ENVIRONMENTS

Falls are a widespread problem among seniors. They are the most frequent cause of seniors being admitted to hospital each year and the sixth leading cause of death in the elderly.[41] In Toronto, in 1999, it was reported that nearly 5,000 seniors were admitted annually to hospital as a result of falls.[42] A study of falls by seniors in Victoria estimated that 69 percent of falls happened outside the home.[43] Moreover, the most frequent sites for falls in public places were, in order of occurrence, sidewalks, crosswalks, curbs, and roads; the reasons ranged from uneven surfaces to icy conditions, and concrete surfaces were by far the most likely to have been involved.[44]

People fall for a variety of reasons that relate to their level of personal competence or the level of environmental press they meet, or a combination of both. If, for example, a senior has limited vision, walks with a cane, or has poor balance, stepping off or mounting curbs and monitoring traffic at a crosswalk make the environment more demanding for him/her. If curbs are not ramped at corners, signal lights too short, sidewalks uneven, or steps unevenly spaced, a high level of competence is needed to negotiate them. Some seniors may avoid these difficult environments, others may be able to adapt, and still others may try to contend with the risks. Like other activity situations, the factors involved are objective, subjective, and consensual. Senior women are more at risk to fall than senior men; those with a history of falls are prone to more falls, and those with sensory or cognitive impairment have a high risk of falling. Subjective factors such as one's tendency to take risks or to hurry when walking can also be implicated in falls.

Brief mention needs to be made of the mobility situation facing seniors who use wheelchairs. About five percent of Canadian seniors are wheelchair users; further, they tend to be those who suffer from several frailties and live alone.[45] Although they are relatively few in number, their mobility is constrained to a greater degree than that of other seniors. The pedestrian impediments listed above become greater problems for the wheelchair-bound and also for those seniors using other assistive devices such as canes, walkers, and scooters.

NIGHTTIME ACTIVITIES

Considerable numbers of seniors undertake nighttime activities: one major study found that well over one-third of seniors were out in their community in the evening once or more times per week.[46] However, as already indicated, many seniors restrict their out-of-home activities after dark. The reasons for this include personal factors such as reduced night vision, practical considerations such as available transportation, and perceptual factors such as fear of crime.

On the surface it might seem as if objective factors (e.g. an individual's visual acuity, frailty, gender) or environmental factors (e.g.

lighting, weather) are the prime impediments of nighttime activity. While these factors do enter into seniors' decisions to pursue activities after dark, they have little effect on these decisions. Among the primary reasons for differences in seniors' nighttime activity patterns are subjective and/or consensual factors: the fear of crime and the psychological meaning attributed to evening activities. That is, those seniors who are active at night have, on the one hand, a strong disposition to seek the stimuli of evening activities (e.g. concerts, theatre, entertainment, socializing) and, on the other hand, strong feelings about being in control of their lives that make them able overlook possible dangers at night.[47] In addition, the availability of transportation at night (an objective environmental factor) can be a strong impediment (or advantage) to nighttime activity. On the negative side this may take several forms such as there being no vehicle available in the household, the absence of public transit, or greatly reduced transit service at night, all of which may make the option of walking impractical and/or dangerous.

The fear of crime has long been identified as an important factor deterring many seniors from participating in nighttime activities, especially those in cities.[48] The likelihood of seniors being confronted by criminal acts, it may be argued, is small, and getting smaller as crime rates drop in Canadian cities.[49] Indeed, the fear of crime among seniors and others is recognized as being more widespread than crime itself, for reasons that are not yet clear.[50] Nonetheless, fear such as this invokes environmental press for many seniors, and decreases their opportunity to participate in after-dark activities in the city. And whether these fears are due to a fear of victimization or are an indicator of the quality of the urban environment, seniors have manifested them extensively. City planners need to pay attention to details such as street lighting, sidewalks, and the design and location of bus stops, if they wish to reduce seniors' anxieties regarding nighttime activities.[51]

MEANING AND COMMUNITY MOBILITY

When it comes to community mobility, or "getting around" as seniors would say, objective factors have always been the easiest to comprehend: the *who, what, where,* and *how* of such trips.

More problematic has been the "why" – the *meaning* (or meanings) involved with making any trip. The grocery-shopping trip is clearly necessary for survival, but how do we interpret those two or three trips every day spent in leisure activities outside the home? Such travel is an activity in itself and culminates in another activity at the destination, both of which will have personal relevance to the individual senior.

A study of elderly women in Winnipeg (reported in 2002) provides useful insights into seniors' mobility.[52] In addition to travel to conduct IADL activities and participate in recreational and leisure activities, these senior women embarked on trips around the city to fulfill *social obligations*. These trips had a special meaning in their lives and included visiting spouses in nursing homes, attending weddings and funerals, visiting sick friends and relatives, and going to cemeteries. Although these trips were not frequent, their cancellation caused significant "worry and concern." The importance placed on these trips reveals the underlying personal meaning of mobility. Moreover, in addition to helping them maintain their sense of identity and relationship, such journeys also gave these women *independence* and a *sense of control* over their lives.[53] When they experienced limitations on their mobility such as not being able to drive and/or having to depend on family members and others for rides, they felt they were being a *burden* on others: something they did not wish to be.

Yet another factor called "risk perception" influenced the mobility of these women.[54] It involves risks the women *perceived* as being associated with their trips about the city that, in turn, influenced the choices they made about the conditions under which they would travel. Two types of perceived risk were identified: (1) continuous, familiar risks and (2) unpredictable risks (see Figure 4.4). The first type included knowledge of unsafe conditions in one's neighbourhood and awareness of one's physical and cognitive shortcomings and had little or no influence on their mobility: because they knew about these risks, they could plan their trips accordingly. However, the second type, the unpredictable risks, did influence mobility in the community. These centred on three aspects of travel around the city: the possible advent of bad weather, uncertainties posed by trips after dark, and possible confrontations with strangers. The

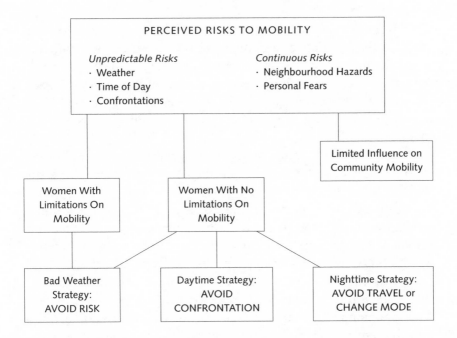

Figure 4.4   Mobility Coping Strategies of Women Seniors
(Adapted from Finlayson and Kaufert, 2002, with permission)

women developed various coping strategies either to minimize these perceived risks or to avoid them altogether. This might involve not traveling at all, say, in bad weather or after dark (which was the prevalent response of those with mobility limitations), or using a different mode of travel such as a taxi or traveling with a friend.

THE MEANING OF PLACE

Everyone has attachments to the places they have lived, to their dwelling, neighbourhood, and/or community. These physical spaces in one's life carry meanings that are constructed out of layers of memory and association: they become *places* as well as *spaces*.[55] For seniors, given their tendency to reside for long periods of time in the same dwelling, the attachment to places is usually very strong.

The layers of meaning about their home and neighbourhood accumulate over the years and reinforce seniors' sense of attachment.[56] The attachment results from many factors: the familiarity they have with their locale from knowing and routinely traversing its space, the social relations that get built up with neighbours and shopkeepers and, not least, the sense of identity and stability that the setting imparts.[57]

Home, especially, comes to acquire a special meaning, to become more than mere shelter. It becomes the key link between the senior and his/her larger environment. Looked at in this way, the notion of "aging in place" takes on additional meaning. It is not simply the expression of inertia or maintaining a status quo. It reflects an on-going relationship – an active *transaction* – between a senior and her/his residential environment that is characterized by changes over time of both the person and the home.[58] Dwellings may fall into disrepair, neighbours may move, or a spouse may have to go to a nursing home: these are just a few of the changes that may occur even though the physical location of the senior remains the same. Thus, attachment to a place is a process that continues throughout a senior's lifetime.[59] It is important to incorporate a temporal perspective in thinking about seniors aging in place so that older persons' transactions with their environments fit with their life course needs.[60]

REFLECTIONS

This chapter began our exploration of the shape and structure of seniors' activities and the everyday geography that emerges in their lives. It has moved us away from viewing seniors' communities from the *outside* toward a view of the community as seniors experience it – from the *inside*. Instead of variables such as population size, age composition, urban type, and location, the community perspective obliges us to recognize a milieu that comprises homes, friends, social ties, and grocery stores, as well as day and night, and good and bad weather. Still, it is some distance from seniors' actual daily lives to be looking at activity patterns, life spaces, and the reach of activities. This is the inevitable dialectic that arises between the observer and the observed, not only in research about seniors but also in those mundane instances in our own lives when we may be visitors or outsiders. Its synthesis lies in realizing that we are all insiders some place, and that those we are observing experience life in much the same terms as ourselves.

Many aspects of seniors' activities touched on above should remind one how complex and multi-dimensional daily life is. The activities in which one engages, for example, not only require one to be physically fit but also involve personal dispositions, needs, and preferences. As we consider the daily life of seniors it is well to remind ourselves that they are *individuals* who have aged into later life.[61] With increasing age the probability increases that some frailty may influence the selection, pace, and difficulty of an activity. But even the same infirmity is not likely to affect all seniors, even those of the same age, in the same way or to the same degree. Differences within age cohorts have shown up persistently in studies of seniors, reminding us that age is only a broad marker of the shape and structure of daily life.[62] Seniors, no less than others, will adapt to the degree that they can to the environmental press they encounter. Some will undertake activities because of the physical challenge, or the social obligation, or both, they need to fulfill. Others will avoid the same activity because of the physical or social risks they perceive. Those seeking to understand activity patterns among older adults should not focus exclusively on competence or vulnerability. Other factors largely unrelated to old age can, and often do, influence their behaviour. Gender is one of these and so are weather conditions, ethnicity, marital status, topography, and transit service.

Lawton and Nahemow's "Ecological Theory of Aging" continues to be a useful perspective through which to consider seniors' everyday geography. Its notion that the elderly person engaging in activities is involved in a "transaction" with his/her environment is borne out time and again in the studies cited above as well as countless others. Thus, each activity a senior wishes to undertake involves a transaction that is, at once, contemplative and overt regarding her/his desire and ability to adapt to the press. Here, again, it is an *individual* senior's attributes and attitudes that will determine the shape and outcome of the transaction. There are, of course, similarities in individual-environment transactions of seniors. (Indeed, the theory itself is proof of this.) Some are associated with age, others with decrements of physical health, and still others with gender, income, or ethnicity, etc. Some come to our notice because of "barriers" in the environment that militate against successful transactions by all seniors or those with certain characteristics. The point to be grasped is that diversity among seniors has to be integral to the stance one takes in examining their daily lives.

In the next chapter, the perspective shifts toward a more holistic view of seniors and their activities within broader community settings. The ideas and concepts cited above, including that of seniors' diversity, will continue to be pertinent. The following question can help maintain that orientation:

What factors enter into the transactions of seniors' daily lives in the community?

Now That She's Away

LLOYD RYAN

Stella Ryan gets out of bed at about 8:30 am and, after morning ablutions, begins to make breakfast. Before she sits at the table, she goes over to the window and looks on to her small patio to see if there are any birds at the feeders. None this morning. It's October. She guesses the birds have gone to warmer climes for the winter. She sort of wishes she could do the same, she tells her almost 85-year-old self.

Stella is living in "her own" apartment in a senior's apartment complex at Marathon, a mining town in western Ontario, on the north western shores of Lake Superior, a long way from the village where she grew up and raised her family on the northern coast of Newfoundland island. She is just five minutes away from her daughter.

She exercises every day by walking through the apartment building, including up the stairs, three times a day. She gets together with some of the other seniors every afternoon for coffee, to play Chinese checkers, or to put together jig-saw puzzles. Almost every evening, a half dozen of them have pot-luck supper together. She reads novels non-stop and continues to write her poetry. When one of the other seniors is not feeling well, she prepares and carries them soup. Her daughter visits almost every day.

Today, on Sunday, she thinks it is too cold to go to church. She'll stay home and read. But she gets up and brushes off her Salvation Army uniform anyhow, just in case she changes her mind. She has been a proud "soldier" of the Salvation Army for almost 71 years! Although staunch in her Calvinist beliefs and religious practice, she has been careful not to impose her beliefs on her children.

Maybe, in the afternoon, her daughter will take her by car to the shopping centre for a coffee. She is planning to suggest that, later on in the month, they go to Thunder Bay – three hours away – for a day of Christmas shopping and stay overnight in a hotel. The phone rings! It's one of her sons in Toronto, just checking in. During the day, she will receive seven or eight other phone calls from her scattered brood. If they don't call her, she'll call them.

Someone is at the door. It's a young man from her home village who works as a miner. He just happened to be in the neighbourhood and dropped in to tell her that his mother is coming from Newfoundland to visit him for a week and she wants to drop over for a cup of tea with Stella. Stella is pleased. A little later, the administrator of the building drops by to check on her. He, also, is from her home village and grew up within sight of her old kitchen window. She is still good friends with his mother, with whom she talks frequently on the phone.

She knows that later on in the day, her 87-year-old sister will telephone her to bring her up to date on the news of home, or her husband's sister will call from the same village. She returns to Newfoundland every second summer for a week or so, but now considers Marathon her home.

STELLA RYAN, 85, was born in the outport of Roberts Arm, Newfoundland, where she lived almost all her life and raised a family of 10 children. She taught herself to read and write, beginning about the age of 38. After her husband passed away, in 1980, she started to write poetry and short stories. At age 70, she learned to operate her daughter's computer and wrote a book about her early life, *Outport Girl*, which sold almost 5,000 copies! She now lives in her own apartment, near one of her daughters, in Marathon, Ontario.

DR LLOYD RYAN, her son, 58, went on from Roberts Arm to earn five academic and professional degrees and pursue a career in public education in Ontario and Newfoundland. He is now in semi-retirement, working on several novels based in early twentieth-century Newfoundland. He lives with his wife, Patricia, in Torbay, Newfoundland.

Chapter Five

Seniors' Community Geography

Seniors' everyday lives unfold as sets of activity patterns and life spaces that encompass the locus of home (with all of its profound meanings) and the larger communities in which they live. Activities that take seniors to different locations, some frequently (as with grocery shopping) and some less frequently (as in visiting the doctor), the routes they take and the modes they use to travel, all teach them the physical form of these spaces. They also experience their community subjectively; locations where activities are carried out and the routes to and from them are infused with feelings.[1] Some of these feelings are communal, because the resources, housing, and modes of travel which seniors use are limited. Other feelings are individual, because each person has different needs, uses, and preferences for these same resources. Thus, each senior's actual geographical experience of his/her community space is different.

The focus of this chapter is a community's space, which consists of its physical facilities and accoutrements in their various arrangements. In the sections that follow, two community environments are explored – the city and the small town. They will act as prototypes of the places where most seniors live in Canada. These prototypes are constructed from a broad array of studies conducted over the past several decades. Thus they are, of necessity, "mosaics" derived from various data from different places and times. They present a rendering of seniors' activity patterns that are indicative rather than substantial. They can, however, provide us with useful perspectives with which to pursue a more coherent view. They also offer the opportunity to assess how well a community's environment facilitates seniors' daily lives. In light of this, a central question for this chapter will be:

How are the transactions of seniors' daily lives facilitated and/or impeded by community environments?

RESOURCE ENVIRONMENTS WITHIN COMMUNITIES

Every community comprises several environments that seniors must negotiate in order to obtain the resources necessary for their daily lives. Lawton pointed this out three decades ago, when he described a community as a "resource environment" for seniors.[2] Every community is a collection of all the physical, cultural, social, and psychological resources available locally to support seniors. (Over and above this is the issue of the sufficiency and accessibility of these resources, to which we shall return later.) In obtaining access to resources, seniors refine and define the community environment in terms that reflect their own needs and perceptions. What occurs is an elaboration of the broad resource environment into four distinctive, but interrelated, domains as follows: (see also Figure 5.1)

· Physical resource environment
· Functional resource environment
· Salient resource environment
· Perceived resource environment

The main characteristics of each environment are described below.

PHYSICAL RESOURCE ENVIRONMENT

This domain is the sum total of *all* resources in a senior's community, whether this is an entire town or city or just an extended neighbourhood. Included here are the physical features of the community such as public and commercial facilities and services (e.g. stores, offices, hospitals, parks, and seniors' centres), the transportation system in all its facets (e.g. roads, transit, and taxis, as well as sidewalks and bus shelters), the communications and utility systems, and the stock of housing by type, affordability, and location. All of these physical features form an interconnected whole. This environment also includes human resources such as family members, friends, and neighbours that, in combination with the physical resources, constitute a baseline of the possible supports for seniors. They can be counted, classified, and located in the community space. They are the resources that are *available* and it is important to know the numbers of resources and their types. However, beyond their availability lie two vital concerns: (1) whether the resources present are sufficient for the seniors who live in the community and (2) whether they are accessible to those seniors.[3]

Availability: The mere presence of an unmediated set of resources in a community at a particular time begs the question of whether these are the kinds of resources actually needed by that community's seniors. Ten to 12 basic facilities and services seniors need most were identified in several early gerontological studies as shown in Table 5.1.[4] Subsequent studies confirm the importance of these resources for seniors' everyday activities.[5] In addition, having many different facilities is not the same as having options for each facility. For example, an urban community with five grocery stores, a bank, four restaurants, three clothing stores, and a drug store, constituting 13 different businesses in all, still has the same number of basic resources – five – as a small town that has only one establishment of each kind. However, the first community provides seniors with greater choice among individual resources. Thus, in defining the dimension of availability it is important to capture both the number of basic resources present and the total number of establishments that constitute these categories. This relationship can be embodied in an *index of availability* as follows:

$$\text{Availability} = \frac{\text{Total no. of establishments offering basic resources}}{\text{Number of basic resources present}}$$

The higher the value of this ratio, the greater the availability of resources in the community *and* the greater range of choice among them. For the example given above, the urban community would

Table 5.1   Basic Resource Facilities and Services Needed by
Seniors in Urban and Rural Communities

Seniors' Resources Needed in Urban Communities*	Seniors' Resources Needed in Rural Communities**
Grocery store	Grocery store
Drug store	Drug store
Bank	Bank
Clothing store	Clothing store
Butcher	Post office
Doctor or clinic	Doctor or clinic
Church (or synagogue)	Church (or synagogue)
Restaurant	Restaurant
Park	Beauty shop/barber
Movie theatre	Social club
Club or organization	Variety store

Sources: * Cantor (1979) for New York City; ** Hodge (1984) for Eastern Ontario.

have an index value of availability of 2.6 and the small town a value
of 1.0.

Accessibility: This dimension deals with the location of basic
resources relative to where seniors live. The measure would be the
preferred distance to these resources by the mode of transportation seniors use. Given the strong propensity for seniors to walk,
the preferred maximum distance (one-way) of four to six blocks or
400–600 metres, as found by studies in New York City and in Eastern Ontario, is adopted here (see Figure 4.3). Caveats are needed
about seniors' walking, of course, in regard to steepness of terrain
and weather conditions. In large communities, alternative modes
include public transit, taxis, and private auto use. Usually in small
communities the only alternative to walking is the private auto.
Whether seniors use autos or transit, it is not so much distance as
time that tends to determine their activities. Studies of both urban
and rural seniors suggest that people prefer services and facilities

they can reach within 15–25 minutes of home.[6] Later in this chapter more detailed examples are provided of how seniors obtain access to basic resources.

Of course, neither availability nor accessibility is a concern in the same way with regard to a senior's human resources such as family members, friends, or neighbours. If such people are identified as support resources, they are, by definition, available. And access to them may be accomplished by telephone or email if distances prove difficult to traverse.

FUNCTIONAL RESOURCE ENVIRONMENT

The domain of those resources that are *actually used* by seniors, individually and/or collectively, is referred to as the "functional resource environment." Effectively, it comprises *all* the resources that a senior finds accessible as well as those he or she utilizes. Its bounds may be the same or smaller than the physical resource environment. This environment is the one in which the senior functions, wherein his/her activity patterns are encompassed. While the measures used here are essentially objective, the outcome reflects personal factors such as competence, gender, and ethnicity (see Figure 4.1). The spatial extent of this environmental domain may change if a senior changes her/his transportation mode(s) to reach resources and/or his or her competence levels change. Bad weather that impedes walking to some resources is an example of both objective and personal factors interacting to affect an outcome in this area. Improved transit service is another example of how a senior's spatial reach may be extended and thereby make a greater number of functional resources accessible.

SALIENT RESOURCE ENVIRONMENT

This environmental domain contains a collection of resources that are especially *valued* by the individual senior. They could include, say, a particular church, a social club, a friend, or a physician to whom he/she feels attached. They may also include the ease of access to services and facilities (e.g. location of bus stops), the amenities of an area (e.g. a local park), and a sense of safety.[7] These resources are "salient" to the individual's needs and values and, thus, form an essential subset of the functional resource environment. They vary, of course, with the individual senior.

PERCEIVED RESOURCE ENVIRONMENT

Seniors, like most people, have a mental picture of the utility and importance of the resources that surround them. Various sources of information (from personal experience, others, and the media) combine with emotional influences to form a "psychological back-drop" against which actual community resources are arrayed and activity patterns are oriented.[8] For example, as we saw in the last chapter, senior women perceived risks in the city and then modi-fied their travel modes and schedules accordingly (see Figure 4.4). Moreover, such perceptions may be very personal and, indeed, are not always accurate. A senior's perception of the environment may be influenced by memories of what the community was like in the past, and some of these memories may be outdated. Changes may have occurred in the physical environment (e.g. new stores or a park or traffic improvements), which long-time residents sometimes overlook (see Figure 4.2). In short, seniors' resources that are con-sidered functional and/or salient are always mediated through per-sonal perceptions as well as through objective means.

THE GEOGRAPHY OF RESOURCE ENVIRONMENTS

From a geographical perspective, the four resource environments that Lawton identified could comprise a set of overlays on a map of the space that encompasses the daily life of a senior. That space could be all or part of a metropolitan area, or a small town and neighbouring towns. Each resource environment reflects a different facet of everyday geography. The first overlay, *physical resources*, identifies and locates all the physical and human resources a senior might be able to access. Next would come the *functional resources* that he/she actually uses. The *salient resources* may then be added to point up the resources the senior highly values. The top layer would show the way in which the senior *perceives* all these various resources (see Figure 5.1). This perspective underlies the following

Perceived
Resources

Salient
Resources

Functional
Resources

Physical
Resources

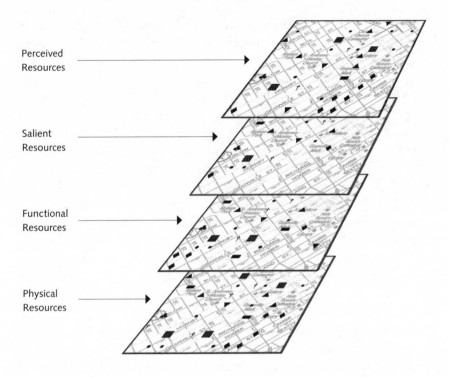

Figure 5.1   Seniors' Resource Environments

sections describing the community geography of first, urban seniors and then, rural seniors.

SENIORS' GEOGRAPHY IN URBAN COMMUNITIES

Most of Canada's seniors are urban dwellers, as we saw in chapter 3. Just over three-quarters lived in urban communities in 2001, or a total of about three million persons aged 65 and older. The urban settings seniors call home range from smaller, independent cities such as Red Deer, AB, and Summerside, PEI, to large metropolitan complexes such as Montreal and Vancouver. Indeed, urban seniors reside mostly in the nation's 27 metropolitan areas – nearly 80 percent of all city-dwelling seniors do so. Half of all urban seniors live in the core cities of their respective metropolitan areas and the rest live in the suburbs (see chapter 3). Several studies conducted some years ago provide "windows" into the everyday geography of seniors who live in metropolitan areas that allow a glimpse of daily life at the community level. The continued importance to seniors of neighbourhood resources and accessibility to them is reiterated in more recent studies.[9] The situation for seniors in central city neighbourhoods is considered first, followed by that in suburban neighbourhoods.

Central City Seniors

The seniors that live in the central, or core, cities of Canadian metropolitan areas share several distinctive characteristics:

- They comprise a higher proportion of their city's population and their level of concentration is higher than for seniors in adjacent suburbs or in the metropolitan area as a whole.
- They tend to be older overall, and concentrations of all seniors' age groups are higher than in the suburbs.
- A much higher proportion of them live alone as compared to suburban seniors.
- Women are a much higher proportion of core city seniors than in the suburbs.

These characteristics affect their activity needs and patterns. For one thing, the fact that so many are 85 and older signals a greater tendency to physical frailty.

SHOPPING GEOGRAPHY

Shopping, or obtaining needed goods, is central to our everyday lives. But obtaining services such as health care, banking, and social and religious services is equally important. For older persons these functions are largely carried out within the neighbourhoods in which they live[10] and which are often considered to be the "central ecological unit" in older person's lives.[11] Early gerontological research undertook to understand seniors' patterns of activities in

ANALYTICAL NOTE ON CENTRAL CITY DIVERSITY: It needs also to be noted that considerable differences can be expected among seniors in the central city, which itself encompasses a variety of environments from high residential densities near the city centre to lower densities, much like the suburbs they adjoin, at the outer edges. For example, within the City of Vancouver it was found that the proportion of seniors living alone ranged from 60 percent in a neighbourhood close to downtown to 20 percent in an outlying neighbourhood.* Similar or even greater variation can be expected in many of the newly enlarged central cities, such as Toronto and Halifax, which now encompass formerly inner and outer suburbs.

* Hodge, Gerald, *The Graying of Canadian Suburbs: Patterns, Pace and Prospects* (Ottawa: Canada Mortgage and Housing Corporation, 1994), 46ff.

their neighbourhoods. Three such studies examined the shopping and services-seeking functions of seniors living in three central city settings: Winnipeg, New York City, and Los Angeles.[12] The basic data derived from these studies comprise the array of activities, the frequency they are undertaken, the distance travelled, and the means of transportation used. Neighbourhoods were self-defined by those living there; in each case they encompassed three to four square kilometres. This relatively small area is indicative of the higher population densities of central cities compared to the suburbs, with the result that stores and services are likely also to be nearby.

The seniors in each of these central city neighbourhoods engaged in approximately the same arrays of activities, with grocery shopping topping the list in all cases. The most used grocery stores were usually nearby and often visited more than once per week. Seniors walked to grocery and other food stores a good deal of the time; this was true for 90 percent of those in Winnipeg and 81 percent of those in New York. The distances walked for groceries varied between one and six blocks, or 100–600 metres. Other stores and services were frequently a greater distance away, although still within the neighbourhood range of 1–2.5 kilometres. Attaining access to these more distant services involved using public transit, driving oneself, or getting a ride. However, if goods and services

Table 5.2   Shopping Patterns of Seniors in Three Central Cities

	Winnipeg	New York City	Los Angeles
Shopping/Service Activities by Frequency of Use	Groceries Clothing Footwear Appliances	Groceries Butcher Drug Store Church/Syn. Park Bank Social Club/Org. Movie Clothing Restaurant Doctor	Groceries Restaurant/Bar Library Clothing Social Club/Org. Medical Clinic Post Office
Spatial Reach Distance Travelled (km)	0.1–2.5 km	0.1–2.1 km	0.1–2.1 km
Transport Modes by Frequency of Use	Walking Bus Car passenger	Walking Bus	Walking Bus

Source: Winnipeg, Smith (1984); New York City, Cantor (1979); Los Angeles, Regnier (1983).

were nearby, seniors preferred walking. A 2002 study found essentially the same spatial parameters among German seniors who, "if they have a supermarket within walking distance," shop in their own neighbourhood.[13] Indeed, up to 75 percent of shopping trips in that study were done on foot or by bicycle.

Each of the foregoing studies revealed additional characteristics of the everyday geography of the seniors involved. The Winnipeg study reported that up to one-third of seniors combined their shopping trips with non-shopping activities such as visiting friends and relatives and/or a favourite restaurant. The New York study identified viable social relations between the elderly and friends and neighbours and, not least, with younger persons in the neighbourhood. These relations provided seniors with help during illnesses, shopping assistance, and social contacts. Personal connections were especially important for those who lived alone.

Additionally, the three neighbourhoods were distinctive in their physical forms as well as in their climates, as one would expect. A major park in the Los Angeles neighbourhood was easily reached and often used for relaxing and socializing. Winnipeg and New York were more likely to face inclement weather in fall and winter, which led seniors to modify their trips by taking the bus rather than walking in those seasons. The New York neighbourhood comprised a diversity of cultures – Jews, non-Jews, African-Americans, and Hispanics – but there were no significant differences in the community geography of the different population groups.

Suburban Seniors

Outside the boundaries of the central city are suburban areas which differ in their age of development, the inner suburbs being the first to experience residential development, followed later by the outer suburbs, and finally by the suburban fringe (see chapter 3 for a detailed discussion). The demographic characteristics of seniors living in the Canadian suburbs tend to parallel the suburbs in which they live. That is to say that the inner suburbs are not only the oldest but also tend to have the largest, and oldest populations; they are followed by the outer suburbs, and the suburban fringe. Suburban seniors, thus:

· Comprise smaller proportions of the total population than central city seniors
· Tend to be younger overall than seniors in the central city
· Are far less likely to live alone as compared to central city seniors
· Have a more equal gender balance than central city seniors

Being generally younger, suburban seniors will also tend to be healthier and less likely to have mobility difficulties compared to central city seniors. They will usually drive to most activities, and of course they need to do so, as we shall see. Cultural diversity does exist among suburban seniors, but less so than in the central city.

Not infrequently, entire neighbourhoods may be home to a single cultural group.

SHOPPING GEOGRAPHY

Shopping for basic necessities and obtaining essential services are important daily activities for all seniors. But while the content of suburban seniors' activities is similar to their central city counterparts, the physical environment is quite different. Most notably, suburban areas are very large compared to core cities (up to 10 times larger) and lower in population densities. To give this some perspective: inner suburbs in the Toronto CMA (using the 1991 definition) have an overall population density that is about 25 percent less than that of the core city, while outer suburbs' density is about 50 percent less, and suburban fringe densities are 80–85 percent less. Similar rates of falloff in density, or even higher ones in some cases, are found in all Canadian CMAs. The effect of this is for suburban neighbourhoods to be larger than city ones, and to get progressively larger toward the fringe leading, as a consequence, to distances between shopping and service facilities and residences being lengthened.

Suburban development and planning since World War II has favoured the clustering of shopping facilities. Plazas and shopping centres have become destinations for shopping and services in the suburban neighbourhoods, in contrast to the more dispersed facilities (including corner stores) available in central cities and older inner suburbs. A study of the grocery-shopping patterns of Winnipeg seniors, some of whom reside in a central city, some in an inner suburb, and some in an outer suburban neighbourhood allows us to compare their community geography.[14] Table 5.3 displays the data regarding seniors' grocery shopping tendencies in each zone. (The central city seniors are the same group referred to in the previous section; see Table 5.2.)

Shopping Opportunities: Seniors living in the three zones have substantially different arrays of stores dispensing groceries. Seniors who live in residential areas adjoining a central business district do not have a chain supermarket within their neighbourhood. On the

Table 5.3   Grocery Shopping Patterns of Seniors in Central City and
Suburban Areas, Winnipeg, 1984 and 1991

	Central City	Inner Suburb	Outer Suburb
PROXIMITY TO GROCERY STORE BY TYPE (KM)			
Chain supermarket	1.60	0.62	1.23
Other supermarket	1.74	0.70	0.78
Dept. store food floor	0.42	1.40	5.02
Corner store/plaza	0.02	0.14	0.42
FREQUENCY OF USE BY GROCERY STORE TYPE (%)*			
Chain supermarket	25	73	57
Other supermarket	4	11	33
Dept. store food floor	54	15	0
Corner store/plaza	17	1	10
TRIP LINKAGES (%)*			
Groceries only	31.5	54.7	37.5
Groceries plus			
Drug store	8.7	14.9	27.4
Bank	30.5	5.5	10.5
Social purpose	14.5	12.7	8.1
Leisure/recreation	9.5	8.5	5.0
Other	5.3	3.7	11.5
TRANSPORT MODE FOR GROCERY SHOPPING FREQUENCY (%)**			
Walking	78.8	52.3	39.7
Bus	63.6	20.5	27.6
Drive car	6.1	29.5	19.0
Car passenger	33.3	13.6	43.1

* Uses mean (weighted) of responses of 65–74 and 75+

** Uses "occasional use" responses and mean (weighted) of 65–74 and 75+

Source: Smith (1984 and 1991).

other hand, they have a corner store a few dozen metres away and several others nearby. Seniors living in the inner and outer suburbs both have a chain supermarket and other supermarkets within reasonable distance. In the higher density inner suburb, these facilities are close to where seniors live (e.g. 600–800 metres on average).

There are also several corners stores available for them to obtain groceries. In the outer suburbs the supermarkets are more widely spaced, as are corner stores/plazas; still, most seniors reside within 800 metres of a supermarket.

Grocery Usage Fields: A useful geographic measure of shopping activity is the *consumer usage field* which looks at the (a) the number of stores patronized for groceries over a specified period, and (b) the mean distance to these stores.[15] In all three zones studied above, two-thirds of seniors took about two shopping trips per week to two stores, a trip of between 1.0 and 1.6 kilometres, with central city seniors travelling the smallest distance. In other words, they all limited the reach of their grocery shopping, and the difference in distance travelled was largely accounted for by the differing spatial densities in the three zones. This study also found little difference in grocery shopping habits between two different ages groups: those 65–74, and those 75 and older.

Accessing Grocery Stores: In the Winnipeg study, seniors in all three zones usually walked to the grocery store (although this may differ in other urban areas; see below). About 80 percent of central city seniors walked to grocery stores at least some of the time, while only 40 percent did so in the outer suburb. Indeed, about half of the seniors in the outer suburb never walked to grocery stores, largely because of the greater distances involved. Very few central city seniors in this study had an automobile and nearly all lived alone, which meant more frequently travelling by bus or being a passenger in a car when going to get groceries. These grocery shopping travel patterns differed little between younger and older seniors, with the exception that those 75 and older in each zone had a greater tendency to use the bus.

The 2002 study of seniors living in suburban areas of Bonn, Germany, referred to above, yielded similar results.[16] Shopping by suburban seniors was frequently done by car in other neighbourhoods. However, those without a car tended to shop in their own neighbourhoods. Again, there was little difference between older and younger seniors in shopping patterns or modes of travel in either the urban or suburban settings.

Grocery Shopping and Other Activities: Almost two-thirds of seniors in all three zones combined grocery shopping with other activities such as going to a drug store or a bank, or even visiting friends, attending a movie, and dining out.

Getting Around in the City

Gerontologists, geographers, and planners talk about the "transportation" needs of seniors, while seniors themselves simply refer to the need "to get around" and carry out their everyday activities. The phrase "to get around" suggests that seniors value the opportunity to keep active physically and socially.[17] For them, transportation is both a means and an end: a means to access services and facilities while satisfying their desire not to be isolated.

At first it might seem that getting around in the city should be relatively easy for seniors since they have a wide range of means available to them. But for as many as half of them, even in the well-served urban situation, getting around does not come without problems.[18] Not all seniors drive; many find the steps on a bus difficult to manage; others fear falling when weather conditions make walking hazardous. In this section, the mobility of urban seniors is examined, along with potential problems such as special transportation needs for frail and impaired seniors.

TRAVEL MODES AND LIMITATIONS IN THE SUBURBS

Automobile Use: A study of seniors living in an outer suburb of the Vancouver metropolitan area provides a further opportunity to consider the mobility of elderly Canadians.[19] As with other recent Canadian studies, it shows that seniors favour automobile travel to get around – three-quarters drive regularly.[20] But this also means that one-quarter do not drive regularly, or at all. Even more crucial is that almost 20 percent of seniors live in households in which *no one* drives. The ability to drive is closely associated with a senior's age, living arrangements, and income. Those aged 75 and older are more than twice as likely not to drive (37 percent) as compared to younger seniors (17 percent).[21] Seniors who live alone and have low incomes are also less likely to drive, especially women seniors.

Table 5.4 Mode of Transportation Mostly Used by Seniors to Get to Selected Destinations, Suburban Vancouver, 1989

Journey To	Mode of Transportation Mostly Used (Percentage)								
	Walk	Drive Self	Spouse Drives	Others Drive	Taxi	Public Bus	Special Bus	Volunteer Driver	Motor Scooter
Family doctor	21.7	58.1	7.9	5.4	1.5	3.9	1.5	–	–
Specialist doctor	10.5	59.9	10.5	8.0	1.2	7.4	2.3	–	–
Drug store	36.8	47.8	6.5	5.0	0.5	3.0	–	–	0.5
Grocery store	27.9	55.2	8.0	5.5	1.0	1.5	–	0.5	0.5
Shopping mall	23.3	57.5	7.9	5.9	0.5	4.5	–	–	0.5
Seniors' centre	17.0	60.6	10.6	5.3	–	4.3	1.1	–	1.1
Church	20.0	58.2	8.2	11.8	–	1.8	–	–	–
Recreation	10.5	61.9	7.1	7.7	–	2.4	0.6	–	1.8
Visit relatives	4.5	65.9	8.9	14.0	–	6.1	–	0.6	–
Visit friends	13.7	62.4	11.7	7.8	–	3.0	–	0.5	1.0

Source: Hodge and Milstein, 1989.

Even among those who drive, nearly one-fifth have problems with driving that limit their mobility. These problems include difficulty with seeing, driving at night, driving on freeways, driving in bad weather, and other limitations due to health. It is common to find similar proportions of seniors in such "transportation dependent" situations throughout the country.

Other Modes of Mobility: Walking is the second most-favoured means of getting around for these suburban Vancouver seniors. On average, about one-fifth prefer to walk to their doctor, drug store, grocery store, and church (see Table 5.4). Obtaining a lift from spouses or others is the third most widely used mode of travel for 12–22 percent of seniors, especially for longer journeys. Public transit buses are not widely used by seniors except for trips that tend to be longer, such as to a specialist doctor or to visit relatives. Taxis, special needs buses, and motor scooters are each used by about one percent of seniors. Regardless of mode of travel, these suburban seniors do most of their travelling within their own community, or within one and a half kilometres of home.

The data in Table 5.4 reveal two important aspects of urban seniors' mobility. First, seniors take advantage of a wide variety of transportation to carry out their various activities. In this regard, while the central tendencies of seniors' automobile use draw one's attention, it is vital to recognize those other means of transport where the use is relatively small. For example, use of public transit by seniors averages about 10 percent and use of a motor scooter is less than one percent. However, in the area in which these data were collected live nearly 15,000 seniors, so buses are used by 1,500 seniors and 150 use motor scooters. These are not only sizeable numbers but they may also represent the best, or even the only, means for these seniors to get around. Similar consideration needs to be given to both the percentages and the numbers of seniors in these and other data involving seniors in a community. Second, about 80 percent get around by themselves: driving, walking, or using a motor scooter. It is safe to infer that this is by choice and reflects the value they place on independence.

Although there have been no empirical studies of Canadian seniors' mobility in recent years, the 2001 National Household Travel Survey showed a similar pattern among American seniors.[22] Location and mode of seniors' shopping travel are also very similar in the 2002 study of German suburban seniors.[23] Lastly, the 2005 General Social Survey of Statistics Canada offers further confirmation that when it comes to seniors' access to and usage of transport modes, past tendencies still prevail.[24]

WALKING ENVIRONMENTS IN METROPOLITAN AREAS

As the elderly are found increasingly in the suburbs, it is important to assess how well these environments support seniors' daily

Table 5.5   The Presence of Sidewalks in Suburban Neighbourhoods in the Vancouver Metropolitan Area Relative to the Core City, 1994

	Geographic Sector		
Neighbourhood Location	East	South	Southeast
Core City (Inner)		—————Full—————	
Core City (Outer)	Full	Partial	Partial
Inner Suburbs	Full	Partial	Partial
Outer Suburbs	None	Partial	Partial
Suburban Fringe	None	na*	None

* No census tract in this sector.

Source: Hodge, 1994.

lives. Walking, as we have seen, is considered by seniors to be both important in itself and as a means of carrying out daily activities. And, in recent years, the role of walking to promote seniors' health has received considerable attention.[25] Sidewalks are the primary physical infrastructure a community provides for its pedestrians. To be effective, they need to be present, in good condition, and promote ease of movement and connectedness.

An exploratory study of neighbourhood walking environments revealed significant inconsistency in the presence of sidewalks in the Vancouver metropolitan area.[26] In general, it was found that the more distant a neighbourhood was from the core city, the less likely it was to have sidewalks. Census tracts were used as a proxy for neighbourhoods: each had populations of 3–6,000 people, including seniors. A dozen census tracts in the core city as well as in three suburban zones and in different geographic sectors were examined in field surveys. The extent to which sidewalks were provided was rated as follows: *Full*, where sidewalks existed on every street (at least on one side); *Partial*, where at least half the streets had sidewalks; and *None*, where few if any sidewalks were provided. The results are shown in Table 5.5.

The general picture in this metropolitan area was that the more distant the suburb, the less well provided it was with sidewalks. Three of the five neighbourhoods examined in the Outer Suburbs and Suburban Fringe were provided with few, if any, sidewalks. However, even some neighbourhoods on the outer edge of the core city had less-than-complete sidewalk systems. Indeed, three-quarters of all neighbourhoods had either no sidewalks or major gaps in their coverage. This is bound to impede seniors' access to nearby stores and services, constrain the use of public transit by those who don't drive, and limit walking for exercise. Moreover, without sidewalks, seniors who wish to walk must walk on the road; this is always unsafe, but especially so for those who may have difficulty walking, hearing, or seeing. Add inclement weather, and the safety and independence of local seniors is further reduced and environmental press increased.[27]

That such great differences in pedestrian infrastructure may be found in the Vancouver metropolitan area suggests the possibility that a similar situation exists in other metropolitan areas. Though shortfalls in sidewalk provision can be a major barrier to senior independence, this is, paradoxically, one problem that is easily corrected.

GETTING AROUND FOR FRAIL SENIORS

Often seniors experience limitations on their everyday activities because of health conditions. Such disabilities, or *impairments,* as they are more properly called,[28] may arise from illness (e.g. cancer, heart disease, diabetes, and emphysema), accidents (e.g. falls, trauma), birth defects, or the so-called diseases of aging (e.g. Alzheimer's, osteoporosis). Overall, 12.4 percent of all Canadians experience limitations in some or all of their daily activities according to the 2001 Participation and Activity Limitation Survey of Statistics Canada (PALS).[29] The rate is much higher for seniors with 40.5 percent having reduced levels of daily activity because of impairments. Moreover, the rate of impairment is age-related among seniors: over half of those aged 75 and older (53.3%) have activity-limiting impairments as compared to less than one-third of those aged 65–74 (31.2%). This is true for both female and male seniors, although women are slightly more likely to report impairments. These figures indicate that a significant number of seniors

have difficulty getting around both inside and outside their dwellings. In 2001, seniors with impairments numbered nearly one and
a half million.

The most common seniors' impairments are: [30]

- Mobility (31.5%), i.e. difficulty with walking a distance,
  up and down stairs, etc.
- Agility (29.2%), i.e. difficulty bending, reaching, using
  fingers to grasp, etc.
- Hearing (16.0%), i.e. difficulty hearing what is said in
  conversation, etc.
- Seeing (8.5%), i.e. difficulty reading ordinary newsprint,
  etc.
- Speaking (3.4%), i.e. difficulty speaking and/or being
  understood

Each of these impairments could have a major impact on one's
ability to get around in the community. Seniors with any of these
impairments could encounter situations in which the environmental
press would prove, at best, challenging and at worst, could exclude
them from many activities. In such cases, a relatively mild impairment could become a real disability. [31] That is, seniors with impairments are not *enabled* but *disabled* in many urban situations.

In 2001, about 65,000 Canadian seniors travelled with difficulty
on local transit systems. A further 60,000 were prevented from travelling on local transportation systems because of their impairments,
and even travelling by car was not possible for many. [32] Over half of
seniors with impairments – about 22 percent of the total number of
elderly people – used assistive devices to get around; women seniors
were more likely to use such devices than men. [33]

Think, for example, how such impairments could affect a senior
using public transportation. Trips are structured like links in a
chain and "must be comprised of links that are continuous, accessible, coherent, and compatible." [34] There is, first, the walk to the bus,
subway, or streetcar stop. Is it within a reasonable distance, say
400–600 metres, and is the terrain flat, and are there sidewalks?
Then there is the matter of boarding vehicles, many of which have

very high steps. Next, if the vehicle is full, is standing possible when the vehicle is moving and/or is it easy to hold on? Add to these questions the matter of directions about transfer points, schedules, etc. Are they posted and legible? These situations might be even more complicated for those who require assistive devices such as canes, walkers, and wheelchairs. It is not over-stating it to say that a senior with a physical or cognitive impairment perceiving "one difficult-to-manage link in the chain" may abandon the trip altogether[35] as was illustrated earlier regarding Canadian senior women.[36] (See also Figure 4.4.)

As mentioned before, loss of mobility because of impairments increases substantially with age: nearly 60 percent of those aged 85 and older suffer a mobility-related impairment, a figure that is two and a half times greater than for those aged 65–74.[37] Seniors with mild or moderate impairments may experience some reduction in the number and/or spatial reach of activities they have access to. However those who are more severely impaired may actually become homebound, unless special needs buses that provide door-to-door transportation are available.

SOCIAL SUPPORT GEOGRAPHY

In addition to the needs of urban seniors for commercial goods and other services, they have social and emotional needs for friends and family, familiar institutions, and, not least, the community environment itself. This renders its own geography, a social support geography, which is unique for each individual. It fits within the "life spaces" framework introduced in chapter 1 (see Figure 1.3). This eight-zone framework was derived by geographer Graham Rowles from his work with rural seniors, but it is also applicable to those in city settings. It is described fully later in this chapter.

Ethnic Seniors in the City

Canada is a country built on immigration, so there have always been ethnic elders in our seniors' population. Although there have always been a few elderly immigrants, most arrived earlier. Many of those 85 and older today were children when they immigrated to

Canada in the 1920s, while younger seniors (65–74) are often those who came as young adults in the 1950s and 1960s. Together they account for most of the 27 percent of seniors who, in 1996, were calculated to be of foreign birth.[38] As we saw in chapter 2, two substantial changes have occurred in the flow of immigration since 1971. The first is the greatly increased number of immigrants, and the second is the ethnic composition of the immigrant population. Whereas earlier immigration was largely European, currently close to 70 percent of Canada's immigrants comprise "visible minorities."[39] The extent of these changes is already apparent in the composition of the seniors' population whereby over seven percent of seniors are now from visible minorities.

Earlier streams of immigration tended to spread across the country in both urban and rural areas. But new immigrants, both visible minorities and others, have mostly been destined for the cities, notably the largest ones. Of the immigrants who arrived during the 1990s, 94 percent went to live in the country's 27 metropolitan areas and of these over three-quarters, or 1.3 million, reside now in just three CMAs: Toronto, Vancouver, and Montreal.[40] Other major "gateway" cities for recent immigrants are Ottawa-Hull, Calgary, Edmonton, and Hamilton. One result of three decades of such flows is the emergence of numerous "visible minority neighborhoods," or "ethnic enclaves," especially in the three largest CMAs;[41] similar clustering is likely in other metropolitan areas still to be studied. In Toronto, the two largest enclaves are Italian and Chinese, and there are also neighbourhood concentrations (measured in terms of census tracts) of Jewish, South Asian, East Indian, Greek, Black, and Portuguese immigrants as well as of those of English origin and those who refer to themselves as Canadians.[42] Such clustering is not unique to the present. In the past, Toronto had two Chinatowns as well as a Little Italy within its centre, and Vancouver had both a Chinatown and a Japan Town close to the downtown core. However, the new enclaves differ from those by occurring mostly in the suburbs of metropolitan areas with their detached-home subdivisions, townhouse complexes, and occasional high-rise apartments. While these new ethnic neighbourhoods are unlike the high-density, inner-city enclaves of the past, they share the same type of commercial infrastructure associated with their forbears. Ethnic malls, restaurants, grocery stores, video stores, and professional offices, along with places of worship and community centres, have become part of the urban landscape in cities across the country.

In these urban settings live ethnic elders; they shop at the local stores, eat at the restaurants, and frequent the mosque, church or gurdawara. Very few work outside the home, although most maintain extensive contacts in the community. There is a paucity of both official and professional literature, even though these seniors now number over one-third of a million and their numbers are growing very fast.[43] However, some useful accounts of their daily activities and living arrangements are emerging. For example, one can extrapolate from the following interview with an elderly Ismaili (Muslim) woman how others like her spend their time:

> I have a busy life. My mother is now 89 and lives on her own ... I do her shopping and take her for all her medical appointments. I visit her two or three times a week. I also take food for her ... when my children come to visit me, I give them lots of food. I go to Jamat Khana [Ismaili palace of worship] quite regularly. I go to morning Khane [worship] ... I get up at nine or ten o'clock and then have breakfast. I then phone my mother, my daughter ... then I go shopping ... I often have to go to the doctor myself. After lunch, I take a little rest in the afternoon; then I cook and prepare dinner. I go to Jamat Khana, and then at night I watch TV and read newspapers.[44]

There is also a similarity in this pattern of daily life to that of other ("non-visible") Canadian seniors described in chapter 4. But broader generalizations cannot be made without more thorough studies of ethnic elders. Moreover, there are cultural and social differences among and within the various ethnic groups that could affect their everyday geography. For example, seniors are often part of extended families of three generations living in the same household, and they may provide much of the childcare, including taking children to school and other activities.[45] The gaps in our knowledge about how their life space activities are formed and articulated is all too apparent and needs to be filled.[46] As we will see below, similar gaps exist in regard to our knowledge of Canadian Aboriginal elders.

Aboriginal Elders in the City

Of Canada's approximately one million persons of Aboriginal ancestry, about one-half (49%) live in cities, according to the 2001 census.[47] And of these, half live in ten metropolitan areas led by Winnipeg and followed by Edmonton, Vancouver, Calgary, Saskatoon, Regina, Ottawa-Hull, Montreal, and Victoria, in that order. Other urban centres with large Aboriginal populations are Prince Albert, SK, and Prince George, BC. Generally, the urban Aboriginal population is young, as is the entire Aboriginal population. Those aged 65 and older account for less than four percent of all Aboriginals, or about 40,000 in total. Of these, 43 percent lived in urban areas in 2001. It must be noted that these urban-based Aboriginal seniors come from three broad groupings of Aboriginal people: North American Indian, Metis, and Inuit. Metis seniors live in urban areas in the greatest proportions (62%), as compared to half that level of North American Indian seniors (33%); even fewer Inuit seniors (22%) live in urban areas. And among these urban seniors, women predominate, especially among those of North American Indian and Metis ancestry.

The above data use age 65 and older to define Aboriginal elders, which provides a ready means of comparison with other Canadian seniors. However, it is not always appropriate when considering the lives and activities of older Aboriginals, according to most researchers and native people themselves. In Aboriginal studies, elders are frequently classified as those aged 55 or older; sometime it is as low as age 50.[48] In part this is because of the lower life expectancy of native people compared to Canadians in general; in 2000, Aboriginal men had an average life expectancy of 68.9 years and Aboriginal women 76.3 years, whereas the comparable Canadian figures were 76.3 and 81.5 years.[49] Only limited study has been given to Aboriginal elders, and most of this has been devoted to issues of health, personal well-being, and care giving. However, such studies do provide a basis for surmising aspects of this group's daily lives. For example, we know that Native seniors are less well off financially than other Canadian seniors and that they tend to live in poorer quality housing often without telephones; furthermore, few own and drive their own vehicles.[50] These limitations, along with a level of physical impairment higher than that of the general senior population, are certain to affect the spatial reach of daily activities for Aboriginal elders.[51] At the same time, it is also known that these elders have a more extensive involvement with family and friends than do non-Aboriginal seniors. It is estimated that Winnipeg Native seniors not only see twice as many relatives as other Canadian seniors do in their daily activities but they also see three times as many friends.[52] Many of these encounters involve care giving, whether it is for the seniors, or the seniors themselves taking care of kin and friends.

SENIORS' GEOGRAPHY IN RURAL COMMUNITIES

Although comprising only 24 percent of the total seniors' population, rural seniors are dispersed over 96 percent of Canada's land space. But though they live in much lower densities than city seniors, rural seniors (except for Aboriginal elders) differ little otherwise in age, gender, education, income, living arrangements, degree of frailty, need for certain goods and services, and so on. It is the spatial tableau on which their life course is played out that mainly distinguishes them from urban seniors. This physical setting, with its low population density, smaller communities, and large distances between communities, affects their everyday geography both in scope and content. A distinctive feature of rural regions is their preponderance of First Nations communities, which are home to the distinctive population of Aboriginal elders.

Small Town Seniors

Rural seniors live in two types of setting: in community clusters and in the open countryside. Community clusters vary from large towns (up to 10,000 in population) down through small towns, villages, and hamlets (of less than 500 inhabitants). They may be called by various names in different parts of the country such as "outports," "reserves," and "parishes"; for our purposes, we will call all of these clusters "small towns." Probably fewer than 20 percent of rural seniors live in the countryside, either on farms or on rural acreages (or what used to be referred to in the Census as "rural non-farm").[53]

DEMOGRAPHIC FEATURES

Small town seniors differ little, demographically, from the overall seniors' population. However, there are two differences which need to be noted: first, they comprise larger proportions of the population in the towns in which they live, regardless of size (see chapter 3). Second, there are greater proportions of elderly males among small town seniors.[54] There is a small counter-tendency for those older than 85 move to larger nearby towns where services are more accessible. Nonetheless, the strong tendency among the elderly to age-in-place is revealed again in these data. It is further reinforced by the movement of many seniors from farm and countryside residences to nearby small towns in order, in many cases, to be close to local commercial, social, and health resources as well as to their long-time community.

COMMUNITY RESOURCE GEOGRAPHY

The small town, like the urban neighbourhood, is the proximate resource environment for its elderly citizens (see Figure 5.2). However, unlike urban neighbourhoods, small towns differ vastly in size and, thus, in the number and kind of resources available locally. For this reason, the physical resource environment may spread over several communities. The smaller the town, the less likely it is to have all of the resources seniors need available within its boundaries. Since over three-quarters of all small towns have less than 500 residents, it can be assumed that most seniors in these places will have to travel to larger towns to obtain things they need.

Since there is a paucity of recent research on seniors' resource geography in rural areas, it is necessary to draw upon a 1983 study of seniors living in nine small towns in rural Eastern Ontario.[55] Populations of these towns ranged from just under 300 to fewer than 5,000. More than 120 seniors who lived in senior citizen housing projects in these towns were interviewed about their activity patterns and means of mobility. Table 5.6 shows the twelve most-frequently used community resources by these seniors. It can be seen that they patronized commercial and service establishments inside as well as outside their own town. Only three of the nine

Table 5.6   Community Resources Used by Small Town
Seniors in Eastern Ontario, 1983

Most Frequently Used Community Resources	Percent Using Local Establishments	Percent Using Non-Local Establishments
Bank	89.5	–
Grocery store	79.8	9.7
Doctor	62.1	37.9
Church	59.7	5.6
Post office	52.4	–
Drug store	49.2	21.6
Beauty shop/barber	49.2	11.3
Restaurant	45.2	8.1
Social club	36.3	1.6
Variety store	22.6	–
Department store	14.4	33.9
Clothing/shoe store	8.9	27.4

Source: Hodge, 1984.

towns – the three largest – contained all of these resources. Seniors living in the other six towns were therefore required to travel to obtain at least some of their desired resources. One could not expect a department store, doctor, drug store, or clothing store in a very small town, for example. The two smallest towns in this sample could provide only half of the listed resources and the remainder could prove only three-quarters. It is important to add however, that the use of non-local establishments also reflects the desire for seniors to have choice among those resources that are available. So, even if a town had a needed resource, a similar establishment in a nearby town might be preferred for price, quality, etc.

Availability and Accessibility of Local Resources: Small town seniors, thus, have two spatial settings in which their activities take place: the first is the community in which they live and the second is the larger region comprising their own and other towns which they visit seeking services and/or social contacts (see the life spaces diagram

Table 5.7   Availability and Walking Accessibility of Community
Resources to Small Town Seniors in Eastern Ontario, 1983

Town Name	Pop'n. 1981	No. Basic Resources	No. Basic Estabs.	Avail. Index	Access. %<400m	Avg. Walking Dist./metres	
Gananoque	4,863	12	46	3.83	83.3	347	(83.3)*
Prescott	4,670	12	42	3.50	0.0	1,041	(66.7)*
Kemptville	2,362	12	31	2.58	0.0	1,048	(60.0)*
Cardinal	1,753	9	20	2.22	25.0	739	(34.8)*
Merrickville	984	8	15	1.87	58.3	342	(73.3)*
Lansdowne	463	9	14	1.55	33.3	812	(63.6)*
Spencerville	434	6	9	1.50	33.3	453	(100.0)*
Elgin	292	8	12	1.50	66.6	382	(93.3)*
Mallorytown	290	5	5	1.00	25.0	546	(91.7)*
ALL TOWNS (median)	984	9	15	1.87	33.3	546	(73.3)*

* Percentage of seniors walking.

Source: Hodge, 1984.

in Figure 1.3). The questions posed earlier regarding the availability of local resources and their accessibility are appropriate to ask in regard to the community environments in these small towns. It was noted above that most of the nine towns lacked some of the twelve basic resources. But, of those available, did seniors have a choice among establishments? And beyond the existence of basic resource establishments, were they accessible to elderly residents of the town? Table 5.7 depicts the situation in the nine Eastern Ontario towns using the dimensions of availability and accessibility.

Although these towns were originally studied with regard to the location of senior housing projects, they also provide an overview of community resource environments with which all seniors in such towns must interact. Clearly, the smaller the town the fewer the needed resources that will likely exist and the fewer will be the alternatives among them, as can be seen in the Availability Index figures below. The housing projects provided a focus for considering accessibility for seniors wanting to walk to stores and other

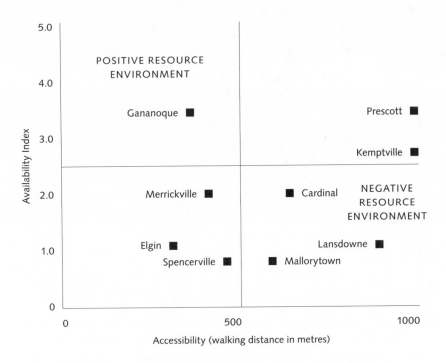

Figure 5.2   Availability and Accessibility of Shopping Resources
for Seniors in Ontario Towns (Source: Hodge 1984)

facilities. Many projects were located at excessive distances and/or were combined with steep gradients on the streets providing access. These factors limited the number of seniors who might have walked and left them to find other means of getting around in what were, otherwise, small communities.

The dimensions of availability and accessibility may be combined, as in Figure 5.2, which depicts the Eastern Ontario situation. This provides a means of evaluating any community environment for its ability to provide sufficient resources within easy access. In this case, an availability index value of 2.5 was selected, which would offer not only all twelve resources but also choices among them. 500 metres was considered an appropriate accessibility level. The graph is divided into four quadrants according to measures of availability and accessibility. The northwest quadrant, where both availability and accessibility are good, is labeled a Positive Resource Environment. All the other quadrants vary from this, with the southeast quadrant being the least amenable in meeting seniors' needs and accessibility.

It is important to acknowledge changes in the structure of retailing in rural regions since the data above were compiled. In general, what has been occurring is the consolidation of retail outlets into fewer and bigger units.[56] This process has meant, spatially, that larger centres have been favoured over smaller ones; this in turn has meant that many rural seniors now have fewer local retail resources. Similar changes have occurred in other service sectors such as banks, post offices, and health care facilities.

Of course, the impact of such changes differs according to the economic and demographic tendencies influencing each community and region.[57] Notwithstanding some variation in how communities evolve, it is reasonable to conclude that seniors continue to require the same resources as before, even though they may now have to go farther afield for them. Given that a walking distance of 500–600 metres continues to be what is comfortable for most seniors, we can only assume that rural seniors are driving more and walking less than they were in 1983. In fact, Availability Indexes will have declined and walking accessibility may have been eliminated for many areas.

Resources in the Regional Community: Due to lack of availability and insufficiency of choice, most small town seniors travel to larger towns and cities to obtain commercial and community services. They must seek their needs beyond the community in a more extensive life space; in this case, the *sub-region* (see Figure 1.3). Five resources tend to be sought in other sub-regional communities: doctor, bank, department store, clothing store, and drug store; with retail and services consolidations, this list may be longer today for some seniors. About one-third of the Eastern Ontario seniors found the need to travel to other centres for some of these resources once or twice per week, and most of the remainder travelled once or twice per month. In most parts of rural Canada the distance between towns is considerable. While nearly half of these seniors had only to travel an average of 24 kilometres, for most of the remainder the distance was 40 kilometres or more. In terms of time required for such trips, the longer trip (40 km.) would require 25–30 minutes in most rural areas of Canada. A recent study of seniors' accessibility in smaller communities in Atlantic Canada found that over half the seniors travelled for 30 minutes or more to obtain a wide range of goods and services.[58] The time their journey took is comparable to that required by urban seniors travelling from the suburbs to the central city to obtain goods or services. However, the distances travelled by rural seniors in this time are significantly greater, up to ten times greater, resulting in their having more extensive life spaces than those living in cities (see Table 5.8).

It is almost axiomatic that seniors who live in a small town will need to travel to another, usually larger, town in the region for shopping and other resources. However, the frequency and the extent that this occurs will vary according to the economic and demographic dynamics of the region. For example, the retail and service restructuring referred to above may not mean fewer stores in rural regions where there is population growth due to resource development, or regions with environmental amenities may experience an influx of retirees, thereby sustaining the local retail structure and even adding outlets such as those catering to recreational needs.[59] Where the opposite conditions prevail, population declines may occur, especially among young people, reducing the retail service population and possibly reducing the number of outlets for the remaining, increasingly senior, population (see Accumulation process and Figure 2.4a).

SOCIAL SUPPORT GEOGRAPHY

The various settings that have been described also perform functions beyond those of supplying commercial goods and other services. They represent, as well, spatial manifestations of seniors' communities with which they identify, of *places* with which they have emotional and social attachments. They are where friends, neighbours and kin often live, where familiar institutions like the church or community hall are located, and where a weekly farmers' market or annual fair is held. In short, these settings form a spatial system of *social* supports for rural seniors.

A nested set of such zones was posited by geographer Graham Rowles in 1983.[60] His construct consists of seven support spaces, or what we have called life spaces, that begin with a senior's home and extend progressively outward (see Fig. 1.3). In these zones are located facilities and/or people that provide both formal and informal support to seniors. Each senior accesses these resources through their modes and routes of travel and other means of communication. Although Rowles rendered these zones from an American rural perspective, they are equally valid for all seniors in every community situation. Allusions to urban situations are included below.

- *Home* (and yard) is the ultimate support zone in which are provided shelter, practical amenities, a stimulus for physical activities and maintenance, a repository for memories, a symbol of personal identity, and a physical connection to the community. Home is the centre of all succeeding zones.
- The *surveillance zone,* the area that can be viewed from the windows of a senior's home, provides for visual and other contacts with neighbours. It extends as far as window placement, topography, visibility and a senior's vision allow. A range of 200–400 metres is common in villages (or urban neighbourhoods); a larger zone may be available to countryside dwellers.
- The *vicinity* zone is an especially important support space for older people; it may encompass an entire small town (or urban neighbourhood) within its 800–1,000 metre radius. This where seniors obtain their groceries and mail, attend church, and make contact with family members, close friends and other age-peers through whom supportive relationships are sustained.
- The *community* comprises all the previous zones within its four-kilometre radius and provides seniors with opportunities to utilize formal resources such as a library, medical clinic, seniors' centre, and seniors' housing, as well as frequent face-to-face contact with others while using services and attending social events. (This is equivalent to a large town or small city.)

- The *sub-region* is a zone extending as much as 40 kilometres from home and typically includes nearby larger towns and cities (or other districts in a larger city or metropolitan area). As well as being the zone for accessing specialized resources such as a supermarket, a hospital, or a department store, this is where family members and old friends live and where socially important activities such as seasonal fairs and sporting events occur. It is an area that is important to rural seniors for the array of personal meanings it holds; meanings that come from accumulated years of doing business, working, socializing, volunteering, etc.
- The *region*, spanning up to 400 kilometres from home, is equivalent, in Canadian terms, to a large province or a group of small provinces as in the Maritimes. Support in this zone is mainly from family such as children who may have migrated to a regional centre to work (e.g. Saskatoon, Halifax) and may involve mutual visits and other kinds of communications. Regional cities may also be visited by rural (and other) seniors to use things like specialized health care facilities, or the airport.
- The *nation*, although other parts of Canada may be visited infrequently, it is a life space in which a senior is likely to have relatives and friends that she/he is in contact with. A typical situation would be seniors who migrated to another part of the country during their working age returning to their hometown to visit children, family or friends.
- An eighth zone, *abroad*, has been added to Rowles' set in order to acknowledge the extent that seniors enjoy travel to other countries. This includes those who reside abroad for extended periods, like the Prairie "snowbirds" who migrate to Arizona, and Quebec "snowbirds" who go to Florida in the winter.

This paradigm pertains mainly to what are called the *informal* or non-organized and non-commercial, social resources that comprise an important part of a senior's (or anyone's) daily life. The components are, foremost, people whom a senior considers important such as family, especially children, and friends and neighbours (especially age-peers). Contacts may be direct, as in visits, by telephone (or even email, nowadays), by casual encounters as when shopping, or simply by sight from home.

The surveillance zone epitomizes a visual kind of contact that is valuable to the elderly person.[61] Many seniors spend time "watching" the space outside their homes; for them, it is a source of contact with their local environment and the people living nearby, a kind of vicarious participation. Along with personal contact with neighbours, mutual support practices may develop from this surveillance, including that of others who "watch out" for elderly neighbours (what Rowles called "visual reciprocity") as well as other forms of mutual assistance (e.g. snow-shovelling, help with shopping). This zone, like all the others, is imbued with subjective aspects (i.e. personal meaning, memories, and emotional attachment) that, for a senior, are usually deep-seated. Such zones are *salient,* rather than *functional,* resource environments.

Getting Around in Rural Areas

Rural seniors have far fewer transportation options available to them than urban seniors. Most regions lack public transportation and few towns have taxis, so the two options for getting around are walking or driving (including getting a ride with another person). These represent less than half the transportation alternatives available to seniors living in Canadian cities (see Table 5.4), and for seniors living on farms or in the countryside, even walking may not be an option to get to stores, doctors, or other facilities. This dearth of transportation alternatives means that the everyday geography of rural seniors is largely articulated by the automobile.[62] They are very heavily dependent upon this single mode of movement in order to access health, recreation, and social services as well as simply to have the freedom to socialize and shop as they wish – that is, to be independent. But many rural seniors do not have ready access to an automobile.[63] This may be due to some physical impairment that prevents driving a car or riding in a car while someone else drives. Some seniors live in households where no one drives, and others may never have learned to drive (especially older women). Still others choose not to drive at night, in bad weather, and/or in highway situations. All of these voluntary and involuntary limitations on a rural senior's use of an automobile represent different degrees of being what is called "transportation disadvantaged."[64] A study of more than 1,000 seniors living in ten small towns in British Columbia found that nearly 43 percent do not drive regularly, and nearly 37 percent live in households where no one drives.[65] Further, it was found that these percentages increased with the age of seniors. Strikingly, the most common source of difficulty seniors cited in getting around was "I don't like to ask for a ride."[66] For transportation-disadvantaged seniors this represents a kind of "double jeopardy" in terms of getting around, because they are limited in their automobile use in a milieu where such transportation is usually the only option.

Despite the mobility limitations that many seniors have, the provision of satisfactory public transportation in rural areas is difficult. This is the result, on the one hand, of the low density of population and small numbers to be served and, on the other hand, of the diversity of destinations that seniors require. In addition, seniors may ignore available services, preferring to get a ride with someone they know. In evaluating the Rural Transportation Assistance Program (RTAP), an initiative to connect five small communities with a larger town twice per week in rural Saskatchewan, it was found that nearly 30 percent of those with "transportation problems" were not aware of the program while only 26 percent of this same group used it.[67] Similar results were obtained in five small British Columbia communities with a local lift-equipped on-call bus service.[68]

This is not to deny the value of such programs but rather to point up the variability among potential senior patrons in their needs and attitudes. In the British Columbia study for example, some seniors wanted service in the evening and on weekends, or regretted the waiting time and having to make advance bookings. Other transportation options, such as Volunteer Driver programs, Mobility Clubs, and taxi vouchers, have been used in rural Canada and the United States. Although none are able to cover all rural seniors' requirements for transportation, or to be profitable, where they are available they provide a needed alternative to the use of the private automobile. They help right the balance in rural transportation modes. And this is an issue that will continue to concern rural

seniors for, as the study in rural Atlantic Canada showed, automobile travel times for many households increased between 1986
and 1998.[69] The further consolidation and rationalization of commercial and professional enterprises in larger outlets, in malls, and
group practice, which one can expect to continue in rural regions,[70]
will exacerbate the travel situation still more.

Aboriginal Elders in Rural Regions

Although large numbers of Aboriginal elders now live in cities, well
over half (57%) still live in communities in rural regions of Canada.
They live in the approximately 1,500 Indian reserves as well as in
numerous communities spread east and west and north and south
across the country. These communities are mostly small, few exceed
500 people, and few have commercial and public resources at hand.
There were nearly 23,000 seniors of Aboriginal ancestry (North
American Indian, Metis, Inuit) living in rural settings as of 2001.
If one were to add the 55–64 age group, which is often included
in studies of Aboriginal elders,[71] the number living in rural communities would be double.[72] Nonetheless, the totals in each place
would be small. Aboriginal seniors live in community settings that,
at best, parallel those of other elderly Canadians in the smallest
rural communities and, at worst, have far fewer resources because
of their size and remoteness.

There is a concordance of daily life activities of Aboriginal elders
in rural communities with their counterparts in urban areas. In
both groups, there is considerable visiting among families (more so
than among non-Aboriginal seniors), and they often live in multi-
generational households. Thus, much of the care and support of
rural elders is provided by family members and friends in lieu of
public sources.[73] Levels of impairment among Aboriginal elders are
higher than reported by other seniors while their access to vehicular
travel is much less; in one study only 46 percent reported being able
to drive, and few owned a car or truck.[74] These conditions keep
many rural elders from being involved in recreational and social
activities such as bingo, dancing, powwows or other tribal celebra-
tions, visiting, and hunting. The picture of the daily geography of
rural Aboriginal seniors provided by these data is, arguably, partial

and sketchy. This is understandable given the great variability in the nature and location of their communities, not to mention their size and cultural differences with other tribal groups as well as with non-Aboriginal communities.[75] But all these aspects must be factored in when designing and providing services or access to services for rural Aboriginal seniors.

REFLECTIONS

The aim of this chapter has been to render seniors' everyday geography; to sketch out their patterns of activities within the communities in which they live. The portraits that have been drawn, of necessity, derive from a variety of studies; some are now two decades old while others are more recent. As we noted at the outset, the renderings are "mosaics" and some pieces may remain to be added. However, the data that are available allow one to glimpse both city and country seniors living their daily lives. The primary difference in the everyday geography of urban and rural seniors is in their spatial *reach* for these goods and services.[76] Rural seniors, in general, must travel far greater distances than urban seniors to obtain the full array of resources they need. Rural seniors also have many fewer means of mobility in these daily activities. Such limitations aside, given that automobile travel in the country is more rapid than in most cities, the *time* involved in the rural senior's reach for goods and services may be in the same general range as for urban seniors, even though the *distance* may be much larger for the former. Essentially, the descriptions of activities presented here fall into Rowles' geographic modality called "everyday action" of "routine service, social and recreational trips" within the senior's community.[77]

The documentation of seniors' activity patterns, as limited as it is, provides a valuable outcome in that the gaps in the data regarding seniors' life spaces and activity patterns are better identified. Though it has been possible to describe broad pictures of seniors' daily activities, there are many facets for which detail is missing. Shopping patterns, for example, are quite clear, but who does the shopping in two-person households? Is it gender-related? Are patterns and routines the same in poorer as compared to more affluent households? In other words, seniors are too often seen as an undif-

Table 5.8   Components of Seniors' Everyday Geography
in Different Residential Settings

| Everyday Geography | Seniors Who Live In | | | |
Component	Cities	Suburbs	Small Towns	Countryside
Preferred modes of transportation to access shopping and other services	Walking Auto Bus	Auto Walking Bus	Walking Auto	Auto
Average walking distance (metres)	500m	500–1,000m	500m	NA
Spatial reach to obtain basic resources of everyday living (kms)	0.1–1.5km	1.0–2.5km	0.5–40.0km	1.5–40.0km

Source: Tables 5.1–5.7.

ferentiated group. Gender, ethnicity, income, living arrangements, education, and even age are often ignored. It is as if there exists a "typical senior" carrying out the activity. Yet one knows from personal experience, regardless of age, that many factors enter into carrying out an activity as commonplace as shopping: when and why we do it, how we get there, and whether we can we afford it, to name a few. It is reasonable to assume that each senior also considers such things from his/her perspective. Recall, then, how little is known about the activity patterns of ethnic and Aboriginal elders. In their case, we are lacking fundamental data such as the meaning of home, identification with place, role in the extended family, daily time-use, types of activities they participate in, the extent (and means) of their spatial mobility, and the personal preferences and satisfactions associated with their activities.[78]

The activity patterns observed in this chapter are an accumulation of individual actions, but how much of this aggregate human agency simply reproduces existing behaviour or represents choice and self-expression? Although there is much to commend in the ways in which seniors' express themselves in their everyday geography, it vital that one not overlook patterns of inequality in Canadian society (e.g. income, gender, ethnicity) that may give an illusion of choice.[79] For example, locational constraints and limited transportation options make rural seniors' lives more difficult than those of urban seniors. A similar case can be made regarding Aboriginal elders and their limited activity patterns, in both urban and rural settings, where poverty is often the root cause. The language and cultural barriers that constrain ethnic elders in their daily pursuits may be as important as their age or health. Then there are the spatial differences in economic vitality and in demographic processes that can affect a region's ability to maintain its retail and service infrastructure.

These perspectives will provide a fuller understanding of the situations faced by older people and what they may mean for their community geography. In the next chapter, the following question emerges for consideration:

How will the everyday geography of future seniors compare with that of today's seniors?

Part Three

Future Seniors and their Communities

Chapter Six

From Baby Boom to Seniors' Surge

The long-forecasted surge in the number of seniors will begin in less than half a decade, as the first of the "Baby Boom Generation" reaches age 65. From 2011–21 the number of seniors will grow by nearly 40 percent, and there will be nearly double the number of today's seniors by 2031. To those who grew up in the 1920s and 1930s will be added those who grew up in the 1950s and 1960s. The new cohort will bring different social and economic experiences as well as different perspectives on growing old. Some of its members will be part of the greatly expanded immigration stream since the 1970s, many of them from Asia. Add to this mix a significant increase in the number of Aboriginal elders and the seniors' population will become even more diversified than it is at present. And finally, seniors will be living longer and surviving into the ranks of the very old in far greater numbers.

Even without this demographic bulge the number of seniors would have continued to increase, but more gradually. The fact that nation's population is aging has implications not only on a host of public policies and agencies but also, and possibly more importantly, on communities and families. As the salient dimensions of this historical surge in seniors are set forth in this chapter, consider the following question:

How will Canada's geography of aging be affected by the coming surge of seniors?

THE BABY BOOM AND AGING OF THE
CANADIAN POPULATION, 2001–31

A nation's population ages just as an individual does – one year at a time. Each year, the collateral processes of *natural increase* (births minus deaths) and net *migration* (in-migrants minus out-migrants) combine to produce not only new numbers of people but also a new age composition within the population. An increased birth rate along with a steady death rate leads to more people and a younger population. An increase in longevity along with a steady birthrate leads to more people and an older population. When the number of people moving to Canada in any year exceeds the number leaving, we have more people; depending upon the differences in their ages, the population could become younger or older than before. These demographic processes repeat themselves year after year, producing a set of "age cohorts" or "birth groups" (e.g. 0–9, 10–19 ... 60–69, 70–79 ... 100+) that comprise the total population. Senior age groups are important to gerontologists because they indicate the current and future size of the seniors' population and also because they indicate differences in social contexts experienced by seniors of different ages.[1]

Origin of the Current Seniors' Population

The current seniors' population originated in birth groups 65 and more years ago. Using 2001 as a baseline, those aged 65–74 were born between the years of 1926–35 while the centenarians (100+), of whom there are nearly 4,000, were born at or before the turn of the twentieth century.[2] These birth groups include mostly those born in Canada in that approximately 35-year period, but also those born elsewhere in the same period. To quote Statistics Canada: "The size of the population at a given age depends essentially on the size of the birth groups."[3] In the period from 1900–14, the number of persons born in Canada averaged 201,000 per year (see Table 2.6). This rate grew in a variable way over the next quarter century, affected by war, the prosperity of the 1920s, and the Great Depression of the 1930s. By 1935, the average number of births per year stood at 236,000. These increases in the Canadian birth groups, plus immigrants born during this period, account for much of the growth in the number of seniors over the past four decades.

Their numbers will continue to grow because the fertility rate of Canadian women increased during World War II, resulting in an average of 280,000 births per year in that six-year period (1940–45). (That birth group started to become seniors as recently as 2005.) Had the size of birth groups remained in the range of 250,000 per year, the number of seniors would have continued to increase at a modest rate well into the future because of increased longevity and despite decreasing fertility rates. However, in the ten years following World War II there was a 70 percent increase in the size of yearly birth groups. This is the first decade of what came to be called the Baby Boom.

Tracking the Baby Boom Cohorts

Although the expanded birth groups that occurred in Canada in the twenty years between 1946 and 1965 are often referred to as the "Baby Boom Generation," they are not a generation of people in the true sense but rather two ten-year age cohorts.[4] They represent a dramatic shift in birth and fertility rates that lasted for a fifth of a century. As noted above, if the average birth group size of 250,000 per year that characterized the previous twenty years had continued for another twenty years after World War II, five million births would have occurred. Instead, there were eight and a half million births! At the time this demographic bulge spurred sudden increases in demand for housing, schools, playgrounds, and health and other social services. Over the ensuing decades, colleges and universities and more housing and health and social services came to be demanded.

As of the 1966 census, the two ten-year age cohorts corresponding to the baby boom (0–9 and 10–19) numbered just over 8.4 million young persons. (This number allows for deaths within the cohorts between year of birth and 1966 and adds in children of immigrants to Canada who were born elsewhere and were still living in 1966.) By 2001, these cohorts were in the age ranges of 35–44 and 45–54 and they numbered just over 9.5 million persons (see Table 6.1). The reason for this expansion of just over one million persons is that,

Table 6.1   Evolving Size and Age Range of "Baby Boom" Cohort,
Canada, 1966–2051

Year	Age Range	Cohort Population*	Seniors' Population	Percent Seniors**
1966	0–19	8,430,000	1,540,000	7.69
2001	35–54	9,521,000	3,889,000	12.96
2011	45–64	9,718,000	4,883,000	14.40
2021	55–74	9,212,000	6,847,000	17.73
2031	65–84	8,015,000	9,136,000	23.41
2051	85+	2,419,000	11,110,000	26.45

* Includes immigrants to Canada born elsewhere in this period.
** Percent of seniors in total population of Canada.
Sources: 1996 and 2001 Census and Statistics Canada 2005, Cat. No. 91-520.

since 1966, immigration has brought a surge of new residents to Canada that were born elsewhere during the 1946–65 period.

In Table 6.1, the baby boom cohorts are tracked as they age over the coming few decades according to the medium projection of population by Statistics Canada in 2005.[5] The size of these cohorts will continue to expand until just after 2011 due to additional immigrants of the same age range, and then they will begin to decline as mortality starts to reduce their numbers. Although the baby boomers won't start to turn 65 until 2011, nearly one million seniors will be added to the Canadian population between 2001 and 2011, bringing the seniors' share of the population to nearly 15 percent. This is due to the aging of birth groups from the five years before World War II and those born during wartime.

By contrast, the surge in both the number and concentration of Canada's seniors that will occur after 2011 is especially notable. About two million will be added to the total in each of the two succeeding decades, 2011–21 and 2021–31. And the concentration of seniors in Canada's population, which indicates the nation's degree of aging, will nearly double in this period, so that by 2031 almost *one-quart*er of Canadians will be seniors. (Dramatic though this seems, Canada will only then reach the level of aging already reached by Italy and Japan in 2002.) The long-term forecasts of

Statistics Canada indicate that the number of Canada's seniors will continue to grow in size and seniors' concentration in the total population will continue to increase until 2051, although at a reduced rate.

To put things further in perspective, it is instructive to note that the size of Canadian birth groups fell dramatically after 1965. The average of 426,000 births per year during the baby boom fell off to 362,000 between 1966–80, a period that came to be called the Baby Bust. There was a slight increase in the size of birth groups as baby boomers themselves started to have children around 1980; births increased to 382,000 per year through to the mid-1990s, a period now referred to as the Baby Boom Echo.[6] Since 1995, the number of births per year has progressively decreased, and for 2004 it stood at 337,000.[7]

Structural Changes Within the Seniors' Population

A surge of population as large as that of the baby boom cohorts can be expected to be accompanied by changes in the structure of the seniors' population as well as in its numbers. The most obvious will be a shift, within the first decade, to an overall "younger" seniors' population. Less obvious will be the long-run effects of increasing longevity among seniors, leading to more people surviving to a very old age. And, since women will continue to outlive men for many decades to come, the gender composition among seniors will also shift.

SHIFTS IN SENIORS' AGE COMPOSITION

"The old-old and the very old, those 75–84 and 85+, have been increasing both in their numbers and their share of all seniors," was the observation made in chapter 2 upon reviewing trends in the elderly in the decades preceding 2001 (see Table 2.2). In the decades ahead, these trends will become more pronounced. Immigration will not slacken and life expectancy will improve further, so that by 2031 it will be 81.9 years for men and 86.0 years for women for those born in Canada.[8] Table 6.2 shows the projected trend in the age composition of the seniors' population through to 2051.

Table 6.2   Projected Changes in Seniors' Age Structure, Canada, 2001–51

Age Cohort	2001 (actual)	2011	2021	2031	2051
65+	3,889,000	4,883,000	6,847,000	9,136,000	11,110,000
65–74	2,143,000	2,644,000	3,992,000	4,846,000	4,940,000
% of 65+	55.1	54.1	58.3	53.0	44.4
75–84	1,329,000	1,600,000	3,045,000	3,169,000	3,752,000
% of 65+	34.2	32.8	29.9	34.7	33.8
85+	444,000	639,000	810,000	1,121,000	2,419,000
% of 65+	11.4	13.1	11.8	12.3	21.8
90+	149,000	217,000	316,000	401,000	1,037,000
% of 65+	3.8	4.4	4.6	4.4	9.3

Source: 2001 Census; and Statistics Canada (2005) Cat. No 91-520.

Because of improved life expectancy, the group aged 90 and over has been added.

The trend to an older seniors' population that has accompanied aging of the population since the 1980s is slated to become more striking as the twenty-first century advances. This is clearly seen in the projections shown in Table 6.2. The very old (85+) will nearly triple in number between 2001 and 2031 and more than double again in the following twenty years. The same is true for those 90 and over: in both cases the rate of increase is far faster than the overall growth of the seniors' population over the same period. The effect of the baby boom cohorts can be seen in the shifting percentage shares of each of the age groups. After 2011, when the first wave of these cohorts becomes seniors, the proportion of younger seniors (65–74) becomes larger and the shares of older seniors decline (although their numbers don't). By 2021, the survivors of the first, and largest, of the two cohorts will have become seniors and by 2031 the survivors of the second cohort will be passing age 65. Thereafter, the effect of their aging will be dramatic on the very old age group: by 2051, all the surviving baby boomers will be 85 and older. At that time, one-fifth of all seniors are projected to be 85+ and nearly half of those will be 90 or older. Extending these trends to include growth in the number of centenarians, those

100+, brings even more striking results. By 2031, their numbers are expected to be over five times those of 2001 levels. Notably, for some time the 100+ seniors have been the fastest growing age groups of all age groups in the population.[9]

The projections cited here are only estimates, and not actual outcomes, of the scale and age composition of the future seniors' population. However, barring substantial and immediate reductions in longevity and immigration and/or catastrophic illness, they present a reasonable picture of the dimensions of aging in Canada in the first half of the twenty-first century.[10] The over-riding implication is that Canada will have a much greater number of seniors in age groups that are significantly more vulnerable to activity limitations due to health problems and who are also subject to changes in living arrangements and lower incomes. The consequences for communities of this surge are examined in chapter 7.

SHIFTS IN SENIORS' GENDER COMPOSITION

Almost a concomitant of the growth of the number of older seniors is that there will be an increase in the number of women seniors, given their greater longevity compared to that of men. This is the case with the baby boom cohorts, as shown in Table 6.3. However, the shifts are not projected to be as pronounced as with past senior cohorts because the life expectancy of males has been improving faster than that of females and is expected to continue to improve in coming decades. The net result is that, as the baby boom cohort ages, women will continue to predominate among surviving seniors, especially among the oldest, but there will also be an increasing proportion of older men.

In Table 6.3 it can be seen that the number of senior women overall (65+) will more than double by 2031. Indeed, this is true in every age group. Of particular note is that in the two decades following, from 2031–51, two kinds of demographic shift happen. First, there is a notable slowing of the growth of women seniors as a result of the aging of the smaller birth groups from the "Baby Bust" period (1966–80), which shows up in the size of the total 65+ group as well as in the 65–74 and 75–84 groups. Second, there is remarkable growth in the number of the very old women seniors (85+ and 90+)

Table 6.3   Projected Changes in Seniors' Gender
Composition, Canada, 2001–51

Female Cohort	2001 (actual)	2011	2021	2031	2051
65+	2,226,000	2,719,000	3,748,000	4,968, 000	6,010,000
% 65+*	57.2	55.7	54.3	54.4	54.1
65–74	1,138,000	1,382,000	2,090,000	2,506,000	2,529,000
% 65–74*	53.1	52.3	52.3	51.7	51.2
75–84	805,000	905,000	1,135,000	1,749,000	2,009,000
% 75–84*	60.6	56.5	55.5	55.2	53.6
85+	313,000	433,000	523,000	703,000	1,472,000
% 85+*	75.2	67.1	64.6	62.7	60.8
90+	113,000	159,000	220,000	271,000	673,000
% 90+*	75.8	73.1	69.8	67.6	64.9

*Percent of the age cohort that is female for each time period (see Table 6.2).

Source: 2001 Census and Statistics Canada, 2005, Cat. No 91-520.

that is attributable to the last of the baby boom cohorts reaching age 85. Nonetheless, as one scans the rows, there is a progressive decline in the proportion of women in each cohort as the century unfolds. This is the result of the narrowing of expected longevity between women and men, and is seen most noticeably among the very old where, by mid-century, there will be 10–12 percent more men than in 2001.

FUTURE AGING IN THE PROVINCES AND TERRITORIES, 2001–21

All of the provinces and territories will experience substantial growth in the number of seniors, and in the concentration within their respective populations, between 2001 and 2021 (see Table 6.4), especially after 2011.[11] In the two decades up to 2021, Canada will experience a gain of nearly 3 million seniors. The four provinces where the bulk of seniors currently live – Ontario, Quebec, British Columbia, and Alberta – will garner nearly 90 percent of the expected total growth, with Ontario's seniors growing by over

Table 6.4   Projected Growth of Seniors in Canadian
Provinces and Territories, 2001–21

Province/Territory		2001 (actual)	2011	2021	Change 2001–21 (%)
CANADA	65+	3,889,000	4,883,000	6,847,000	76.1
	%	12.96	14.40	17.73	
Newfoundland and Labrador	65+	63,000	81,000	118,000	87.3
	%	12.29	15.80	23.10	
Prince Edward Island	65+	19,000	22,000	31,000	63.7
	%	13.73	15.43	21.28	
Nova Scotia	65+	127,000	153,000	213,000	67.7
	%	13.94	16.12	22.00	
New Brunswick	65+	99,000	121,000	171,000	72.2
	%	13.56	15.16	22.25	
Quebec	65+	960,000	1,226,000	1,666,000	73.5
	%	13.27	15.64	20.37	
Ontario	65+	1,472,000	1,857,000	2,602,000	76.8
	%	12.90	13.88	17.61	
Manitoba	65+	156,000	171,000	227,000	45.4
	%	13.97	14.06	17.62	
Saskatchewan	65+	148,000	151,000	192,000	29.8
	%	15.07	15.38	19.65	
Alberta	65+	308,000	410,000	627,000	103.6
	%	10.37	11.77	16.32	
British Columbia	65+	533,000	685,000	988,000	85.3
	%	13.64	15.06	19.60	
Yukon Territory	65+	1,700	3,100	5,200	205.9
	%	6.03	9.75	15.90	
Northwest Territories	65+	1,600	2,900	5,500	243.8
	%	4.38	6.25	10.76	
Nunavut	65+	1,000	1,400	1,500	150.0
	%	2.22	3.23	4.62	

Sources: 2001 Census and Statistics Canada, 2005, Cat. No. 91-520.

one million. Alberta will add more than 300,000 seniors, more than doubling its population, the fastest rate of growth among the provinces. British Columbia will add more than 450,000 seniors. The remaining six provinces and three northern territories will also see their seniors' numbers expand greatly in this period. The four Atlantic provinces are projected to have average growth rates of 63 percent or more; Newfoundland and Labrador will exceed 80 percent. The lowest rates (still in the 39–45 percent range) will be in Saskatchewan and Manitoba and will result in 44,000 and 70,000 additional seniors respectively. The three northern territories will have multi-fold increases in their seniors' population, the largest growth rates in the country. Their new numbers will still be small, of course, given their initial base, but by 2021 they will begin to have sizeable concentrations of seniors. For example, the Yukon Territory at nearly 16 percent will start to rival Alberta, and the Northwest Territories will qualify as having an aging population.

The demographic bulge attributable to the baby boom (and adjunct immigrants) is also largely responsible for expected increases in the number of seniors at the provincial level. (In the northern territories this is much less a factor.[12]) All the provinces experienced the expansion of birth groups from 1946–65 but this, in itself, does not explain present-day and projected numbers and concentrations of seniors. The reason is the effect that inter-provincial migration has on the distribution of people within the country. Baby boomers remain within the nation as they age, but they may not remain in the province where they were born or where they landed as immigrants. In other words, they may have aged elsewhere in Canada. Furthermore, inter-provincial migration can affect the concentration of seniors in a province.

All of the provinces are projected to have concentrations of seniors above 16 percent by 2021. Newfoundland and Labrador will, by that time, be the "oldest" (at 23.1 percent seniors), followed closely by New Brunswick and Nova Scotia. Past trends in the out-migration of younger residents, along with the increase in seniors, have contributed to the high levels of aging in these three provinces, and in Prince Edward Island and Quebec as well. The two oldest provinces at the beginning of this century, Saskatchewan and Manitoba, are not expected to age as fast in coming decades as their already-old population passes on. And while the numbers of seniors in Ontario, Alberta, and British Columbia are projected to grow dramatically, each will continue to attract more young migrants than seniors from other provinces, and this will moderate their levels of aging.

THE VISIBLE MINORITY SENIORS' SURGE

Within the population bulge that contains the surviving Canadians born during the baby boom is another demographic component. Among the several millions of people who have immigrated to Canada since the end of World War II are many who were born in the same period. For example, the number of people born in Canada between 1946–65 was about 8.5 million. Yet in 2001, the number of people in the corresponding age cohorts grew to 9.5 million (see Table 6.1). There were upwards of one million immigrants in each of the 1970s and 1980s and 1.8 million in the 1990s who entered the country. Since at least one-third of these immigrants have now lived here between 25 and 35 years they are, or soon will be, senior citizens.

Source and Scale

Not captured in these numbers, however, is "the face" of these immigrant flows. Since 1971, over 70 percent of immigrants have comprised "visible minorities" from South and Southeast Asia, China, Africa, the Middle East, the Caribbean, Latin America, and the Pacific Islands, compared to less than one-quarter prior to that time.[13] They, too, have aged in Canada and many have become seniors. By 2001, visible minorities constituted over seven percent of the seniors' population. In fact, the visible minority population, including its seniors, is growing twice as fast as the rest of the population. The outcomes of these trends are discussed below and shown in Table 6.5.

In 2005, Statistics Canada prepared projections of the future size and age distribution of the visible minority population up to 2017.[14] In Table 6.5 it can be seen that high rates of growth for visible minority seniors are projected to continue to 2017 at an annual

Table 6.5   Projected Numbers and Proportions of
Visible Minority Seniors, Canada, 2001–17

	Total Visible Minority 65+	5-Year Growth Rate (%) of Visible Minority 65+	Percent Visible Minority 65+ of Total 65+
2001	268,100*	na	6.8
2006	364,700	36.0	8.7
2011	473,600	29.9	10.0
2017	683,400	44.3	11.2

* Denotes actual values from census data; all others are projections.
Sources: Statistics Canada, 2005, Cat. No. 91-541-XIE.

average rate of over six percent. This rate is twice as fast as that for the seniors' population as a whole and has the effect of creating a bulge within the baby boom bulge. By 2011, visible minority seniors could constitute 10 percent of the seniors' population and by 2017, over 12 percent. An extrapolation of this projected trend to 2021 indicates that there will then be nearly one million visible minority seniors, and they will constitute 14 percent of the total. There will be a smaller proportion of visible minority seniors aged 75+ than other seniors but gender composition is projected to be about the same, with women constituting 55 percent. Although this surge in visible minority seniors is not expected to affect the overall number of seniors, it will significantly amplify the diversity of the seniors' population, especially at the community level.

Spatial Parameters

One cannot speak with certainty about where visible minority seniors live within Canada or the type of community in which they live. Although Statistics Canada has published a number of helpful studies dealing with changing ethnocultural patterns, they do not address the age composition and residential locations of seniors.[15] Assuming visible minority seniors are distributed in the same way as younger members of their ethnic groups, however, it is possible to infer several spatial dimensions as of 2001:[16]

- Across the country, 94 percent of the visible minority population is concentrated in the four largest provinces: Ontario (54%), Quebec (11%), British Columbia (21%), and Alberta (eight percent).
- British Columbia has the highest concentration of visible minorities at nearly 22 percent with Ontario (19%), Alberta (11%), and Manitoba (eight percent) following.
- Nearly three-quarters of Canada's visible minority population lives in the three largest metropolitan areas: Toronto, Montreal, and Vancouver.
- Other metropolitan areas with large visible minorities are Winnipeg, Calgary, Edmonton, Abbotsford, Ottawa-Gatineau, and Halifax.
- Within the Toronto, Montreal, and Vancouver metropolitan areas, especially since 1991, there has been an increased tendency for the formation of visible minority neighbourhoods.[17]

Regarding the last point, so-called ethnic malls and new religious edifices have become part of the urban landscape in Surrey, BC, and Markham, ON, for example. They are new iterations of the ethnic neighbourhoods established in the wake of previous waves of immigrants, such as the Chinatowns, Little Italys, and the Jewish, Greek, and Portuguese communities. But the difference is that, for the most part, recent immigrants are culturally different and more varied and their numbers are much larger. The result has been the more frequent and widespread congregation of a single visible minority in city neighbourhoods, especially in Toronto, Montreal, and Vancouver. Statistics Canada's studies of this phenomenon indicate that in 2001 there were 254 "visible minority neighbourhoods" in these three metropolitan areas as compared to only 6 in 1981.[18] These congregations exist when, using census tracts as proxies for neighbourhoods, 30% or more of the population is from a single visible minority group. Other researchers employ criteria on a scale from 20%, when a group has a substantial presence, to 50%, when it forms a majority.[19] However, more important than statistical aggregates of these residential areas, is whether they have become "imprinted with activities and institutions of a particular group," at which stage it is said that they have become an "ethnic enclave."[20] This can only be determined empirically in each neighbourhood or census tract.

From the perspective of this book, ethnic enclaves are important spatial domains because visible minority seniors live there. These emerging neighbourhoods are widely scattered across the Toronto and Vancouver metropolitan areas, while Montreal's few such neighbourhoods are located near the downtown area. While the tendency for minority populations to congregate in relatively large numbers has been the most obvious outcome of recent immigration, there are several other spatial aspects that merit attention. First, emergent visible minority neighbourhoods account for only half of the immigrant population; of the rest, half live in neighbourhoods where they are not a significant presence and/or which they share with other population groups. Second, even ethnic enclaves do not comprise a "singular culture and class."[21] For example, the use of broad classifications of immigrant populations often obscures how groups within these areas differ from each other (e.g. economically, educationally, linguistically, or by religious orientation). Third, ethnic enclaves have formed in both the inner and outer suburbs (in Toronto and Vancouver especially), with their characteristic low-density settings of single-family homes.

THE SURGE IN ABORIGINAL ELDERS

Also within the baby boom population bulge is an upsurge in the number of seniors of Aboriginal ancestry. Although not large in numbers relative to the main baby boom, it represents a large increase in Aboriginal elders. Projections made by Statistics Canada in the mid-1990s indicate a growth to 113,000 by 2016 compared to 40,000 in 2001, an increase of nearly three times.[22] The expected trend is shown in Table 6.6. It can be seen that the growth in the number of Aboriginal elders will likely be between four and six percent per year, on average, through to 2016. This is much faster than the growth of the overall baby boom cohorts and very similar to the growth rate of visible minority seniors. The concentration of seniors within the Aboriginal population will double as a result, so that by 2016 they could constitute two percent of Canada's seniors' popu-

Table 6.6   Projected Numbers and Proportions
of Aboriginal Elders, Canada 2001–16

	Total Aboriginal Elders (65+)	Five-Year Growth Rate (%) of Aboriginal Elders	Elders as a Percent of Total Aboriginal Population
2001*	40,000*	na	4.1*
2006	62,000	55.0	4.4
2011	81,000	30.6	5.4
2016	113,000	21.0	7.0

* Denotes actual values from 2001 census data; all others are projections.

Sources: Statistics Canada Cat. No. 91-539-XPE, and Census of Canada, 2001.

lation. In other words, what has previously been a very "young" population will begin aging very quickly over the coming 20 to 30 years. This is the result of declines in both fertility and mortality rates, which are expected to continue. However, because their mortality rates are still relatively high, future Aboriginal elders will include fewer of those aged 75 and older than the general baby boom cohorts.[23] Older women will constitute the bulk of Aboriginal elders, 57%, about the same as for other seniors' groups.

AN EMERGING NATIONAL GEOGRAPHY OF AGING

The forecasts to 2021 discussed above show several distinctive tendencies underway to redefine Canada's geography of aging. First, the degree of population aging among provinces is increasing. Second, aging among the provinces is tending to a noticeable East-West division. Third, aging in the northern territories is quickly accelerating. Fourth, virtually every community, whether large or small, can expect more seniors. And, fifth, within metropolitan areas, neighbourhoods with a substantial presence of visible minority seniors will become commonplace. Each of these tendencies is discussed below and broadly indicated in Table 6.4 and Figure 6.1.

Provincial Population Aging. Population aging at very high levels is occurring in every province. In 2001, the median concentration of

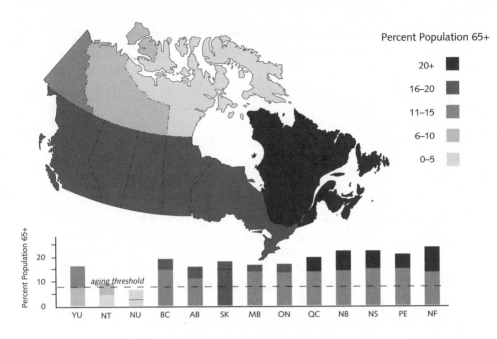

Figure 6.1   Emerging Geography of Aging in Canada,
2006 and 2021 (Source: Canada Census)

seniors among the ten provinces was 13.6%; by 2021, it will reach
19.5%. Alberta will still be the youngest province (16.3%) but with
an increase of six percentage points since 2001, it will differ little
from neighbouring provinces. Indeed, Canada's two oldest provinces in 2001, Saskatchewan and Manitoba, will further age but
only to the median level. The four Atlantic Provinces will each
experience dramatic aging in the period up to 2021 such that more
than one in five of their populations will be seniors, as will also be
the case in Quebec.

East-West Population Aging. A tendency for the new provincial concentrations of seniors to be regionally selective is also occurring.
Eastern Canada, from Quebec eastwards, is becoming the oldest
part of Canada: all five of these provinces will have an average concentration of seniors of almost 22 percent by 2021 (see Table 6.4).
Westward, from Ontario to the Pacific coast, the average provin-

cial concentration of seniors will be significantly lower, at just over 18%. This marks a distinct shift from 2001, when there was a more variegated picture of aging levels from coast to coast. This marked shift can be seen by comparing Figures 2.2 and 6.1.

North-South Population Aging. In 2001, Canada's geography of aging showed a band of provinces in the south with high levels of population aging, bounding three northern territories in which the concentration of seniors had reached six percent in only one. This spatial distinction will dissipate as all three territories experience dramatic increases in aging in the coming decade or so. Both the Yukon Territory and the Northwest Territories will surpass the 7-percent level that is considered to mark an aging population.[24] Yukon, with almost 16%, will reach a level in 2021 that would have been among the highest in Canada at the turn of the century. Even Nunavut, the youngest demographically, will see its degree of population aging more than double. The majority of this change in the north is due to the surge in Aboriginal elders described above.

Community Aging. The profound tendency of seniors to age in place in their own communities – 91% did so from 1996–2001 – is unlikely to change much, if at all, in coming decades. Combine this with a doubling of the seniors' population by 2031 and *every* community will see its seniors' numbers grow strongly, regardless of location. Indeed, mobility of all Canadians, seniors included, has been declining since at least the mid-1980s.[25] Of course seniors will move in the future, especially those who rent, but mostly between dwellings in their own communities and/or between communities in their own province. Migration to other provinces was an option for only 1.2 percent of current Canadian seniors, a level similar to that in the United States (which has seen no increase in fifty years).[26] The numbers (even if not the proportion) migrating for amenity and other reasons will grow. However, even doubled or tripled, the much-publicized amenity migration of seniors to coastal British Columbia, rural Ontario, and other attractive recreation regions will change the general distribution of seniors very little.

The outlook for the bulk of Canadian communities is that their senior population will grow in numbers, probably doubling, and its members become progressively older. Seniors will continue to have their primary residence in the same communities that they have lived in for some time. Seniors will stay on in Sackville, NB, Kitimat, BC, and Moose Factory, ON, for example, as well as in metropolitan suburbs. It can also be expected that they will travel periodically around the country and abroad in increasing numbers and return to their home communities; some may even have secondary homes elsewhere in which they spend several months of the year.

Diversity in Metropolitan Aging. Metropolitan areas, especially the largest, will continue to attract the bulk of future immigrants to Canada. Moreover, that migration stream will continue to comprise mainly the so-called visible minorities. Local geographies will often be transformed by the formation of ethnic enclaves and their commercial and cultural accoutrements. By 2021, minority seniors will often be grandparents, and their children will start becoming seniors too. Further, this will occur in all parts of metropolitan communities – in core cities, inner and outer suburbs, and the suburban fringe. And the suburbs, overall, will come to be where most metropolitan seniors live.

The Geography of Aging in 2021

Broadly speaking, these five tendencies will, by 2021, further articulate Canada's geography of aging. What we saw as recently as 2006 (see Figure 2.2) is already in the process of changing at all levels from the nation down through the provinces and regions to the community. By 2021 (see also Figure 6.1):

· Canada as a whole will have aged to a level of nearly 18%, almost 50% higher than in 2001.
· All ten provinces will also have aged to a median level of 19.5% and have a more uniform distribution around the median of about plus or minus 3.0%.
· The provinces will divide into two broad regions of aging: (1) from Quebec to the east will be older, with an average concentration of seniors of 22% and (2) from Ontario to

the west coast will be younger, with an average concentration of seniors of 18%.

· As a result of the dramatic aging of the Aboriginal population, the North will display signs of aging across two of the three territories and become much more like the provinces.

· Communities of all types, sizes, and locations will experience a doubling in the number of their seniors' population, in its concentration, and in the proportion of the very old.

· Metropolitan areas will further develop neighbourhoods with a substantial presence of visible minority seniors and many will become ethnic cultural and commercial enclaves.

REFLECTIONS

The seniors' surge that is forming in Canada as a result of the Baby Boom of 1946–65 (and the upswing in immigration during the 1971–2001 period) is often portrayed as having calamitous effects on the lives of older people, their families and communities, and social policies and programs. Mostly, the focus has been on the sheer number of seniors that will be present in Canadian society and, indeed, the projected numbers are noteworthy. Over nine and a half million people will begin to join the ranks of the seniors' population in 2011 – twice as many as there will be seniors at that time (see Table 6.1). Within another decade, nearly two million seniors will be added and, by 2031, an additional two million more will be seniors. Nonetheless, it is important to realize that the seniors' population has steadily grown for three decades and would have grown larger regardless of the baby boom cohorts: mortality rates continue to decline and life expectancy continues to grow. The impetus of the baby boom cohorts simply means that the numbers of seniors will now increase much faster.

Not infrequently, the surging numbers of seniors after 2011 are portrayed as a social problem of catastrophic proportions for the country's pension system and health care institutions. This perspective has been branded "apocalyptic demography" by Canadian and other gerontologists, who point out the fallacies of looking only at the numbers of seniors and drawing dire conclusions.[27] Many other factors are at work, such as the productivity of the economy, the uses of medical technologies, the increasing good health of seniors themselves, etc., which need to be taken into account in reckoning the consequences of an aging population.[28] This is not to say there will be no ramifications of the seniors' surge. There will be more old people everywhere in the country, there will be greater numbers of the very old, and the whole seniors' population will be ethnically and culturally more diverse than it has ever been. These prospects will present a host of challenges, not least at the community level.

What we can expect in the not-too-distant future is the ubiquity of seniors – east and west, south and north, in small communities and large. The projections discussed above bear this out. No longer will just a few provinces be demographically old – they all will be. No longer will the North be very much younger than the South. No longer will high concentrations of seniors be found just in small Saskatchewan, Manitoba, and Prince Edward Island towns, or in amenity destinations like Qualicum Beach, BC, and St Andrews, NB. Resort communities and resource communities, both previously home to young populations, will also age substantially, as will remote Native Indian, Metis, and Inuit communities. The impact of the seniors' surge will be felt profoundly in all the communities in which seniors live, for this is where shortcomings in housing, transportation, home support, recreation, personal safety, physical infrastructure, and so forth will have to be confronted on a daily basis.

One other important point should be made about the people constituting the seniors' surge. The bulk of them, the Canadian-born, grew up in a different social and economic milieu from today's seniors, so they will bring to their "golden years" a different set of life experiences that could affect their needs, preferences, and attitudes about aging. Others, who could soon constitute one fifth of all seniors, are immigrants and their life experiences will be different again. Gerontologists refer to such differences as "cohort effects"; a discussion of their ramifications is the thrust of the next chapter. Thus, it will be helpful to keep in mind the following question:

> How is the everyday geography of seniors likely to be affected by the baby boom cohorts?

Getting To Be A Senior

MOHAMMAD QADEER

My awareness of being a senior came to the surface almost overnight. Of course, I had been growing old, but the thought that I was a senior had not taken hold. Seniors were those elderly persons who sat silently, with blank looks, in the food courts of shopping malls. My first encounter with 'senior-hood' was from a VIA rail ticket agent's suggestion that I could claim a senior's discount if I was 60 years old. I laughingly accepted the discount. "Dad is senior" was the family joke for a while. But it was my retirement from almost 30 years of university teaching that brought home for me my passage into the life of a senior.

I had been preparing for retirement for a year, shedding administrative responsibilities, silently withdrawing from the deliberations of new appointments, programs, and decisions whose consequences I would not be bearing. Yet retirement was a jolt. Suddenly I became like a visitor in the house where I had been a member of the household. The familiar became strange; nothing changed on the outside, yet within me feelings turned upside down.

Retirement seemed like a moment to make a new start in a new place. I had raised my family in a smaller, picturesque town; I had come to like the unhurried life and the easy access to the country. But coming from a family who, for seven generations, had been city dwellers, I am at home in big cities. My wife, a New Yorker, concurred and together we decided to 'try' Toronto.

A big city is not normally thought to be a good place to start later life. Yet after a year of feeling a 'stranger,' I began to have a sense that Toronto was home. I developed a social network in the city largely made up of co-ethnics, unlike my previous 'community' that was predominantly constituted by persons with whom I shared professional and political interests. Although I had been happy in my interest-based community, in the big city I fell back on the ethnic identity for my social sustenance.

I found that outside of one's workplace, there are few opportunities in Canadian society to meet people and form close relations. I volunteer in community organizations, but acquaintances in those situations rarely turn into friendships. However, introductions in ethnic circles have frequently led to animated conversations and personal closeness. Ethnicity provides a path for meeting people and exploring mutual relations. With more of my life spent in Canada than in my home country of Pakistan, I do not regard myself defined by my birthplace.

But I now meet my current needs for companionship primarily through my ethnic network. This, for me, is a paradox of modern Canada.

Toronto, the city, is also my companion. It keeps me entertained and engaged. I have a weekly circuit of restaurants where I go for lunch: an Afghani meal on Monday, an Italian sandwich or a Dim Sum on Tuesday, and South Indian cuisine on another day. I enjoy discovering cheap ethnic eateries that offer delicious food. This is my new hobby. My 'finds' become recommendations for friends.

The city also offers concerts, exhibitions, and lectures aplenty. One cannot be lonely even if one is alone. Further, I live in the central part of the city and am not dependent on a car. Interestingly, being in a hub city has meant that I get to see many more friends and relatives, some passing through, something I did not have living in a small town. Later life so far has been a journey of discovery for me made possible by the big city.

MOHAMMAD QADEER, 71, is professor emeritus of Queen's University, Kingston, where, for 30 years, he taught and wrote about urban planning. He grew up in Pakistan, went to the U.S. for doctoral studies, and then immigrated to Canada in 1971. This began for him a life-long experiment of combining his formative culture with his adopted culture. When he is asked: where are you from? he says: "I wonder, am I not a Canadian?" Even in these golden years his identity appears to be ambiguous.

Chapter Seven

Impact of the Seniors' Surge
on Communities

The baby boom bulge will increase the absolute and relative number of older people at all geographic levels in Canada. The increase will happen gradually and will occur along with the continued aging of earlier cohorts. Its impact will be evident in communities big and small within a decade of 2011. From the perspective of this book, there are two essential questions to ask in response to this phenomenon: *what difference will this increase in seniors' numbers make to the communities in which they live and to their functioning?* And *will communities be prepared to offer environments that enable seniors to achieve independence?* Other issues underlying these questions include the increasing suburbanization of the elderly, seniors' tendency to age in place, seniors migrating for amenity reasons, and the effects of better health and delayed retirement. We will also need to consider the effects of gender and ethnic differences in regard to these issues.

Understanding what this surge of seniors will bring to Canada's elderly population requires looking at several dimensions: cohort effects, demographic parameters, and societal trends. The knowledge about seniors reviewed in previous chapters will also be needed. Taken together, these will provide broad brushstrokes of a profile of tomorrow's older people, among whom there will be many exceptions. Even within these limits it is still important to pursue the question:

> How will communities be affected by this surge in the seniors' population?

COMPARISONS WITH PAST COHORTS

Every population, be it national, provincial, or community, comprises a set of age cohorts, and each cohort brings to later life particular values, attitudes, experiences, and resources that will have an effect on their and others' aging. One of the important ways that gerontologists look at a demographic shift such as the aging of the baby boom is by comparing the "cohort effects" of different age groups.[1]

Cohort Effects

Differences in period-of-birth direct our attention to an important aspect of aging: the *time path*, the period of time in which each person's life course is played out. For example, members of the youngest Canadian cohort (aged nine or younger) will, on average, live a further 70–80 years and will experience and absorb the evolving values, social and economic forces, technology etc. of the current century. In contrast, the members of the oldest cohort (100 years old and older) have lived through the social, technological, and economic changes of the last 100 years. Except for a possible brief overlap at the beginning and ends of their lives, they do not share the same time path. Concomitantly, older and younger cohorts in between these extremes have already shared or will share some of the time path of both the oldest and youngest.

A senior of age 75 in 2006 had a childhood embedded in the economic circumstances of the Great Depression, followed by adolescence during wartime with its exigencies. He or she probably began raising a family in the relatively prosperous (and tumultuous) late 1950s into the 1960s. That same senior likely entered old age with a workplace pension (at least if he were male) and other social benefits such as Canada Pension, Old Age Security, and a national medicare program. He/she could expect to live considerably longer and to be healthier than his/her parents and grandparents, and to live in relative security among other elders who were not ethnically very diverse. Seniors from this 1930s cohort are the ones who established the importance of "seniors' independence" and of aging-in-place, as well as undertaking extensive amenity migration. As we consider the latest cohorts to become seniors, the question that needs to be asked is *will their life experiences confirm, negate, or modify the perspectives of older seniors?*

COHORT SIMILARITIES

It is evident that three conditions characterize later life for Canadian baby boom seniors: health and impairment, age structure, and diversity.[2]

- *Health and impairment.* Seniors will continue to experience the risks of acute and impairing illnesses, but healthier lifestyles and diets will prolong an active life for some, while advances in medical technology may also help others. Both these factors may also forestall impediments until later in life. However, old age will continue to bring a variety of ailments that will require personal and community supports for older people.
- *Age Structure.* The future seniors' population will have at least as wide an age span as exists among today's seniors. The striking differences between young and old seniors will endure along with their implications for health-related matters, income, and housing. Despite increases in male longevity, the very old will continue to be predominantly women.
- *Diversity.* Tomorrow's seniors will be just as diverse a group as today's, indeed probably more so. Differences in age, gender, health, income, education, ethnic origin, lifestyles, family relationships, and language will continue. Communities need to consider the impact this diversity will have in order to provide support.[3]

A concomitant of these enduring features of later life for the baby boom cohorts will be the increased size of the seniors' population. Although physical impediments may not occur until later, they will affect a much larger number of seniors than today. Similarly, there will be many more very old requiring support, as well as greater numbers within each distinctive ethnic group. From the community point of view, the press in the various aspects of community environments will be tested more frequently and by more seniors.

COHORT DIFFERENCES

While sharing several important attributes with today's seniors, those from the baby boom cohorts are products of the watershed post-World War II era with its momentous changes in "social values and mores ... sexual freedom, increased empowerment of women and minorities."[4] Some variation will mark those who have immigrated to Canada more recently but all have experienced the great changes of the latter half of the twentieth century, especially those related to electronic communications and biomedical technology. This social context will be reflected in the behaviour and attitudes of tomorrow's seniors as well as in their longevity, family supports, education, and approach to work, health, economic security, and ethnicity. Thus, we can expect seniors in this surge to differ in the following ways:

· *Behaviour and Attitude.* Born and raised in an era that flouted many of the older mores associated with sex, women's roles, and deference to authority, baby boomers will likely be not only more confident about being old but also take more control over their own health, and refuse to tolerate the ageism of others.[5]
· *Longevity.* Tomorrow's seniors will live longer because of improvements in medical technology and workplace procedures. By 2031, it is expected that Canadian women will see a gain in life expectancy of four years (over the 2001 level) to 86 years and men will see a gain of 4.8 years to 81.9 years.[6] On the other hand, this will serve to expand the numbers of the very old, who are most prone to physical impairment and dementia.
· *Family Supports.* It has been observed that baby boomers have "set records for a variety of living arrangements that reshaped the definition of families and household composition."[7] These challenges to traditional relationships may mean that the ability and responsibility to provide care to

elders and receive care as elders is blurred at best. In short, family support for the very old will be considerably reduced or even unavailable.

· *Education and Work.* On average, these cohorts are better educated and more affluent than today's seniors. They are generally skilled users of computer technology and some have even experienced different approaches to work, such as home offices and flex time. A much greater proportion of women will have worked outside the home and they, like the men, will have varying attitudes toward retirement and many may continue working.

· *Health.* The baby boom cohorts will live longer and remain vital because of lifestyle and diet changes and greater attention to problems of disease and physical impairment. They will be more aware of the need for preventive health care, less accepting of impairment, and more demanding that health care systems respond in kind.[8]

· *Economic Security.* While generally more affluent during their working years than their predecessors, baby boomers may suffer due to diminished private pensions, business downsizing, forced early retirement, etc. Differences in economic security will exist between older and younger halves of this cohort with younger baby boomers (1956–65) being at more economic risk during retirement.[9] Further divisions will occur due to differences in education, gender, and immigration status, resulting in substantial income disparities among baby boom seniors in their later years.

· *Ethnic Makeup.* Among the surging seniors' population are visible minorities and Aboriginal people who are aging faster than the majority (see chapter 6). Up to one-fifth of the baby boom cohort will be from these groups who frequently experience restrictions on economic and social mobility. Ethnic and/or religious differences cut across these populations creating still more diversity. They will arrive at old age with "different customs, family structures, and social mores about growing old."[10]

Seniors from the baby boom cohorts will comprise a complex picture involving all the various facets described above. Diversity will be the hallmark of Canada's seniors of tomorrow. But from province to province and, especially, from community to community, the configuration of diverse elements will vary. This is already evident in the 2001 census, where it can be seen that the living arrangements of seniors vary among provinces and size of urban area.[11] For example, many more of the very old (85+) lived alone in Manitoba and Saskatchewan than in Newfoundland and Labrador and Prince Edward Island. It will be necessary to be aware of such differences among the elderly when considering community support.

DEMOGRAPHIC PERSPECTIVES

There are several demographic perspectives that can assist in further assessing the size and nature of the changes that the baby boom cohorts will bring to the communities they live in. One of these is associated with the projected size of the elderly population. Others are related to the retirement of older workers, the expectations regarding the institutional care needs of tomorrow's elderly, and the geographic mobility of future seniors. Each is discussed below.

Size of the Elderly Population

In the last chapter the expected numbers of future seniors was derived by using Statistics Canada's "medium" forecast; nonetheless uncertainties surround any population projection. Indeed, Statistics Canada offered two other projections, "low" and "high," which differed according to assumptions regarding fertility, morbidity, and immigration (see Table 7.1). The low projection assumed lower birth rates and lesser life expectancy, the high projection assumed the opposite, and the medium projection assumed intermediate levels between the two.[12] In terms of the number of seniors in 2031, when the last of the baby boom cohorts will have reached age 65, the lowest and highest forecasts differ by seven percent, or more than 600,000 seniors.[13] Such a difference would have significant ramifications for pension and health policies among other considerations.

It is at the provincial level that broad policies are translated into actual facilities, and forecast variations begin to make a difference to daily lives and activities. It is here that health, housing, and trans-

Table 7.1   Range of Forecasts of the Seniors' Population, Canada, 2031

Subject of Forecast	Low Forecast	Medium Forecast	High Forecast
Total population 65+	8,848,000	9,136,000	9,441,000
Total population 85+	1,068,000	1,121,000	1,184,000
Institutionalized population 65+*	654,800	676,100	696,100

* Based on 2001 Census level of 7.4%.

Sources: Forecasts by Statistics Canada, 2005, Cat. No. 91-520-XIE, Tables 8.1, 10.1, 13.1; Institutionalized 65+ by Statistics Canada, Cat. No. 96F0030XIE2001003.

portation policies aimed at seniors are translated into allocations of resources among communities in terms of hospitals, assisted living units, and special transit buses, for example. How, then. is the variation in the total seniors' population distributed among the provinces? Statistics Canada offered the same three projections for the provinces and territories for 2026; these forecasts reveal the range of uncertainty in seniors' numbers for each province and territory.[14] For Alberta the difference between high and low forecasts is about 48,000 seniors, while for Ontario it is over 244,000, and for Newfoundland and Labrador only 7,500. Each of these numbers represents the range of possibilities that these provinces must plan for. In other words, it is known that each will have more seniors in 2031, but just how many more remains uncertain. The same uncertainty applies to other provinces and territories.

This immediately raises the question of *how will the difference between high and low projections be distributed across any province or territory?* Take Alberta as an example: will the possible 48,000 additional seniors be located in the province's large cities, or in the small towns, or in both places? Just 50 additional seniors in a town of 1,000 persons could impose a significant burden on community and family resources, for it is at this level that decisions come to the fore such as whether more seniors' housing, home care, or special transportation is required. Unfortunately, large-scale forecasts like these are seldom disaggregated to the community level. Communities are generally left to make their own forecasts,

but few do. Given the quickly advancing surge in the seniors' population everywhere in Canada, communities would do well to monitor their own seniors' numbers and characteristics. These implications are discussed in more detail in the concluding section of this
chapter and also in the next.

Retirement Patterns

Canadians have been retiring at younger and younger ages for at
least three decades. Whereas age 65 was the norm for a long time,
the median age of retirement dropped as low as 61 years for both
sexes in 1997. In 2003, the median age of retirement was 60.4
years for women and 63.3 years for men.[15] Several factors have
contributed to this decline in retirement age, including corporate
downsizing, government cutbacks, incentives for early retirement,
and access to pension plans. Given the large numbers who will be
making the transition to retirement over the coming two decades, a
look at retirement tendencies can aid in understanding the seniors'
surge.

It will be useful to begin by considering the term *retirement*. It
is an ambiguous term that pertains, generally, to older people and
whether they are actively participating in the labour force. Thus,
when they stop working, with no intention of returning to work,
they are considered retired. In any case, labour force calculations
includes persons only up to age 64; those aged 65 and older are
statistically considered retired. Then there are situations such as
a widowed woman who has never worked outside the home and
who lives on her husband's pension. She will also be referred to as
"retired." Statistics Canada's definition is based on the variables of
age, labour force activity, and sources of income: "Retired refers
to a person who is aged 55 and over, is not in the labour force, and
receives 50% or more of his or her total income from retirement-
like sources."[16] "Retirement-like sources" include Old Age Security
and Canada and Quebec pensions, as well as private pensions and
investment income.

Nonetheless *retirement* and *aging* are not synonymous although
they may coincide.[17] Yes, retirement is associated with the latter
part of people's lives and many people retire at or before age 65,

but many other people continue to work well past age 65 and still others return to work after initial retirement. People retire for many different reasons: some because they can afford to, others because they want to do something else, and still others because of health problems, job loss, or family demands. The time of retirement varies according to the characteristics and personal situation of the individual and his or her work environment; moreover, retirement timing is becoming increasingly varied among Canadians.[18] Although surveys of non-retired Canadians in late middle age suggests that there seems to be a "culture of early retirement," actual retirement times are frequently later than preferred because of personal circumstances. Adequacy of savings and pension coverage and home ownership are primary concerns, and these may be magnified for those widowed, divorced, separated, or never married, as well as for those in poor health and many recent immigrants.[19] Indeed, as many as 30 percent of non-retired persons indicate that they either do not intend to retire or do not know when they will retire. While many more people will retire in the coming two decades, the paths they take to that stage will be extremely varied, like so many other aspects of contemporary aging.

And what can we expect about the daily lives of tomorrow's retired seniors, given that seniors today are already living longer and living better than their forbears?[20] Data for current seniors, as we have seen in chapter 4, shows that both men and women have nearly eight hours per day of "free time" which they use for leisure, active recreation, socializing, and volunteering. Very little of their time is spent alone and some, especially men, have even returned to paid work full or part-time. Others assist in caring for their grandchildren, friends and neighbours, or their parents. The amount of free time was not very different for all age groups of seniors, although at age 85+ the time previously allocated to household chores, shopping, taking care of family members, and volunteering shifts to personal care and more sedentary activities. Baby boom seniors will not only live longer themselves, but many will also find that their parents and other close relatives are still living to an age requiring considerable care. This will affect their activity patterns during retirement and, possibly, their living arrangements and housing location as well.

Tomorrow's Very Old

Among the three age groups (65–74, 75–84, and 85+) that comprise the seniors' population, the numbers of those aged 85 and older – the very old – will grow the fastest over the coming few decades. This is the result, initially, of the continued aging of present-day seniors who comprise largely the parents of persons born during the baby boom era. They will then be followed by the oldest of the baby boom cohorts (those born 1946–55), who will begin to reach age 85 in 2031. Beyond that date, *the seniors' surge caused by the baby boom will become the surge of the very old.* Indeed, by 2041, the number of seniors aged 85 and older is expected to increase by a further 62 percent from a decade earlier and total 1.8 million.[21] Even more striking is that 38 percent of the 85+ group will be aged 90 and older. The import of this surge of the very old is twofold. First, it is in this stage of life that health problems increasingly lead to physical limitations affecting daily activity patterns inside and outside the home. Second, institutional care is required for a large proportion of those aged 85 and older.

For the first two decades after the baby boom cohorts start to become seniors in 2011, their own health will be good, but many will need to care for their very old parents, other relatives, and friends. The nearly 650,000 persons aged 85+ in 2011 will grow to well over one million by 2031 (see Table 7.1). Every one in two persons at this age reports being limited in daily activities by a long-term health problem.[22] It is well known that younger family members provide the bulk of care for elders living at home: one study estimated that 2.1 million Canadians cared for a senior family member or friend in 1996.[23] Many from the baby boom cohorts, especially women, will already be providing such care. The prospects are that this need will expand as more and more people live to age 85 and beyond.

In 2001, nearly one-third (32%) of those 85+, or 131,000 people, required institutional care.[24] If the Statistics Canada high forecast proves accurate, by 2031 that number could rise by 240,000 to a total of 372,000. Since the number and location of future continuing care facilities will depend upon the numbers of persons requiring them, there is no question that additional spaces will be needed for very old seniors; the only question will be how many. How these spaces are distributed across the country will depend first, upon the number of seniors in each province requiring such care and then, upon which regions and communities they live in. At issue here is both the expenditure of many thousands of dollars for each space and the location of such facilities, i.e. in which community will the expenditure be made?

The location of continuing care facilities is more than a functional decision, for it has implications beyond their cost and operation that extend into the community. Family, friends, volunteer agencies, community groups, and churches are part of the support network for most frail seniors. When access to continuing care is only available in another community, this support is reduced by distance and possibly disrupted almost entirely. Rural seniors and their families commonly face this situation. Consideration must also be given to the differing levels of care that need to be provided. For example, as many as one-half of the institutionalized very old suffer dementia (from Alzheimer's and Parkinson's diseases) and they require the most complex and costly care.

Across Canada, a measure used to estimate the number of residential care spaces is the "bed rate," the number of such beds per 1,000 seniors aged 75 and older. In 2004, the average bed rate was 95.7.[25] Using the medium forecast, there will be 4.3 million seniors aged 75 and older in 2031 and they will require approximately 410,000 residential care spaces – 225,000 more than existed in 2004! It must be noted that the 2004 bed rate is lower than it was in 2001 (99.8); indeed, every province except Ontario made a policy decision to reduce its bed rate in this period, although each of them was experiencing growth in the number of their seniors aged 75 and older.[26]

In addition, approximately 23 percent of seniors aged 75 and older require home health services such as nursing, physiotherapy, palliative care, and support to assist in activities of daily living.[27] Personnel providing these services must be able to reach a senior's home with minimum travel, which means that they must come from local government, non-profit, or contract agencies. Communities must be prepared for the surge in the number of seniors who require home health services and institutional beds that will occur soon after 2011.

DIVERSITY WITHIN THE BABY BOOM BULGE

The diversity among seniors that has been referred to numerous times in this and previous chapters is important for two reasons. First, it points up the limitations of using only chronological age to identify and describe seniors and their needs. All of those aged 65 and older do not have the same personal capacity and experience: age is only one of several dimensions of social location and is best seen as a marker for the increased likelihood of need. The second reason is that diversity among seniors may make a difference in how their needs are responded to by their communities, and by people in general. It will be important for communities to know the economic status of their seniors, for example, as well their gender, living arrangements, mobility, and perhaps their predispositions to seek support when in need.[28] Any group of seniors is more likely to have diverse characteristics than uniform ones.[29]

Several characteristics of the baby boom cohorts will accompany them into old age and impact them, their families and their communities. One is the diversity of family structures that have abounded among them; the other is the much wider array of ethnic differences among tomorrow's seniors as compared to today's seniors. Another, somewhat generic aspect, is that diversity increases with aging. Each is discussed below.

Diversity of Family Structures

That portion of the baby boom cohort born in Canada has been reshaping the definition of families and the composition of households in the last half of the twentieth century. "They have had children later, have divorced and remarried more frequently, have raised more children in single-parent households, have had smaller families, have households with two adults working, and have a larger number of persons never married."[30] These tendencies, which have reconfigured families, will result in more complex relationships between older and younger generations in the future as well.

The diverse family structures that have emerged have important implications for the provision of support to senior family members.

Smaller families of the baby boomers mean fewer family members available to provide care for them in later life.[31] Similarly, the much greater participation of women in the workplace reduces the availability of those family members most often involved in such care. Dissolution of marital and common-law unions among baby boomers tends to create two smaller households. As well, there are sizeable numbers of baby boomers that never married, or were childless if they did. And the children of this generation, fewer than those of earlier generations to begin with, are likely to reprise these same family situations.

Of course, seniors today are already facing the consequences of weakened family support and the changing relationships among the generations that accompany it. When their children are single parents, seniors often become the caregivers for their grandchildren. Some of them may still be providing care for their own parents at the same time – one version of the "sandwich generation." Other seniors may be providing care while receiving care themselves, whether from family members or age peers who are their friends and neighbours.[32] A host of reciprocal relationships have emerged in the lives of today's seniors. These will no doubt multiply both in number and variety as the baby boomers age. Probably the most hopeful outcome for seniors of extended family structures will be stronger bonds with their peers; this will be especially important to the one-third or more who live alone.[33]

Diverse family structures impact the incomes and other resources of seniors. Many seniors providing childcare for their grandchildren may see this evolve into co-residence with adult children, a common situation among Aboriginal elders. Seniors are often expected to provide financial support to kin, especially their children, thereby reducing their own financial security. This, in turn, may limit a senior's choice of housing. It may mean not having sufficient funds to migrate to an amenity location, for example. If combined with caregiving of the younger generation, aging-in-place may be the only choice seniors have. The various configurations of family structure and ties are social attributes of all parts of Canada, urban and rural, and likely to be a factor in responding to seniors' needs in all communities.

The New Ethnic Elderly

In all the attention given to the aging of the mostly white baby boom generation, it has been overlooked that the large influx of mostly "visible minority" immigrants since 1970 has aged too. By 2031, they could number one million, or one-seventh of the nation's elderly.[34] An important facet of this trend lies in the spatial distribution of these elders within the country. Provincially, both Ontario and British Columbia are expected to be home to 77 percent of visible minority populations in 2017, according to recent projections.[35] At the community level the distribution will be equally concentrated, with 95 percent of visible minority groups living in metropolitan areas. Within these places, "visible minority neighborhoods" with senior members will become much more evident.[36]

Although it is not possible at this time to link the population projections to the age composition of the emerging ethnic enclaves, it seems safe to assume that this is where most ethnic seniors now live and will continue to live. However, beyond this assumption, little is known about their everyday geography, the types of activities they participate in, the extent (and means) of their spatial mobility, and the personal preferences and satisfactions associated with their activities.[37] Will ethnic seniors follow the tendency of the majority of Canadian seniors to age-in-place? If this is so, as seems probable, how will it manifest itself in terms of living arrangements? Communities will be faced with such questions in making decisions about housing, transportation, and personal support for these seniors. In regard to housing, much still needs to be known about tendencies toward multi-generational households.[38]

It must be emphasized that the questions posed above will have to be considered numerous times because of the diversity within visible minority populations. Statistics Canada uses ten broad categories of visible minority groups and these encompass a variety of groups with differing characteristics including language, religion, and national origin. Thus, the ethnic enclaves that form are also likely to be diverse in culture and economic circumstances. For example, enclaves of South Asians (one of the broad categories) emerging on the western side of the Toronto CMA are composed of groups such as East Indians, Punjabis, Pakistanis, Sri Lankans, and others.[39] It is within reason to expect that the seniors in such neighbourhoods differ from each other. The challenge will be to meet their needs in ways that are accessible to their linguistic and cultural differences, a topic that will be further discussed in the next chapter.

The Aging of Diversity

Aging is a process. This seemingly obvious statement holds within it some keys to understanding diversity among the baby boom cohorts and among seniors in general. To say that seniors are a diverse group refers, essentially, to the composition of a seniors' population *at a particular point in time* (e.g. its age structure, gender, ethnicity, health status, etc). To say that seniors are becoming more diverse may mean that new elements have been added, such as the values accompanying visible minority seniors, or those of the most recent seniors' cohort, or it can mean simply that more seniors are living to be centenarians. Diversity among seniors also changes with time.

When the baby boom cohorts join the ranks of Canada's seniors in 2011, the seniors' population will begin to be infused with a set of values, expectations, and experiences that may differ markedly from those held of existing seniors, especially those now 75 years or older; in other words, something akin to a "generation gap" will exist. As well, the age structure of the seniors' population will become not only more numerous but also more diverse, younger, and with more male seniors added to the mix. For a further twenty years there will also be an infusion of ethnic seniors.

Not only is a whole cohort of seniors changing, but also there are great differences between individual seniors within the cohort. Some will retain the ability to carry out a wide variety of activities well into later life while some will not - many seniors are able to drive a car quite safely, for example, while others may have difficulty. In other words, they are not all afflicted by some incapacity at a certain age; indeed, some are not afflicted at all. Thus, making policy decisions based just on age is unwise, and cannot be implemented satisfactorily.[40]

The implications of this may be seen at the community level. A program to provide special transportation for frail seniors is likely to see its needs change over time; the program could become inadequate or, alternatively, no longer needed. Programs to house seniors to live independently may see them become impaired with increasing age and no longer able to care for themselves.[41] New seniors migrating to a community, or even just the aging of those already within the community, will bring a variety of new needs to be served. While some needs can be predicted, such as linguistic support (e.g. translation and signage) for minority groups, it is still necessary to monitor and review a program's clients frequently and be attentive to new demands. Community size, or at least the size of the seniors' community, may make a difference in assessing needs. Larger communities will generally have a larger base of seniors and therefore be able to sustain a more diverse range of programs. By comparison, smaller communities may have difficulties sustaining programs, and the situation is likely to differ from community to community as well. Thus, the advent of a surge of seniors into a community's population in the next decade or so is a signal, but only a *general* signal, that community support may be needed. It seems certain that tomorrow's seniors will be diverse and their individual needs diverse.

COMMUNITY RESPONSES TO FUTURE SENIORS

Soon after 2011, almost all communities in Canada will experience a substantial change in the size of their seniors' population. For most this will be the result of people aging in place; other places, such as those sought out for amenity reasons, will experience in addition an influx of the elderly from elsewhere. In both situations the increase in numbers will be large, amounting to 50 percent or more within five years. Meanwhile, the current seniors' population will have aged further, resulting in a greater number of the old and very old. Both populations will make demands on a community's resources.

Two paradigms can assist a community in structuring its response to the coming surge of seniors. The value of these models is their universal application and their relevance for seniors in any time period. The first derives from the perspective of *seniors' independence,* which was discussed in the opening chapter and now may be brought forward to show how it applies to communities. The second is based on the concept of a *continuum of care* for seniors.[42] Each model has its role in determining the nature and extent of support needed by a community's seniors.

Supporting the Independence of Community Seniors

The basic question for every community to ask itself in regard to each of its various policies and programs is: *how will this sustain and promote seniors' independence?* There is general agreement that seniors' independence (SI) is the prime concern of the elderly. Although SI is rendered in personal terms for each individual senior, the essential parameters are clear. In chapter 1 these were identified in terms of two sets of factors: *generic factors* concerned with the need for security in health, income, and housing, and *community factors* where housing, transportation, and community support are the concern (see Figure 1.1). A central feature of both sets of factors is that each individual component is inter-linked with each of the others in its set and that the two sets are linked in the area of housing.

The second set of factors – community factors – provides a basis for a community to appraise its approach to policies and programs for seniors (see Figure 7.1). This is a paradigm that is both universal in its application to all types of communities and practical in its identification of the key community elements, and their interconnections, that are essential to consider in regard to seniors' well-being. It starts by saying that *housing, transportation,* and *community support* are each important elements, but goes beyond this to emphasize that each element is connected to each of the others (as indicated by the double-headed arrows). Thus, for example, if a community is being urged to make provisions for senior housing, it needs to ask whether provision ought to be made for transportation and support services at the same time.

The basic relationships captured in this paradigm will be as relevant tomorrow as they are today. The outcomes may differ with future innovations in housing, transportation, or support, but the fundamental categories and relationships will not. It is a heuristic model, one that evokes our understanding of the relations among the three elements, rather than one that describes their mutual

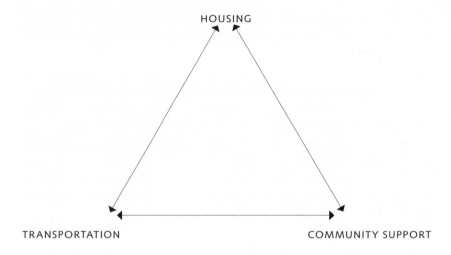

Figure 7.1   Community Factors in Seniors' Independence

causes and effects.[43] It could be likened to a simple checklist that can be used by communities in any time period. By its nature, it is general: each of the elements is a broad category containing many different aspects. In actual use, the diverse nature of each will be revealed, as illustrated in the following sections.

HOUSING FOR SENIORS

This key element in a senior's independence carries with it attributes of both "shelter" and "home." The former represents the objective aspects of housing, the structure and location, and the latter its subjective aspects, the social and personal meaning embodied in it.[44] Although seniors live in a wide array of housing situations, from single-family homes to apartments, mobile homes, and condominiums, it is not the building itself but the subjective side of a senior's home that provides much of the incentive for her/him to age in place. There is a continual "transaction" between the person and his/her housing milieu towards a "congruence" between his/her personal capacity and the housing resource.[45] If there ceases to be congruence or fit, a person may seek another dwelling, as when a senior living in a two-storey house finds that climbing stairs is increasingly difficult or when another senior finds home and yard maintenance too burdensome. Other changes could include loss of a partner, increasing frailty, reduction in income, or some combination of these and other issues, each of which may force a senior to reassess the appropriateness of her/his existing housing (see Figure 2.5) and whether they have to leave it. Increasing frailty may be offset by the provision of home care services on a scheduled basis, allowing seniors to remain in their own homes. Loss of a partner may leave the survivor with no one to drive, but transportation alternatives might allow him or her to stay home. A reduction of income might require a senior to seek more affordable housing, unless accommodation in publicly or privately provided supportive housing were made available.

The point to grasp is that what starts as a housing problem may require transportation and/or community support to solve it satisfactorily. Suppose, for example, a community wishes to provide designated housing for seniors: this paradigm points up the need for access to appropriate transportation as well as home care for frailer residents.[46] And, as residents grow older, further enhancements may be needed in transportation and home care, as well as in the design and furnishings of the housing itself.

TRANSPORTATION FOR SENIORS

This second key element in seniors' independence is more properly thought about in terms of mobility. It covers walking, driving one's own car, riding with others, using public transit and taxis and, more recently, mobile scooters. Mobility is both a *means* to accomplish daily activities and an *end* in itself for the sense of autonomy it evokes (see chapter 4).[47] The most important mode of getting around is driving an automobile, and Canadian seniors consider maintaining the ability to drive to be vital for their independence.[48] But, as with housing, there is also the matter of congruence in regard to a senior's personal capacity to drive. Driving ability is not age-related, although medical conditions that could affect ability to drive occur more frequently as people get older. If a senior is unable to drive, there will be both a functional and emotional loss for him/her.[49] The household could be left with one less driver, or perhaps none. In an urban area, there will be other forms of transportation to compensate for such a loss, but public transit may require a long walk, taxis a higher cost, and even getting a ride with a friend may be limited if there is difficulty getting in and out of a car. In suburban areas, where most urban seniors live, shopping and other services may not be within easy walking distance and, even if they are, the sidewalk system may be incomplete. In rural areas and small towns, substitute modes may not even be available and walking may be impracticable.

In many instances, even where a senior's dwelling is suitable in other ways, the inability to get around turns a transportation problem into a housing problem and/or one of community support. To maintain seniors in their homes, options include providing services such as meals on wheels, volunteer drivers, and/or shopping. Having alternative housing available in a pedestrian-friendly, transit-accessible location is another option.

COMMUNITY SUPPORTS FOR SENIORS

Supports for seniors in a community involve, on the one hand, *informal* support provided by family, friends, and neighbours and, on the other hand, *formal* support provided by government agencies and non-profit and community volunteer groups. It is important to look at each of these options separately because of the differences in support they provide and the structural arrangements they involve.

Informal Supports. Family, friends, and neighbours play a major – indeed a vital – role in the care and support of seniors. The 2002 Statistics Canada General Social Survey found that more than 1.7 million adults aged 45–64 were providing support of various kinds to almost 2.3 million Canadian seniors (or 60 percent of all seniors).[50] Slightly more than 90 percent of these caregivers were family members looking after either their own or their spouse's parents. Nearly one-quarter of all informal caregivers provided help to close friends and neighbours as well; indeed, many provided help to more than one senior. It also needs to be noted that about eight percent of seniors are themselves caregivers for their spouses, friends, and neighbours. The type of assitance provided by informal care-givers ranges from emotional support and personal care to general housekeeping, running errands, household maintenance, gardening, and giving rides to appointments and shopping. Health care is generally provided by trained non-family members.

The support provided by family, friends, and neighbours is crucial in enabling seniors to remain in their own homes. It has been estimated that as much as 80 percent of the support seniors receive in the community comes from these informal sources. Assistance varies in intensity and in the numbers and kinds of people (or "care networks") involved at the different levels.[51] A wide network of "social support," including neighbours, helps seniors to take part in community activities. A smaller "support" network of close friends, spouses, and children provides assistance with instrumental tasks such as house cleaning, shopping, and transportation. When seniors are frail and have health-related problems a third level of "care-giving support" is provided by an even smaller group comprising mainly family members. Some researchers point out that demographic and social changes, such as fewer children in families, high divorce rates, and competing job and caregiving demands, reduces the ability of the informal sector to provide support.[52] Despite the importance of informal support in the care of seniors, communities cannot assume it will be available in all cases and will need to be aware of the limits of such resources.

Formal Supports. Formal support plays a complementary role to the informal care provided to seniors. It includes services by trained personnel through provincial and local government programs such as home nursing, home support, adult day care, seniors' centres, recreation programs, and transportation services. As well, it includes services provided by non-profit and volunteer groups such as friendly visiting, grief counseling, emergency response systems, and meals-on-wheels.[53] They may overlap with very supportive forms of housing such as assisted living residences and transportation such as Para-transit bus services.

The community support seniors require is, thus, *multidimensional* and *holistic*.[54] It requires the involvement of both informal and formal caregivers, and has as much to do with assisting seniors to maintain a role within the community as with their physical health.[55] Communities face a complex task in weaving the various formal and informal strands together given the diversity of seniors and their needs. In the following section we shall see how they fit into a "continuum of care."

The Continuum of Care

The *"continuum of care"* model, which originated in the health care field, suggests how one might provide services for seniors of differing levels of need in an integrated way. We see in Figure 7.2, below, the resulting spectrum of care ranging from informal and community support at one end (e.g. family help, meals-on-wheels, and seniors' centres) to acute hospital care at the other (e.g. surgery or intensive care).

The continuum has five columns related to the degree or level of wellness of seniors, starting on the left:

1   the *well elderly* for whom general family and community support are usually sufficient
2   the *frail elderly living at home* who require more targeted informal care and community supports
3   the *functionally impaired elderly living at home* who require home care services
4   the *functionally impaired elderly living in facilities* who require round-the clock medical care
5   the *ill elderly* who require intensive medical care[56]

Each of these columns represents a distinctive domain of care with its own standards and professional training, although there is, and needs to be, considerable overlap among them. In the continuum of care, the primary principle is that each domain is linked to its neighbour and, ultimately, to the complete array: that is, they are *functionally integrated* so as to respond to the diversity of seniors' needs among individual seniors.[57] For example, a senior experiencing a serious fall will usually access the continuum utilizing the acute care services of a hospital. This is often followed by various rehabilitation services in continuing care, or possibly nursing and other support in the home. The extent of the latter support

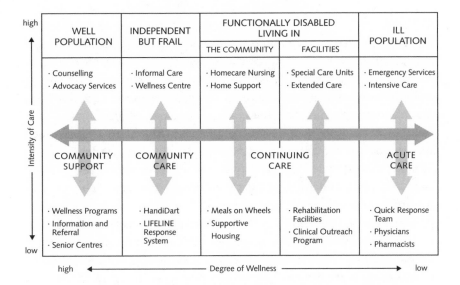

		FUNCTIONALLY DISABLED LIVING IN		
WELL POPULATION	INDEPENDENT BUT FRAIL	THE COMMUNITY	FACILITIES	ILL POPULATION
· Counselling · Advocacy Services	· Informal Care · Wellness Centre	· Homecare Nursing · Home Support	· Special Care Units · Extended Care	· Emergency Services · Intensive Care
COMMUNITY SUPPORT	COMMUNITY CARE	CONTINUING CARE		ACUTE CARE
· Wellness Programs · Information and Referral · Senior Centres	· HandiDart · LIFELINE Response System	· Meals on Wheels · Supportive Housing	· Rehabilitation Facilities · Clinical Outreach Program	· Quick Response Team · Physicians · Pharmacists

Intensity of Care: high ↑ low

high ◄——————— Degree of Wellness ———————► low

Fig. 7.2   Community Continuum of Care for Seniors. Routes to the integration of the continuum of care (examples are used for illustration purposes only) (After Havens 1995)

will depend upon the availability of family or friends to provide informal care. In this not-uncommon scenario (falls are the most frequent reason for seniors entering a hospital), the senior is moving along the continuum from right to left. Yet another senior may experience gradual physical impairment over a long period of time to the point where the care provided by family and friends needs to be supplemented by formal home support and home nursing and eventually care in an institution. Here, the senior is moving along the continuum from left to right.

For the majority who rank as the well elderly, the left-hand domain of the continuum may be the only part they and their families need and/or come in contact with. The supports they may require must be integrated vertically within the domain. Much of the practice within this domain works informally between seniors, their families, friends, and neighbours, along with voluntary programs such as those at seniors' centres, churches, and recreation centres. An important component in this area is an information and referral service that can direct seniors and their families to available supports in the community.

The ideal continuum of care is a dynamic system of services, facilities, procedures, and persons that are interdependent and integrated and able to respond to the variable needs of seniors collectively and individually. This means that information about clients and the services required for them flows between the care domains and between the agencies that comprise them, and also includes the families of seniors receiving care.[58] Thus, at the point that a senior requires assistance within the continuum of care, all the other points along it are informed of immediate and prospective needs, and the family is fully informed of the care choices available. This crucial linking function is often referred to as "one stop access," or single-point-of-entry, for seniors and their families to receive information and be referred to the appropriate point in the continuum for their needs. In 1998 Ontario instituted a version of this with a system of Community Care Access Centres providing health care.[59] However, without a system that links services and programs between *each* domain, a great deal of uncertainty faces seniors and their families.[60] In addition, it is necessary that services within each domain also be considered so they operate as sub-continuums coordinating their efforts as the needs of senior clients change.

The value of the continuum of care model for communities concerned about their seniors' needs is that it provides a base map of the components required. Following this model, one could use a map overlay and plot the services for seniors' care and support that exist within the community. By comparing the base map and the overlay, one would have a general idea of the parts of the community's continuum that may be missing. Of course, not all components would, or could, exist within all communities. A large city or metropolitan area is more likely to have all the components, perhaps even in multiple forms. Smaller urban areas will tend to be lacking, say, a major hospital for specialized acute care services. And small towns and rural communities may lack community-based services as well as facilities for long-term care.

A counterpart to the basic continuum "map" is to geographically map the location of facilities, services, and programs comprising the continuum (see chapter 5 and Figure 5.1). Seniors in smaller communities have to accept the fact that components may be dispersed within their region. The crucial factor in making such a dispersed continuum function satisfactorily is the *accessibility* of facilities to seniors and their families. Access may take several forms including transportation, telephone, and mobile services. While this is essential for seniors in rural regions it is also true for seniors in metropolitan areas. In the latter, distances may not be as large but accessibility may still be difficult. For example, specialized transit may be needed for seniors who do not drive and/or cannot utilize public transit and, where this is not feasible, alternatives such as volunteer driver programs or grocery delivery services may be practicable. One realm of the continuum that applies to all communities regardless of size involves the care and support of the well and the frail (but still independent) elderly. On the continuum this covers columns one and two, community support and community care. These two domains, indeed, cover most of the seniors' population in any community who are not yet among the very old, and even many who are. Most of the support in this area is provided by family members; in addition, community groups offer programs involving large numbers of volunteers. Programs may include rides for seniors to medical appointments, meals-on-wheels, shopping assistance, grief counseling, home and garden maintenance, and so on. Community support is more complex in these domains than in the other more structured and professionalized domains (to the right). In many ways, support needs at the left hand side of the continuum defy easy coordination of the many distinctive needs of seniors and the resources and availability of family caregivers, friends, and neighbours as well as of community volunteers.

Recent studies of rural Canadian seniors have pointed up the diverse ways that are used to connect people and services.[61] Their findings further emphasize the importance of the two left-hand domains, or what is sometimes called a "social" model of care. The social model emphasizes openness between and within domains in order to be sensitive to the idiosyncratic needs of seniors as well as to involve the families and friends of seniors and other members and groups in the community in that care. That is, seniors (and their families) are linked to various support resources, their preferences are considered, and their choices are respected. This contrasts with, especially, the two right-hand domains with their "medical" model of care that is much more hierarchical and guided by professional norms and standards. Making the continuum of care fully functional requires that the social and medical components of the continuum be bridged so that their respective strengths are maintained. And this needs to be accomplished so that the continuum functions to support and maintain the independence of senior clients.

REFLECTIONS

In the 1990s, the City of Vancouver's Social Planning Department instituted a program called "Ready or Not!" in anticipation of the surge in seniors' population that the city would experience in the year 2011 and beyond. It was designed to motivate city departments, politicians, and community groups to plan for greater numbers of seniors in their activities and services, and its message was that major demographic change was about to happen regardless of their readiness. All communities in Canada would do well to heed this same message. By 2016, and certainly by 2021, it will be evident from the increased incidence of grey heads everywhere that the seniors' population has grown significantly. The increase is likely to be 50 percent or more in all communities by that time.

With that will come changes in the mix of the seniors' population. At first, the age structure will tend toward younger, healthier, and better-educated seniors. For most communities, the source of these new seniors will be from the ranks of the current population who have recently turned age 65, that is, the aging of one's own neighbours – they will be undergoing what can be called *indigenous* aging and become what have been called "naturally occurring retirement communities" (or NORCs).[62] A select group of communities will also experience an inflow of new seniors wanting to share the amenities of the locale; they will experience *itinerant* aging as well.[63] In a few places in Canada, especially in the metropolitan areas, the ethnocultural mix of seniors will also change. These changes will be gradual but substantial, affecting both the numbers and composition of seniors' populations (see chapter 6).

While we know a lot about the general changes that will occur in amongst the senior populations of communities such as numbers, age composition, and ethnicity, knowing what is appropriate support in each community will have to be assessed locally. Communities can confront such prevailing uncertainty by, on the one hand, monitoring changes in the numbers and composition of community seniors and listening to seniors when they express their needs, and on the other, by employing the paradigms of community SI factors and the continuum of care. With the help of the latter and the knowledge of the former a community will be in a better position to respond appropriately to the seniors' surge. There will still remain the actual implementation of facilities, programs, and services for present and future seniors so that communities are sensitive to their graying population's needs, so that they are "Senior-Smart." As we proceed to outline such measures in the next two chapters it will be helpful to review the positive and negative aspects of seniors' activity patterns identified in previous chapters and consider them in regard to the following question:

In which ways do community environments impinge on the independence of seniors?

Many Faces of Aging: The Journey Continues

NORMA STEVEN

So this is what the rusty years feel like. My earthbound years will total 70 this year. I must admit to being somewhat amazed at how exciting, interesting, productive and rewarding this phase of life has been and continues to be. I believe I was programmed to expect, at best, a rather uneventful, relaxed, leisurely daily routine devoid of clock-watching activities.

In my youth I recall convincing myself that when the years of career and child-raising were done, there would be time enough to do all the things I didn't then have time to do. Of course I also didn't really entertain the idea of growing old, growing ill, weak, diseased, or frail. I intended to become much wiser, more knowledgeable, more experienced, more effective, and, in short, well-seasoned and deliciously desirable.

As throughout most of life, I now find that we get *some* of what we wish for and expect. But we also receive much of what we do not desire or expect and, perhaps, some of that which we have inadvertently sown as we hurried, somewhat unconsciously, through our youth.

The years as a senior were barely digested as I grabbed at every new opportunity which presented itself. The freedom from structured responsibilities of a career evoked an almost giddy sensation. It was an amazing and unexpected ego boost to find my time, talents, and presence were desired. The community had need of me. At the end of a crushing 28-year marriage, I felt nurtured and valued. I became involved as a director on many boards, hosted and produced a weekly cable talk show, and facilitated workshops for several caregiver support groups. It was during these busy years that I married again, this time to a partner as involved in the community as I was.

At some point I realized that it probably was not so much a tribute to my personal attributes that my services were desired, but rather that there simply is a great need for volunteers. The seniors of a community have the time and experience these days to fill the many necessary and important positions. It is pleasant and enormously rewarding to give back.

However, in my recent years as a senior citizen I have experienced more "oxidizing" or "rusting out." A bout with cancer, disruptive digestion problems, some activity-limiting hip and knee discomfort, a minor accident resulting in painful whiplash, and the beginning stages of macular degeneration have slowed my pace, and I have sought less responsible and more pleasurable activities. These years, much of my time now is devoted to my personal growth, painting and presenting my art in several art shows each year. For two recent Christmases I indulged my passion for giving voice to the written word by producing and performing an evening of readings of Christmas stories with carols performed by a children's choir. I have added a home-based business which, along with art sales, excites my bank account and my palette.

So, I enter my seventieth year with much anticipation. There are so many choices of things to do. I have subjects to study, books to read, a husband to cherish, family and friends to enjoy, grandchildren to encourage and get to really know, and poems to read and paintings to finish. And I have gained so much wisdom I want to share. So I guess I'll just polish the rust 'til it shines like the gold it really is.

NORMA STEVEN, born 1935 in Vermilion, Alberta, was raised and educated in Victoria, BC. After graduating from high school and being presented as a debutante that same year, a teaching career followed that spanned 30 years. Interest in theatre, voice, and elocution enhanced her career and continues to provide much pleasure in her senior years in Comox, BC. She acts as a facilitator for caregiver workshops, works as an artist, and is married to the love of her life, Frank Steven.

Part Four

Preparing Communities for the Seniors' Surge

Chapter Eight

Developing a Seniors' Planning Perspective

In the years after World War II, as the population of Canada surged, there was also a surge in the development of cities and towns to provide housing, schools, and parks. Suburbs grew as never before, and they were largely shaped by planning principles that favoured families and children.[1] Neighbourhoods were centred on elementary schools, dotted with playgrounds, had street patterns that discouraged through traffic, and sidewalks were often considered unnecessary. In those communities six decades later, the dominant age groups are seniors and near-seniors – and there are more to come. Those same suburbs and cities now need to serve seniors in their planning. Designers of communities today need to recognize that *what went around has come around.*

It is not necessary, however, for communities to wait until the baby boomers have surged onto the scene looking for different housing or transportation options, or putting stress on community support services. Indeed, there are probably significant unmet needs among today's seniors. The latter are already a sizeable group in most communities, and they too will continue to age. So communities can begin *immediately* to create environments that enable their senior citizens to sustain their independence, environments that are "Senior-Smart." At the outset, what will be needed is to appreciate the everyday lives of seniors and the geographies these generate. Next, there will be the need to grasp the many ways that community environments exert press on seniors as they conduct their daily activities. Then, communities will need to develop an approach to planning that encompasses this understanding. The operative question for communities (and readers) to consider at this juncture is:

How can communities prepare themselves to plan for seniors?

SENIORS AND COMMUNITY ENVIRONMENTS: AN OVERVIEW

To begin to answer the question above one needs to review what is known about the everyday geography of Canadian seniors. This must include our knowledge about seniors' activities, their mobility, and the composition of the seniors' population that shape these activities. In addition, one must allow for differences among communities in location, size, topography, and economic performance. With this knowledge in hand, a basic checklist can be developed to which community officials, service providers, and seniors alike can refer in their efforts to establish enabling environments (see Figure 8.2 below). Two other general factors need also to be considered: the first is the widespread tendency among seniors called *aging-in-place,* and its effect on housing supply and demand; the second is the widespread use seniors make of the automobile, and its effect on mobility and safety for them and others.

Activities and Mobility

Seniors, in general, consider a select number of activities as central to the maintenance of their independence. Research shows that this holds true everywhere except for very remote communities in Canada.

ACTIVITY PATTERNS

Besides the activities within their homes, their yards, and close-by surroundings, seniors pursue activities within the larger community that are necessary for daily living, as well as those that provide for leisure and community involvement (see chapter 5 for a detailed discussion). A list of destinations seniors commonly cite as important (roughly in order of importance) includes:

· Grocery store
· Drug store
· Bank

- Doctor or clinic
- Restaurant
- Post Office
- Visiting friends
- Church or other religious institution
- Seniors' centre
- Library

Other normal activities they mention include taking walks, going to the movies, playing badminton, watching ball games, going for drives, and doing volunteer work.[2]

The list is useful in showing various destinations and their frequency and spatial reach. In the upper part of the list are destinations visited most frequently by seniors (usually every one to three days) while those further down are visited less frequently (often weekly). For most urban seniors these destinations are located within two to two and a half kilometres from their homes. For rural and small town seniors the distance traveled is usually much greater, not infrequently 10 times or more, especially for those destinations on the lower part of the list (see Table 5.8). The situation for seniors living in remote and northern communities is, of course, not comparable; for this reason, each community would have to be examined individually.

It is evident that this list of destinations and the spatial reach associated with them (with the exception of the seniors' centre) could apply just as well to younger adults. Everyone shops and has the need for services, health care, recreation and leisure, preferably within one's local community, if not in one's immediate neighbourhood. It's important to acknowledge this because too often, seniors are portrayed as a "problem" population needing special treatment. But 93% of seniors live in their own homes and apartments and, like other householders, seniors have the same needs and desires to conduct everyday activities.[3]

MOBILITY

Differences do exist between seniors and others because of physical changes associated with aging (e.g. vision and/or hearing loss, slower movement, and memory reduction). These impairments, however, are most likely to affect the mobility of seniors rather than their choice of activities or desire to do them. And most seniors get around like most of the rest of the population – by automobile. As previously noted, more than half of Canadian seniors drive regularly.[4] Just as important to recognize is that even seniors who do still drive may not use cars all the time or for all their daily activities. Almost all seniors, including drivers, highly value walking. And for one-fifth of all seniors walking is the prime means of mobility.

Nominally, urban areas have a fairly wide array of transportation options while smaller centres and rural areas do not, and this is an important consideration in facilitating seniors' mobility. However, in both situations, the key factor is *accessibility* to transportation. In rural regions the issue is usually one of adding modes of transportation beyond those of driving and/or walking. In urban areas, accessibility often is constrained, even though several means of transportation are available. For example, sidewalks systems may be incomplete, transit stops too widely spaced, parking too difficult to maneuver, and taxis too expensive. In both urban and rural situations, planning for transportation and activity patterns should be considered jointly, thus pointing up the integral role of transportation for seniors' independence as was discussed in chapter 7.

Seniors' Characteristics Affecting Everyday Geography

Each community desiring to create an enabling environment for seniors must be aware of the background characteristics of its seniors' population, of its age, gender, ethnicity, income, and so forth. These social location variables shape the kinds of activities in which seniors participate, as well as their ability to carry out the activities and receive satisfaction from them (see chapter 4). One type of recreation program or transportation system or housing may be more appropriate than another, depending upon those who it is attempting to serve. The most important characteristics for making such assessments are set out below. Although these characteristics are only "markers," or general indicators, of tendencies, they do allow one to chart the general contours of a community's seniors' population in both statistical and spatial terms. In fact, the City of Regina has carried out such analyses by tabulating and mapping their seniors' data at the census tract ("neighbourhood") level for the entire city.[5] It is also well to keep in mind that these characteristics seldom function singly. The seniors' population is complex and several characteristics (a cluster) are often needed to more fully describe it.

AGE

As discussed earlier, age alone will prove to be a weak predictor of seniors' needs. Neither driving ability nor mental ability is simply age-related. Age in numerical terms is best thought of as an indicator of a *context* within which a senior's life is currently unfolding or will unfold (see chapter 1). It can act to signal a community that a segment of its citizens may require support of various kinds by family, friends, and the community.

In addition to the basic marker of age, gerontologists use *age groupings,* cohorts such as 65–74, 75–84, and 85+, to signify different life contexts for seniors as they age. The first cohort includes those who are generally healthy, more affluent, and living with a partner and thus less likely to require support. Those in the third cohort are more prone to frailty, less affluent, more likely to be without a partner, and be female. Again, these are general attributes that signal to a community the possible kinds and levels of support required by citizens falling into these age groups. Activity patterns tend to diminish in spatial scope, but not necessarily in content, with increasing age, as does physical capability in conducting them. Walking and/or dependency on others for rides also increase with age, and points up the need for a community to consider, for example, its sidewalks and other means of transportation. Also associated with advancing age is increasing concern over personal safety.

GENDER

The need for support by women and men seniors differs little at the younger age levels. However, the greater longevity of women results in a significant shift as the seniors' population reaches 85 and older. Not only is there a greater proportion of women seniors (as many as 70%) at this age, but also they tend to live alone. As well as exhibiting increased frailty, they frequently have low incomes and are renters, all characteristics leading to increased vulnerability in the community regarding housing and mobility (see Figure 4.4, for example).

LIVING ARRANGEMENTS

Knowing seniors' living arrangements offers a way of distinguishing potential needs and vulnerability among households. The primary distinctions are seniors living with a spouse/partner, living alone, or living with others (including family members). Those living alone tend to be more vulnerable to situations within the home where they may need help, and also within the community where they may need assistance getting around. To obtain a more complete picture, these various living arrangements need to be considered along with the age composition of seniors, their gender, income, and health. For example, while close to 30 percent of seniors live alone, the proportion of women living alone is twice that of men in each of the age groups. By the age of 85 and older, nearly 60 percent of women live alone.

HEALTH

Although the senior years hold the prospect of various health impairments for both men and women, all but a small proportion (about seven percent) continue to live in their own dwellings, and most in their own communities, until the end or near the end of their lives. Three-quarters of seniors describe their own health as "good" or better.[6] In other words, despite the presence of one or more health conditions that may limit daily activities, most seniors are able to live independently. This does not mean that their health limitations can be ignored in considering community environments or in providing personal support. Rather, those specific limitations associated with aging (e.g. reduced agility, vision decline, and hearing loss) constrain activities in the community and should be taken into account. Consideration must be given to walking surfaces in public spaces, traffic signalization, accessibility of public transit, and transitions between different levels (including stairways in senior housing). A special consideration is that seniors make up more than half of all persons who, although wheelchair-bound, are involved in activities outside the home.[7]

INCOME

Seniors, on average, have lower incomes than younger adults, and income continues to decline with increasing age. Senior men in general have higher incomes than their female counterparts, and those who live alone or in non-family households fare worst, especially women. Lack of money limits seniors in their choices of housing and their means for getting around in the community. It is also closely correlated with poor health, with the consequent need for family and community support.

ETHNICITY AND CULTURE

As already discussed (in chapters 5 and 6), there is a paucity of knowledge about the activity patterns, mobility, housing, living arrangements, and so forth of Aboriginal and ethnic elders, especially those from visible minorities. However, what is known suggests their needs may differ significantly in some respects from that of the larger seniors' population. Family visiting patterns among Aboriginal elders and the attraction of ethnic shopping and cultural areas for visible minority seniors are two such examples, each leading back to considerations of housing and mobility.

Aging in Place

In various studies in the early 1980s, it began to be noticed that the rates of mobility of older Canadians were very low compared to younger age groups. Moreover, such mobility tended to decrease further as seniors aged. From this observation grew the concept of *aging in place*. With seniors, the importance of staying in one's own home is heightened because of the security it represents, the memories it holds, and its proximity to friends and familiar neighbourhoods and their services. Further, when seniors do change dwellings, it has been found there is an equally strong tendency to find another home within the same neighbourhood or community. Relatively few move far away. Thus, every community's seniors' population is largely (75% or more) made up of those who have lived there for some time (see chapter 2). When seniors are asked how long they have occupied their present dwelling, it is common to find that it is 20 or more years. And aging in place also occurs with those seniors who do move long distances to high-amenity locations like Whistler, BC, and the Laurentians in Quebec; their new homes become the places they want to stay.

Aging in place by seniors presents a community with a special set of challenges. Seniors may seem to be familiar with the environment and may be supposed to cope with it. But it is too easily overlooked by the community, and often by seniors themselves, that because they are aging, new problems and needs are arising all the time. In other words, their relation to the environment they've known so long is changing, perhaps revealing new levels and kinds of environmental press.[8] A community presented with this kind of situation – and all of them are – has two challenges ahead of it. The first is to learn *where* its seniors live and in what concentrations, and the second is to be aware of their *aging* by continually monitoring it. With this knowledge, a community can work to achieve an enabling environment, including those inter-related factors – housing, transportation, and community support – described in chapter 7 and shown in Figure 7.1.

Central to the notion of aging in place is housing and the implications such housing has for communities. They are many. In the first place, it is likely that most of the housing seniors occupy was not designed for their use and therefore will not be able to meet the exigencies of increased frailty, which can often occur suddenly.[9] Programs for modifications to individual dwellings offer one solution to assist seniors better.[10] A second issue is that the housing stock occupied by seniors is also aging. Because their housing is held out of the housing market for long periods of time and not subject to periodic renovation, it may not be fully maintained, a situation often found among low-income seniors. A third and related problem occurs when seniors desire to move into more manageable, usually smaller, dwellings and discover that there are few alternatives in the neighbourhoods they know and favour. This may force them to move at a difficult time of life. Fourth, and possibly most important, is the often-overlooked nexus between the housing of seniors and the support they need to maintain their independence. Aging in place will be perfectly tenable for most seniors when support services are planned and delivered on a neighbourhood-by-neighbourhood basis. These should include safety strategies to allay the frequent security concerns of seniors, an issue described more fully below.[11]

Seniors Behind the Wheel

For several generations the automobile has been the main means of mobility for all Canadians. Studies of Canadian senior drivers in 1996 showed that about two-thirds of those who lived in cities held drivers' licenses; for rural seniors the proportion was nearly three-quarters.[12] Women seniors were less likely to hold licenses in both areas. These findings reflect the situation for senior cohorts of a decade ago; there are clear indications that the propensity to drive will be much higher for the baby boomers, most of whom have always driven. Thus as baby boomers become seniors, they will expand the number of senior drivers at a faster rate than the total seniors' population will be growing[13] Regardless, driving will still decline with age – by choice and/or necessity. And there will continue to be differences between rural and urban seniors, with the former having to rely more heavily on their cars for getting around.

Reduced vision, hearing problems, and impaired agility due to arthritis or rheumatism are medical reasons that cause seniors to reduce or cease driving; to these should be added a prominent non-medical reason: low income, which may impede automobile ownership. On the physical/health side three facts about sensory and cognitive changes that occur with aging are important to recognize because of their effect on driving.[14]

1   Speed of response becomes slower with age, affecting sensory functions, mental activities, and motor activities.

2   Sensory and cognitive performance become more closely associated, especially where the senior driver is negotiating new or unclear road environments.

3   Relatively more sensory information is required by older drivers, such as higher quality lighting and more readable signs.

Such facts, which are widely documented, can be the basis for interventions to improve the driving environment and/or improve the capacity of seniors to adapt to it. While it is important to reiterate that driving ability is only weakly correlated with age, the onset of medical conditions among the oldest drivers could impair driving and needs monitoring by licensing agencies, physicians, and family members.[15]

RECOGNIZING ENVIRONMENTAL PRESS IN COMMUNITIES

When considering how community environments can be more enabling, it is useful to review the ways in which they may impinge, or press, on seniors' everyday geography. The three broad areas of environmental press that need to be assessed in community planning for the elderly are housing, mobility (including walking environments), and neighbourhood safety and security.

Housing Environments

Housing environments constitute the primary source of environmental press on seniors within a community because of the central role the home plays in their daily activities and because housing occupies the greatest amount of a community's land. Community housing encompasses the space in which seniors spend most of their time (and which has its own internal "topography" to be negotiated), and is the origin and destination for seniors' activities in, around, and beyond the community. Two aspects of housing need to be considered: one is the *stock* of dwellings, that is the type and composition of housing extant in a community, and the other is the *spatial pattern* of the housing stock. Each of these exerts its own variation of environmental press on seniors' activities singly and together.

INDIVIDUAL DWELLINGS

A senior's dwelling exerts a constant environmental press each and every day on its occupants. Although few dwellings were designed with this age group in mind, most seniors have sufficient levels of competence and/or have adapted their behaviour to deal with the press. Problems often arise, however, when infirmities associated with aging occur so that they can no longer make adaptations. A typical situation occurs when climbing to an upstairs bedroom or bathroom, or to a basement laundry, or even to the yard and street outside, become impossible because of loss of strength and agility. Another might be when a senior is released from hospital after a fall to discover that the dwelling's doorways are too narrow to admit a wheelchair. Less dramatically, the necessity of keeping a dwelling maintained and in repair may exert a press beyond a senior's competence, as in having to shovel snow in winter or mount a ladder to clean eavestroughs. These kinds of environmental press in mundane in-home activities of seniors may go largely unnoticed except by family and friends because of the numerous adaptations that seniors make personally in "navigating" the home and yard. This may include physical modifications, such as improving lighting or installing grab bars in the bathroom. Nonetheless, all of the dwellings in which seniors live have the potential to exert a degree of environmental press to which they cannot adapt any further. This may occur due to decreases in a senior's level of competence, decreases in the condition of the dwelling, declines in income, or all three. Housing modification programs, such as one sponsored by Canada Mortgage and Housing Corporation, can improve the situation, allowing frail seniors to get out and visit others, and/or receive physically impaired seniors peers for visits in their homes.[16]

HOUSING STOCK

An array of choice in housing stock is important to seniors seeking to move within, or into, the community. In general, the larger the community the more variety of housing stock. However, even where the choice is wide in the larger community, inner city elderly residents, especially poorer ones, may find themselves in areas of decline and/or gentrification for which both their financial resources and support networks are insufficient.[17] Such seniors may feel the press of having to stay in their unsatisfactory dwellings because a suitable alternative is not available in their neighbourhood and/or it is unaffordable. Renters are particularly vulnerable: they comprise upwards of one-third of all seniors and generally they have the lowest incomes.[18] Noticeable among senior renters are women living alone who are aged 80 and older. Senior renters often lack long-term security of tenancy – a one-year lease or no lease is common – and may be subject to inflationary changes in rents.

Another vulnerable group are those requiring assistance in daily living. Housing where care is provided is unavailable in many neighbourhoods, and to access it seniors may have to leave their communities. The housing stock in an enabling environment will have a wide variety of housing types available across all neighbourhoods that are both for rent and purchase, accessible to a range of incomes, and suitably designed to accommodate seniors of all ages and cultures.[19]

SPATIAL PATTERNS

The spatial arrangement of dwellings in a community may also exert environmental press on seniors by affecting the extent of their activity patterns and ease of mobility. The low-density, single land use suburbs created mostly since World War II clearly have different implications for a senior's everyday geography from the older, prewar suburbs and core areas of cities. In most new suburbs activity patterns are more extensive and depend almost entirely on the automobile. Sidewalk systems are often incomplete as well, to add to the press. Most of the older housing districts have the advantage of closer services, public transit, and sidewalks, but may lack suitable housing alternatives as well as be more subject to concerns over safety and security.[20] By contrast, small cities and towns benefit their seniors by being more compact but frequently have the disadvantage that many services can only be obtained by traveling long distances (and usually only by automobile). Although these are broad generalizations, they should serve as an alert to housing's environmental press on seniors.

Community Mobility

Mobility is crucial to senior independence. Mobility means making choices about how to get around: whether to walk, drive, or take public transit. When those modes provide access to desired activities, senior independence is further enhanced. Although driving is the prime means of mobility for seniors, it is seldom the only one. Their choice of mode may involve consideration of the weather, time of day, degree of congestion, sense of safety, healthfulness, or level of income, as well as personal predispositions. Not least, each form of mobility implies an assessment by the senior of the environmental press it presents and her/his competence to adapt to it.

WALKING ENVIRONMENTS

Every activity a senior engages in involves some walking. It may only be walking from a parking place to a doctor's appointment or getting to a bus stop, or it may be walking farther to stores, cafés, etc. There may be a high level of environmental press even in the first example, if reaching the appointment involves crossing a busy street where there is no signal light or marked crosswalk. Reaching the bus stop may involve a high level of environmental press if the distance is unduly long and/or up hill. For those who habitually walk to nearby destinations, environmental press may be exerted in the form of uneven pavements or when curbs that haven't been ramped are encountered. These may be the source of falls, and falls are the most frequent cause of seniors being admitted to hospital as well as being a leading cause of death in the elderly (see also chapter 4).[21]

There are numerous instances where the level of environmental press may increase for a senior in the mundane activity of walking. Signals at intersections that don't accommodate the slower walking speed of the average senior are one example; discontinuous sidewalk systems are another, and the lack of clearly marked walkways in large parking lots yet another.[22] Falls and missteps may occur when a senior's level of competence is reduced or compromised relative to the environment's press, when they simply become "tired, confused or distracted" by traffic or noise, etc.[23] The inclusion of benches along walkways allowing seniors to rest and/or assuring clear signage may help in these situations. This kind of attention to the needs of senior walkers is important in small communities as well as large ones.[24]

DRIVING ENVIRONMENTS

Although seniors will usually voluntarily reduce the amount they drive, and when and where they drive (e.g. avoiding nighttime and bad weather situations), communities can expect considerably more senior drivers than in the past. Several aspects of driving associated with visual acuity exert high levels of environmental press for all drivers, but especially for seniors. They are listed below in order of the degree of difficulty they pose:[25]

· Glare, from the sun or lights at night, which is distracting and/or reduces legibility of signs
· Signs, in terms of their own legibility and in being recognized amidst other street signs
· Speed of vehicles, judging both one's own and that of other vehicles, especially in making left turns
· Unexpected merging of vehicles appearing in a senior's more limited field of view
· Dim instruments, especially if there is a difference between the light outside and inside the vehicle
· Windshield haze, which may be both a distraction and result in a reduction in view lines

Given the sensory and cognitive changes that occur with aging, this increase in environmental press should not be unexpected. Interventions in the driving environment to reduce this press include clearer signage, better lighting, and legible road markings. Left turn situations involve considerably more press for older drivers than younger drivers because of the greater complexity of perceptions and movements that are involved. This results in proportionately more accidents and injuries for seniors. Seniors who live and drive in small communities and rural areas are blessed, so to speak, with not having traffic congestion to contend with, but they still know they are obliged to deal with the environmental press of driving itself because it is often the only means of getting around (other than short-distance walking).

TRANSIT ENVIRONMENTS

The use of public transit is considered second best by most seniors, compared with driving one's own car or getting a ride with family or friends.[26] The fact that transit cannot serve all places or provide service all the time entails environmental press. There are also several other sources of this press. (1) Transit use requires physical and cognitive abilities that may exclude some seniors as, for example, the walking distance needed to get to the bus or streetcar stop and to the destination if those distances are long and/or involve steep grades. (2) There is the need to climb the (usually) high stairs into and out of the transit vehicle, as well as the ability to maintain balance when the vehicle is in motion. (3) There is also the need to wait for the bus in various kinds of weather, frequently without shelter.[27] Most urban communities now have special services that provide curb-to-curb service for those who cannot use ordinary transit. However, though the routes of the latter systems are more flexible than those of public transit, there is the need to book ahead, and service is not usually provided in the evening or on weekends.

Many seniors are transit users of necessity, because of low incomes and/or because they cannot or choose not to drive. There have been improvements made to transit vehicles in some communities, such as the low-floor buses used in Victoria. But as well as the press of accessing and riding in transit vehicles transit users, especially in cities, must cope with the press of urban pedestrian environments in ways that drivers do not. Transit users cannot determine where the stops are located and must accept the environment that exists where they wish to board or leave the bus, streetcar, or rapid transit. Two pedestrian environments that transit riders typically encounter are transit exchange points, with their busyness and complexity, and bus stops in locales that appear unsafe. The latter may occur in areas of what are termed "negative land uses," such as liquor stores, bars, pawnshops and so on, which show signs of neglect or misuse with graffiti and excess litter.[28] These situations can lead many seniors to fear for their personal safety and to avoid transit use.

Neighbourhood Safety and Security

Safety and security in seniors' neighbourhoods is an aspect of the broader factor of community support. As the city planners in Regina found out, many seniors (35% in their case) acknowledged that safety is one of the most important issues for them; only health is more important.[29] Another study of seniors' quality of life covering seven Canadian cities found that safety and security was a major issue in all of them.[30] Urban seniors are particularly prone to voice such fears and in doing so are identifying another form of environmental press exerted on them. For example, they often feel that it is unsafe to walk alone in their neighbourhoods after dark. To this may be added fear of burglaries and home invasions, crimes that could result in serious financial impact and even personal injury for them. All these fears will be more pronounced among seniors who are older, as well as those who need to use a cane, walker, or wheelchair to get around. Although fear of crime is more widespread than crime itself, seniors' fear of victimization and/or of vulnerability due to age remains a pervasive form of environmental press for many.

Conditions which separately and combined produce the sense of a neighbourhood being unsafe include inadequate street lighting, ill-located bus stops, and areas of poor visibility. Other concerns may revolve around the sufficiency of the police presence both in providing patrols and in community participation. Still others may be associated with traffic congestion, pedestrian activity, or noise. Each of these conditions fall within a community's responsibility; a community's response to them, or not, constitutes an aspect of support for seniors.

With regard to the typical, but by no means comprehensive, instances of environmental press cited above, we should remember three things. (1) Even though we have emphasized the importance of maintaining physical structures such as stairs, signs, sidewalks, and housing, each senior approaches them according to her/his own bodily competence, social awareness, and personal goals. Thus, identical situations of environmental press may be experienced differently by different seniors.[31] (2) Identical situations may present their environmental press differently depending upon *both* the conditions of the moment (e.g. day, night, summer, winter) and the personal competence and predisposition of the individual involved. Seniors are involved in a *transaction* with the environment and will make decisions that suit them, including avoiding or changing the situation (e.g. changing a route, making housing modifications). And, (3) people perceive the environments they encounter in terms that reflect not only present conditions but also their memories of the past and their goals for the future. The environment is never just physical. Thus, planning for seniors, at whatever scale, must be cognizant of how they perceive that environment and the environmental press embedded in it.

PREPARING FOR SENIORS' PLANNING

Communities wishing to become Senior-Smart must know their seniors' population and its needs, and minimize the environmental press exerted on seniors. However, a community wanting to reach this goal must face the fact that there is very limited experience to draw upon. Very few communities in Canada – or elsewhere – have initiated plans for their seniors' populations, and there is no accepted format for preparing such a plan; nothing like a "municipal plan" or "official community plan," as they are variously called across Canada.[32] Nonetheless, principles and approaches from the field of community planning can be of assistance. When they are combined with the knowledge of seniors' activities and needs compiled in this and earlier chapters, it is possible to for communities to become Senior-Smart.

Such planning should incorporate four basic components to assure both its relevance and its success. These components encompass substantive understanding about seniors, as well as the administrative, technical, and political aspects involved in planning. Each of these is addressed briefly below.

Figure 8.1   Seniors' Quality of Life Factors
(Source: University of Regina Seniors Education Centre 2000)

The Substantive Perspective. Seniors' planning should be essentially *holistic* and appreciate all the facets of seniors' activities and community needs. Its starting point, therefore, should be the mutually supportive paradigm of housing-transportation-community supports described in the last chapter (see Figure 7.1). Planning approached this way will ensure not only that *all* the basic elements of seniors' independence at the community level are taken into account, but also that their fundamental interdependence will not be not lost. Planning for one element obliges consideration (and possibly planning) of each of the others. An elaboration of this paradigm was used in Regina during the preparation of its Seniors' Action Plan, and is shown in Figure 8.1.[33] Vernacular in its use of terms such as "getting around" and "belonging" yet comprehensive in its scope, the diagram conveys the need for an integral perspective in seniors' planning. It reprises the several domains contributing to quality of life identified in a study of Toronto seniors: "physical, social, and spiritual well-being, physical, social, and community connections, and opportunities for satisfaction in daily activities, leisure activities and maintenance or growth activities."[34]

Administrative Scope. An inherent part of seniors' planning is the *multiplicity of responsibility* involved. One must recognize the broad scope of groups and organizations – public, private, volunteer – that will need to be involved in making plans and accomplishing them. This is evident in the Regina planners' diagram above. A number of agencies of different kinds must be involved such as local government (e.g. police, health, housing, roads, recreation, and planning), provincial agencies (e.g. for home support and income assistance), and local non-profit groups (e.g. friendly visiting, volunteer drivers, hospice). Planning for seniors requires a far greater scope than for other areas such as parks or transportation. It will involve a high degree of cooperation, and not infrequently barriers are encountered in achieving this.[35] Still, a large number of organizations are stakeholders in the planning process and it is vital that they be part of the process from the beginning.

Technical Knowledge Base. Planning should not begin before assembling a base of knowledge about the seniors' population through a variety of objective measures such as numbers, age composition, gender composition, living arrangements, income levels, and housing conditions. Most of these are available through the regular census of Statistics Canada. Other local data on health, traffic accidents, and home support are also available. Such a knowledge base will prove indispensable when plan-makers wish to know which seniors' issues to focus on and/or which neighbourhoods require support. The next chapter discusses various methods for establishing a knowledge base about seniors.

Involving Seniors. Another way to get to know a community's seniors is to involve them in the planning process. There are various ways of doing this, including neighbourhood meetings, general surveys, focus groups, and personal interviews. In addition, provision should be made for seniors to have an active role in making the plan by including them as part of the planning team or instituting a seniors' committee to advise the local council. The World Health Organization is only one of many advocates of such "active aging" as being a great benefit to seniors' well-being.[36] Canadian health care providers are examining ways in which seniors could not only be involved in planning services but also in providing services to others in the community.[37] In 2000, Health Canada sponsored a study of the quality of life of seniors in eight cities – Halifax, Quebec, Montreal, Ottawa, Toronto, Regina, Whitehorse, and Vancouver – that showed this factor's importance. In the final report of the project, *A Nation for All Ages?*, a prime barrier to change was "seniors' sense of powerlessness in influencing government decisions. Seniors lamented the inability to make their voices heard."[38]

These four components provide a necessary foundation for seniors' planning. Beyond this, a structure is needed to formalize policies and programs for seniors' wellbeing; such a structure is described in the next chapter. However, the importance of the preparatory level cannot be overemphasized. Given that there are no legislative requirements for Canadian communities to prepare seniors' plans, it is vital that they make a commitment to proceed. That commitment should be made by the primary legislative body in the community such as the municipal council (or other body such as a regional district or county). Once that is done, a simple checklist such as the one shown in Figure 8.2 can be helpful both in indicating the scope of the planning that will be necessary and in beginning to mobilize the needed organizational and other resources.

REFLECTIONS

Virtually all communities in Canada will experience a surge in their seniors' population beginning in 2011. Most will see their elderly population double or more in subsequent decades. They have no choice about accepting this demographic transformation. But they do have a choice to plan for the seniors' surge and for the continued wellbeing of community elders. The task of making a community seniors' plan is discussed in the following chapter. It should be considered an opportunity for a community not only to address

Where Do Seniors Live?	How to Communicate with Seniors?
❑ Identify community neighbourhoods	❑ Establish a Seniors' Committee
❑ Identify neighbourhood shopping facilities	❑ Identify seniors' meeting places
❑ Determine public transit services	❑ Identify neighbourhood meeting venues
❑ Assess sidewalk quality/coverage	❑ Inform by appropriate media
❑ Identify different housing types	
	Who Should be Involved in Seniors' Planning?
Who are the Neighbourhood Seniors?	
❑ Numbers	❑ Seniors and families
❑ Age composition	❑ Municipal departments
❑ Gender composition	❑ Provincial agencies
❑ Living arrangements	❑ Health care sector
❑ Income levels	❑ Community support groups
❑ Ethnic/cultural composition	

Figure 8.2   Preparing for Seniors' Planning: A Checklist

seniors' needs but also to see them in association with the needs of all residents. This perspective has received considerable attention. Eight municipalities across the county participated in a study entitled *A Nation for all Ages*?[39] The Province of Alberta conducted a government-wide study of the impact of their aging population under a similar title.[40] Although stimulated by the anticipated surge in seniors, these efforts and others have recognized the matter of equity in the use of community resources among all age groups because of the focus on seniors.[41] Somewhat offsetting this issue is recognition that those improvements made for seniors will be available to later generations. More choice in housing, better access to transportation and more accessible support services will benefit all, now and in the future.

The concept of "lifecycle communities" is one response that has arisen to the foregoing issue.[42] These are communities that are sufficiently flexible in physical infrastructure and service and social resources to accommodate the changing needs of all residents as they age. A community in Canada that has incorporated this concept into its planning is Okotoks, Alberta, on the fringe of Calgary. Its 2006 community plan authorizes up to 30 percent of its housing units be "non-traditional" including apartments, second units, housing over garages, and so forth.[43] In this way, there will be a choice of housing for seniors needing to move but wishing to remain in the same community and/or for younger people wishing to move in. As we move now to discuss how communities can prepare plans to become Senior-Smart, this question should be central:

What knowledge should be brought to bear in preparing a Senior-Smart Community Plan?

Chapter Nine

Planning and Designing
Senior-Smart Communities

Even as the surge of seniors approaches communities – in less than five years for most – very few have turned their attention to planning for it. As urgent as the demographic data seem, they do not have the insistence (or visibility) that other community problems have. There is no rush of new subdivisions, or traffic gridlock, or marshes to protect confronting community planners. Population aging occurs one person at a time in individual dwellings across the community. Increases in requests for accessible transportation or for supportive housing accumulate gradually, and usually seem unrelated. For these reasons, it is perhaps understandable that communities have not responded as quickly as they need to.

Nonetheless, if a community wishes to provide its aging population with an enabling environment, one that will help maintain their independence, it needs a plan at the community-wide level. Accomplishing this plan requires a viable framework to be in place. This chapter presents such a framework for communities to follow. In addition, a number of planning tools and approaches are also described. The aim is to enable communities throughout Canada to provide their seniors' populations with environments that are Senior-Smart. To achieve this, a pivotal question to consider is:

*What factors related to seniors' everyday geography
should be central in a community's seniors' plan?*

SENIOR-SMART PLANNING FRAMEWORK

A community that intends to make a seniors' plan needs to follow the steps used in other community planning efforts. It needs to know, first, about seniors and their needs. Next, it needs to appraise that information and lay out goals for addressing its seniors' needs. Subsequently, it needs to identify and mobilize the means by which the goals are to be attained. And, following good community planning practice, the seniors' plan needs to be monitored for its progress, and updated on a regular basis. Among the few communities that have developed a seniors' plan, those of Regina, SK, and Sierra Madre in California have followed this process; their experience will be drawn upon and supplemented.[1]

Seniors' Planning Process

Putting the above steps into formal terms, a planning process for Senior-Smart communities should have four basic stages:

1 *Seniors' Plan Assessment*: (a) determining the needs and preferences of community seniors and (b) acquiring demographic and other background data about them.

2 *Seniors' Plan Development*: establishing goals for the well-being of community seniors and developing an action plan to implement those goals;

3 *Seniors' Plan Implementation*: taking the necessary steps to carry out the plan;

4 *Seniors' Plan Review*: reviewing at regular intervals the success of the plan, the appropriateness of goals, and changes in seniors' needs and characteristics.

The general planning process for community seniors is illustrated in Figure 9.1.

Assessments for the Seniors' Plan. This phase, which might be called "getting to know the community's seniors," has two parallel avenues of assessment. The first is, literally, getting to know seniors personally by inviting them and their families to participate in the planning process and seeking their views and observations. The second is about getting to know the demographic and other characteristics of seniors who comprise the aging population. Each of these probes is equally important. Together they provide the information necessary to "diagnose" the situation with regard to seniors in the

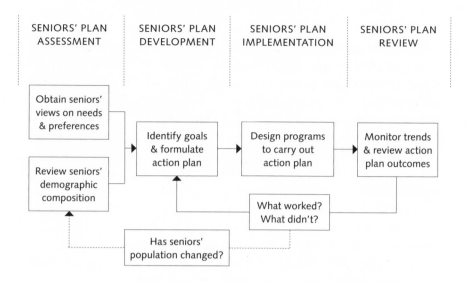

| SENIORS' PLAN ASSESSMENT | SENIORS' PLAN DEVELOPMENT | SENIORS' PLAN IMPLEMENTATION | SENIORS' PLAN REVIEW |

Figure 9.1   Stages in the Seniors' Community Planning Process

particular community, for each community's situation is likely to differ in age structure, living arrangements, income levels, etc. This follows the approach advocated by pioneer community planner Patrick Geddes in his classic tenet: "survey and diagnosis must precede treatment."[2]

Assessing Seniors' Needs and Preferences. It is a given today in community planning that citizens are entitled and encouraged to participate in their community's planning. The same approach needs to be followed in seniors' planning; indeed, seniors frequently voice concerns about being left out.[3] They are a diverse population with a range of incomes, skills, and physical impairments, as well age differences that span one-third of a century. It is only prudent for planners to take these differences into account when seeking seniors' participation.

This could include holding meetings in neighbourhood settings, during daylight hours, in venues that have adequate acoustics; providing special transportation for physically impaired seniors; and using graphic and printed materials that are easily read by older people with diminished vision as well as by those accustomed to other languages. [4] These procedures will help make seniors more comfortable, improve attendance, and enhance the information gathered. Besides the public meeting format, information may be sought through participatory research using smaller advisory committees and focus groups; the qualitative principles indicated above would also apply in these formats. The City of Toronto tried to adhere to them when it convened The Mayor's Roundtable on Seniors as part of its process for determining seniors' needs. [5]

Survey research is another valuable method for gathering seniors' views of community environments. This technique is complementary to, not a substitute for, hearing from seniors directly in meetings. Survey approaches such as direct mail or door-to-door interviews have the advantage of reaching more seniors and achieving results that can be subject to statistical analysis when the survey is rigorously constructed. An essential prerequisite for such surveys in larger centres is to establish the boundaries of neighbourhoods in which the senior respondents live. The most convenient way is to adopt Statistics Canada's census tract designations, which tend to approximate the neighbourhoods known locally. In this way, survey data can be compared with the demographic statistics gathered in the statistical area of assessment (as described below) and thereby provide a more complete picture of a community's seniors.

In addition to locational information, these surveys need to collect other basic information such as the age, gender, living arrangements, income, type of dwelling, and ethnicity/culture of the respondents. Surveys of seniors, as well as complementary meetings, may be conducted for a variety of purposes. These could include determining a community's needs for housing, transportation, health services, safety, and home support; alternatively, a comprehensive survey could cover all of these issues. A guide to the preparation and conduct of a broad-based seniors' survey was developed by the author for Canada Mortgage and Housing Corporation for use in small and rural communities; it has also been used in urban centres.[6] An example of a more focused survey is that conducted by Peel Region in Ontario in 2002. A region-wide sample of 1,300 older adults (55 and over) was surveyed regarding their plans for moving and the housing options they would consider. The results were combined with information obtained through focus groups.[7]

This survey also paid attention to the ethnic composition of the region's older population, a facet of the region that has been diversifying rapidly in recent decades. An example of a survey aimed at examining environmental press related to falls among seniors was developed in Victoria, BC. In this "Falls Prevention Audit," seniors were asked to identify hazardous places such as sidewalks, streets, crosswalks, pay phones, benches, buses, and stores where falls might occur.[8] Such locally specific information often reveals facets of a neighbourhood not readily evident to planners.[9]

Another requisite of this assessment phase is to identify the organizations that provide services and/or operate facilities primarily for seniors in the community. The array of such organizations will usually include government agencies (local, regional, and provincial), volunteer organizations, commercial firms, non-profit groups, churches, and service clubs. Most communities, even small ones, have a considerable number of programs and services. These may include home support, special transit, seniors' centres, shopping assistance, home nursing, community policing, fitness programs, friendly visiting, volunteer drivers, home maintenance, and education.

There are two important reasons for identifying community-based programs. The first is that these organizations have direct knowledge/data of seniors' needs through their responses to their clients, and these perspectives will make a valuable addition to the information being gathered. The second is that these organizations need to be included in formulating an action plan, for they will be vital in its implementation. Their partnership is essential for the success of seniors' planning.[10]

Assessing Seniors' Demographic Composition. The second component of the assessment stage of seniors' plan-making is the assembly of a statistical picture of the population. The primary source of such information is Statistics Canada's census, which has the advantage of breadth of content about seniors (see chapters 2 and 3), comparability over time and between communities (it is available every five years), and a great deal of spatial detail. Virtually every community in Canada can obtain a wide array of data concerning their seniors at the level of the census tract, a statistical spatial construct covering about 5,000 persons. Census tracts are established within local parameters that tend to approximate locally recognized neighbourhood boundaries. Thus they are very helpful, especially in places with populations of 10,000 or more, in recognizing differences between the seniors in different parts of the community.[11] The essential data to gather from each census tract comprise the following:

- Age groups: 55–64, 65–74, 75–84, 85+, as well as 65+ as a whole
- Gender, within these same age groups and including the variables below
- Living arrangements for those 65+
- Housing tenure for those 65+
- Income levels for those 65+
- Aboriginal population 65+
- Visible minority population 65+

The data provided will help create a statistical picture of a community's seniors. A number of different descriptive statistics would be produced for each neighbourhood, such as total number and concentration of seniors, their division by age group and gender, the number and percent of seniors living alone, average income levels, proportions of home owners and renters, and the number and percent of Aboriginal and/or visible minority seniors. Visual representations of the data may form *senior profiles* for the whole community and/or for each census neighbourhood to allow for easy comparison between areas, and over time. Simple bar charts (such as used in Figure 2.3) utilizing data on percentages of seniors by age group, gender, living alone, renters, Aboriginal elders, and visible minority elders would accomplish this.

Age group data for those aged 55–64 also need to be gathered, because this cohort comprises those who will be seniors within the next ten years. These data will indicate the extent and pace of aging. All these data should be updated every five years with each subsequent census, but in the meantime, planners can use analytical methods such as the cohort-survival technique to make projections of future seniors' numbers and age composition. These forecasts can also be made with data disaggregated by gender to learn the expected numbers of male and female seniors. This method uses survival rates to estimate the population of each age group over a specified period.[12] The mobility of seniors, even within the same community, must also be taken into account, as this could change the numbers as well.[13] The supply and demand for housing is also affected by the tendency of seniors to move from single–family houses to smaller multiple dwellings as they age.[14]

Census data by themselves provide only a partial picture of a community's seniors. To obtain a more complete picture other sources need to be accessed, such as data gathered by organizations that provide services or programs for seniors. For example, home support programs may provide data on numbers and locations of seniors receiving in-home assistance, and this can be a way of identifying those who are frail. Local agencies and groups providing special transportation for seniors will know the neighbourhoods (or communities in rural regions) where mobility needs are being served. Libraries, recreation centres, and school boards often provide programs for seniors and may have useful information about their clients. Although data from these sources may not always be statistically consistent with census data, it is important to acquire them for the additional completeness and local immediacy they provide. This task may be aided in a number of communities which have local committees that coordinate the activities of several agencies serving seniors; Victoria, BC, has one such organization.[15]

DEVELOPING THE SENIORS' PLAN

The results of the assessment stage provide the basis for a diagnosis of seniors' current needs and future prospects. At this point, the general concerns and aspirations of seniors and their specific problems within the community environment will have been identified and a demographic picture of the population obtained. Attention now needs to be turned to identifying *goals* that address these concerns. Goals provide the rationale by which the community proceeds to plan for its seniors as well as a commitment to do such planning. They will range from general aims for seniors' well-being to specific aims that address a particular community's situation. A few hypothetical examples will help to illustrate the content and range of seniors' planning goals:

- To ensure that all seniors in the community are adequately housed and have transportation to all necessary facilities and services
- To provide a safe and secure environment for all seniors within their homes and neighbourhoods
- To provide a barrier-free environment in all community facilities
- To ensure that seniors from all cultures will be able to obtain information about community services and resources

The Seniors' Action Plan flows directly from such planning goals. Essentially, every plan is an articulation of its goals into a set of *objectives* that the municipality and its departments and collaborating agencies propose to achieve in reaching their goals. The role of the action plan is to provide a context for the proposed actions. Thus, besides containing a statement of the basic goals at its outset, the action plan should contain a summary of concerns found from meeting and surveys, the results of demographic analyses, and the views of key providers of services to seniors. The heart of the plan lies in the recommendations it makes and the objectives it sets out to achieve. These will be stated in more specific terms than the basic goals, but will still need to be refined into programs and projects. The objectives are, in effect, *targets* for various agencies and organizations to strive for. Again, a few examples can illustrate the form that such senior objectives might take in an action plan. Some of these are drawn from actual seniors' action plans:

- To establish a committee of senior citizens to advise the municipal council on housing and transportation for seniors in the community
- To expand "the Dial-a-Ride service to enable seniors to attend many of the special events that occur on Sundays and after current operating hours" (Sierra Madre, CA)
- To "encourage safety planning for any new housing development ... [including] built-in security systems, alert sys-

tems for vulnerable persons, and social, recreation and health maintenance programs that prevent persons from becoming isolated in their homes" (Regina, SK)

· To "dedicate some housing program resources to older Aboriginal people" (Regina, SK)

· To "collect data obtained from fire and police personnel on the locations of health and safety incidents involving seniors to determine what patterns, if any, exist in the frequencies and locations of various types of incidents" (Sierra Madre, CA)

Objectives such as these acknowledge a community's awareness of the most pressing matters that need to be confronted and dealt with to develop a more enabling environment for its seniors. It is important to recognize that they are cast in *measurable* terms so that progress toward their achievement can be determined.

IMPLEMENTING THE SENIORS' PLAN

The preparation of the action plan is essential, but there still remains the final step of realizing the plan, of actually improving the daily lives of seniors. Carrying out the plan, as noted earlier, is the task of multiple agencies and organizations (for example the transit service, health agency, police department, building department, library, etc.). The action plan serves as a way of directing their resources more effectively, but it remains to them to mount programs and carry out projects. Both the ease and the speed with which the various initiatives can be mounted are likely to vary among the groups involved. For example, collecting data about "health and safety incidents" may proceed fairly quickly, as could the establishment of a committee of seniors to advise council, whereas changing the "Dial-a-Ride" bus schedules could take longer, as would altering a housing resource program to better serve Aboriginal elders.

Crucial to implementing such a diverse plan is establishing a focal point of responsibility. This could be the original steering committee that developed the plan, or the committee of seniors that advises the council. In either case, it is important that seniors be involved. Their task would be facilitated by having a program of the planned activities of all the organizations involved, including a schedule of expected outcomes. This program would constitute a further commitment to the community's seniors, and it is a vital element for the next stage of the planning process.

REVIEWING THE SENIORS' PLAN

The seniors' planning process constitutes a continuous feedback loop so that the plan can be reviewed as it is being implemented. The two aspects that require review are (1) the progress that is being made toward achievement of the basic goals and objectives and (2) changes that might have occurred both within the seniors' population and the community environment since the plan was prepared. As Figure 9.1 indicates, the review would be looking to the program of planned activities and asking such questions as "what worked?" and "what didn't?" In other words, the review is concerned with whether planned activities are actually carried out, and whether they have the desired effect. As well, the demographic picture should be monitored as the census is updated, in order to determine changes within the seniors' sector. Changes will occur in the aging of seniors, but they could also occur in their numbers and ethnic composition, or even in their living arrangements as a result of immigration and mobility. Such shifts may require changes in the action plan and a revision of activities and programs, so this is a logical extension of the task of the steering committee that prepared the original plan. Reviews should be scheduled to occur at least once every two years.

PRINCIPLES FOR SENIOR-SMART PLANNING

At the heart of any plan for the community lie a set of principles that those making the plan believe will achieve the desired outcome. These principles are primarily normative in nature as distinct from being administrative and technical. They say, essentially, this is what "ought" to guide the making of a plan. In our case, this means these are the important concepts that should be embodied in the plan to achieve an enabling environment for seniors. A set of planning principles for seniors' community environments may be derived from the discussions in this and previous chapters. Think of them as preceded by the words "the plan should":

1   *Facilitate seniors' independence.* Planners need to be guided by the National Advisory Council on Aging's definition of seniors' independence: "To be able to carry out life's activities within a normal community setting, to be able to make choices about these activities and to have a degree of control over one's life."[16] Seniors' desires for self-determination and choice as their life advances have been reiterated in numerous surveys.[17]

2   *Recognize the diversity of the seniors' population.* From the outset, planning for seniors must accept that the elderly are not a homogenous population. They differ by age, gender, education, income, frailty, ethnicity, and so forth, each of which may be a factor in shaping their everyday geography.

3   *Reflect the progressive aging of the seniors' population.* The age composition of the seniors' population is not static. It is continuously changing, with current cohorts growing older and new cohorts being added. Thus, the needs of the elderly require ongoing review.

4   *Respect the everyday lives of older people.* Just like younger people, seniors experience a flow of daily life that takes place in a variety of settings and is marked by numerous interactions.[18] They have various roles, and these roles change as do their homes, families, bodies, friendships, and communities, among other contexts.[19] Plan-makers need to see seniors as older *people*, not as a "problem" requiring attention.

5   *Embody the integral relationship among housing, transportation, and community support.* All three cornerstones of seniors' independence (see Figure 7.1) need to be considered in planning for any one of them.[20]

6   *Provide a balance of options.* Seniors are a diverse group and their needs in housing, transportation, and community support will be diverse. An array of options should be provided where possible, to allow them to exercise choice.

SENIOR-SMART PLANNING DIMENSIONS

At its most basic level, seniors' planning is about creating a good "fit" for older *people* with their *community* environment (both built and natural). Thus, one must consider (1) a set of People dimensions and (2) a set of Community or physical dimensions (see Figure 9.2). This Senior-Smart perspective differs from conventional community planning, where the primary concerns are with allocations of land and the facilities and other physical development that occur on it. In seniors' planning, the primary concern is with the senior *users* of facilities and services.

(Older) People Dimensions

Nine basic dimensions encompass the characteristics of the senior population of a community. Although they parallel the demographic information described in the planning assessment section, here they may be thought of as the application of those variables when making a seniors' plan. These dimensions should be applied when considering the activities encompassed in seniors' everyday geography and the spatial reach required in accessing them. Further, as it will be seen, they frequently interact or combine with one another.

1 *Number of seniors*. This dimension provides a sense of scale for the needs of seniors. Knowing, for example, *how many* require assistance in the home or transportation to medical appointments is important in planning the use of resources. This dimension is also used in association with each of the dimensions below (determining, for instance, how many seniors in a particular age group are living alone).

2 *Age structure*. One of the most important dimensions is the age of seniors in the community, whether the old (65–74), the old-old (75–84), or the very old (85+). Age is a good indicator of different *contexts* of life experiences of seniors that might affect the geographical scope and level

of participation in community activities. As well, increasing age often brings with it the increased risk of health problems, although their incidence and effect on activities varies considerably.

3 *Gender.* This dimension is associated with a senior's place and role in society, because the life experiences of women are different from those of men. Moreover, the majority of seniors are women, nearly 60 percent in 2001, and this increases with age. Older women are among the least affluent citizens in Canadian society, and they most often live alone.

4 *Living arrangements.* Seniors' living situations can greatly affect their ability to obtain social support and participate in activities in the community. Those who live alone lack the support of another in the household, which may manifest itself in reduced mobility outside the home. Women seniors are more prone to be in this situation.

5 *Housing tenure.* The two broad types of tenure are home ownership and renting. Each type tends to limit residents to specific parts of a community, thereby constraining their activity patterns. Renters, who comprise one-third of seniors, are usually less affluent, and predominantly women.

6 *Cultural composition.* It bears repeating that the seniors' population is increasingly diverse and will become more so in the future. Visible minority seniors are a significant part of this diversity and, not infrequently, find it difficult to access many community services. They often prefer services and facilities that are culturally and language-friendly that may, in turn, engender distinctive activity patterns. In some communities, parallel concerns emerge with Aboriginal elders.

7 *Income distribution.* Overall, seniors' incomes are lower than the national average, which itself affects choices of housing and transportation. Among seniors, there is further disparity such that one-third requires income supplements to their basic public pensions. Women seniors are prominent within this group.

8 *Health status.* Seniors have a much higher incidence of physical impairment than younger populations, which can affect their ability to get around. Despite this, over 90 percent are able to continue to live in their own homes even though their activity patterns may be constrained. Physical impairment does increase with age, thereby requiring planners to be aware of accessibility may vary among its seniors' population.

9 *Transportation mobility.* The importance of being able to get around for seniors' independence and well-being is internationally acknowledged.[21] In planning community transportation it is necessary to know to what degree seniors are transportation dependent.[22] It is also useful to know whether seniors have cars and driver's licenses, or can rely on others for rides.

While communities exert environmental press on all seniors, planners need to be particularly aware of those for whom the press tends to be highest. Applying these dimensions in concert will help identify them. Neither age, nor income, gender, homeownership, or any other dimension on its own will sufficiently identify the vulnerable, for many 80-year-olds are able to drive their own cars while younger seniors may be wheelchair bound, and so forth. Usually this may only be determined by direct contact with seniors and the agencies that provide support to them.

Community Dimensions for Seniors' Planning

The community dimensions for seniors' planning are essentially physical in nature but reflect a more human scale as compared to those subjects normally dealt with in municipal planning. For seniors, it matters whether facilities such as a grocery store or drug store are located within their neighbourhood (i.e. are *available*). Similarly, it matters to seniors whether such facilities can easily be reached (i.e. are *accessible*). *Location*, too, is important both in terms of ease of access and proximity to other facilities and services. Attention must also be given to *safety and security* both on neighbourhood streets and in accessing services in busy locations.

COMMUNITY DIMENSIONS

PEOPLE DIMENSIONS	Availability	Accessibility	Location	Safety
Number of seniors		e.g., sidewalk coverage	e.g., nearby seniors' centre	
Age of seniors				e.g., road crossings
Gender composition			e.g., bus stop locales	
Living arrangements				e.g., neighbour-hood safety
Housing tenure	e.g., variety of housing		e.g., transit service	
Cultural composition	e.g., ethnic malls			e.g., transit signage
Income distribution	e.g., transit for non-drivers			
Health status		e.g., wheelchair accessible		
Community mobility		e.g., within walking distance		e.g., street lighting

Figure 9.2   Planning Dimensions for Senior-Smart Communities

These dimensions are described further below, and shown in Figure 9.2 along with examples as to how they might be applied.

1   *Availability.* Seniors require that a number of basic facilities and services be present within their neighbourhood (if in a city) and their town (if in a rural region) to facilitate their everyday activities. Several studies have identified 10 to 12 basic resources seniors need, including a grocery store, drug store, doctor, bank, and restaurant (see Figure 9.3). When these resources are present, a community has a basic level of availability. If two or more of any of these

resources exist the community has a higher level of availability, because of the greater choice this represents. Thus,
in defining availability one needs to capture both the
number of basic resources present and the total number of
establishments in these categories (see chapter 5). Availability is a dimension that can be applied to housing as
well as stores and services. Seniors often require a range
of housing options to match their needs at different stages
in their lives and, preferably, within their own neighbourhoods and towns.

2 *Accessibility*. Beyond the sheer presence of facilities
and services in a neighbourhood or town is the issue of
whether seniors can reach them readily, i.e. their accessibility. The measure would be the preferred time and/or
distance to these resources by the mode of transportation
which seniors use. Since seniors have a strong propensity
to walk, one could use their preferred maximum walking distance (one-way) of four to six blocks, or 400–600
metres, in planning neighbourhoods.[23] In applying this
standard, it is necessary to take into account the steepness
of terrain and weather conditions. In communities that
have transit service, a similar standard of distance to bus
stops should also be used.

3 *Location*. The situation of facilities and services is also
important. In applying this dimension consideration needs
to be given to (a) the *walking environment,* for example,
crossing busy streets, (b) the *traffic conditions* that senior
drivers might face, (c) *transit access* for seniors seeking
alternative modes, and (d) *proximity* of basic facilities and
services to one another. The location of seniors' housing
projects also needs to be subject to the same considerations.

4 *Safety/Security*. One of the prime concerns of seniors is to
feel secure in their houses and to be safe in their journeys
around the community. This invokes the need for attention
to design in terms of traffic, sidewalk conditions, street
lighting, location of bus stops, and street signage.[24] It

also concerns perceptions of adequate security in terms of police and fire protection.

In Figure 9.2 both sets of dimensions are presented in the form of a matrix because they must be considered together when planning for seniors. Accessibility or safety, for example, needs to be considered in light of the age structure of seniors and their living arrangements. Different age groups of seniors will have varying needs for accessibility, while different cultural groups of seniors may have different views about what services and facilities should be available. Seniors' planning should not proceed only from one side of the matrix because their everyday geography comprises both dimensions and the interactions between the two.

COMMUNITY PLANNING AND DESIGN GUIDELINES FOR THE SENIORS' SURGE

The foregoing sections provide a basic process, principles, and dimensions for developing a Senior-Smart plan. They are applicable to any Canadian community concerned about planning for their current seniors and preparing for the surge that will begin soon after 2011. However, in each community there will be differences from the norms described above because of their location, size, housing stock, etc., not to mention the characteristics of their present and future elderly. Although there can be no single recipe for a seniors' plan it is possible to render guidelines for several broad types of communities such as city and suburban neighbourhoods, small towns, and retirement communities. These are provided in the following sections.

Planning Senior-Smart Neighbourhoods

The residential focus of future seniors will, for the most part, be the neighbourhoods in which they now live, for people's tendency to age in place is not likely to diminish.[25] Furthermore, next to a senior's home, the neighbourhood is the locus of activity in the geography of in his or her daily life. It provides a social context for activities as well as a physical setting for their conduct and for this reason it deserves concerted attention in seniors' planning. Indeed, as one study of retirement moves observed: "the best place to retire is in the neighbourhood where you spent your life."[26]

What, then, constitutes a good neighbourhood to retire in? Figure 9.3 presents a pro forma scheme for rating neighbourhoods according to their capacity to meet seniors' needs. It deals with two dimensions of amenities in a neighbourhood – availability and accessibility – and also with the quality of the environment. Availability and accessibility are elaborated here in concrete terms related to actual facilities and the means of getting around. Quality of the environment deals with more subjective aspects of a neighbourhood. Too much complexity or busyness can be daunting, but very little activity may make the neighbourhood uninteresting; much the same is true for too much diversity and noise. These attributes are probably best rated by those who already live in the neighbourhood.

Planners could begin by rating neighbourhoods (with the help of seniors living there) according to this chart, thereby determining their capacity to meet seniors' needs. In this way they could also make comparisons between neighbourhoods. In fact, in small towns, the chart could be used to assess the entire community in terms of availability, accessibility, and environmental quality. Such a chart would provide a basic checklist of desirable attributes in a neighbourhood or small community. And then, when new suburban neighbourhoods are being planned, it could be used to ensure they are Senior-Smart. Even if the initial residents are not seniors, seniors will live there in the future, and in the mean time these attributes will be beneficial to all ages. This kind of planning ahead for generational change is now being couched in terms of creating "life cycle communities."[27] The same attributes should also be included when planning the redevelopment of old core city and suburban neighbourhoods.

PLANNING FOR CITY SENIORS

Three-quarters of Canada's seniors presently live in cities, and their numbers will undoubtedly continue to grow, along with their

NEIGHBOURHOOD FEATURE	SCORING	SCORE
Available within walking distance:		
Grocery store(s)	0 = none; 1 = 1–4; 2 = 5+	_____
Drug store	0 = none; 2 = any	_____
Bank	0 = none; 2 = any	_____
Post office	0 = none; 2 = any	_____
Medical clinic	0 = none; 2 = any	_____
Seniors' centre	0 = none; 2 = any	_____
Park	0 = none; 1 = any green area; 2 = park	_____
Indoor recreation	0 = none; 2 = any	_____
Library	0 = none; 2 = any	_____
Church	0 = none; 2 = any	_____
Accessibility to facilities:		
Sidewalks	0 = none; 1 = partial; 2 = total	_____
Sidewalk condition	0 = none; 1 = poor; 2 = good	_____
Terrain for walking	0 = steep; 1 = mod. grade; 2 = flat	_____
Traffic on walking routes	0 = busy; 1 = moderate; 2 = quiet	_____
Bus service	0 = none; 1 = hourly; 2 = 1/2 hourly	_____
Bus stop distance	0 = 4+ blocks; 1 = 1–4 blocks; 2 = 1 block	_____
Bus shelters	0 = not sheltered; 2 = sheltered	_____
TOTAL SCORE		_____

Quality of environment

Complexity _____

Diversity _____

Noise level _____

Safety – physical _____

Safety – emotional _____

Sense of belonging _____

Score these factors as:

+ = good; 0 = tolerable; – = poor

Figure 9.3   Rating Seniors' Neighbourhoods

cultural diversity. Urban seniors live in both the central city and the suburbs. Each environment poses its own set of challenges to achieving independent living. They are discussed separately below.

In the Central City. Although the seniors who live in a city's core are as diverse as the general seniors' population, they are more likely to be older, live alone, and be less affluent than those in the suburbs, and they are likely to be more culturally diverse than rural seniors. The urban milieux in which they live generally offer a wide array of commercial, health, recreational, and transportation services. Yet cities are also varied and comprise different districts, each with their distinctive functions, physical characteristics, housing stock, and populations. Some may be decrepit and others not; some may be considered unsafe and others not; some may have many seniors, and so forth. Central cities tend also to have considerably higher population densities and a greater intermixing of land uses than do suburbs. Further, most were constructed on a gridiron of streets, which, though it enables greater connectivity and enhances walking opportunities, brings with it the dispersal of traffic and attendant safety problems. In cities that are older, these same characteristics apply also to older, inner suburbs.

Cities are complex, as are the seniors' population that live in them, and neither and can be planned as if they were uniform. Therefore, it is important to pay attention to two aspects in particular: the composition of the elderly population in different districts and the physical attributes of these districts, including their connections to other parts of the city. With regard to the first, it is imperative to assess seniors on a district-by-district basis for their age and gender composition, income levels, mobility, and so on, as was done in Regina and described in the last chapter. Regarding the second aspect, a fundamental task is to assess the built environment of each district, especially the housing options, as well as the quality of walking surfaces, street lighting, areas that generate perceptions of risk and fear, and automobile traffic/pedestrian interfaces.[28] One study sums it up this way: "if a neighbourhood is walkable but unsafe, residents, and especially women, will be far less likely to walk extensively."[29] An example of this concern for detail in city walking environments is the Urban Braille System, developed by planners in Hamilton, Ontario. It is designed to assist the elderly, severely visually impaired, and infirm in "navigating" public spaces such as sidewalks and bus stops.[30] It is one solution toward enabling environments for city seniors; others include:

- Designing street crossings that enable seniors ample time to cross safely
- Repairing sidewalks that have cracks and rough surfaces to prevent falls
- Involving seniors in a safety and security audit in all neighbourhoods and then addressing their concerns
- Establishing a "council of elders" to advise the municipal council on matters that concern seniors
- Developing senior citizen "playgrounds" which could include such activities as giant chess boards and bowling, etc.[31]
- Ensuring that signs for streets and businesses are legible
- Expanding housing choices within each neighbourhood
- Assessing public transportation so that routes serve areas where seniors live; also ensuring that vehicles are able to be boarded and transit stops are accessible to seniors with a range of functional abilities
- Providing home maintenance services
- Establishing a single-point-of-entry information and referral service for seniors and their families

In the Suburbs. Today, more than one-third of Canada's seniors live in suburban settings, arguably their most common residential situation.[32] Suburbs are no longer just extensions of central city residential areas as they were in the 1960s and 1970s. They may contain major shopping complexes, office and other employment centres, and groupings of high and medium density housing. Still, their dominant feature remains the large tracts of single family housing set within curvilinear street patterns bounded by arterial roads. Shopping and other services exist in widely separated clusters and getting to and from them is inextricably linked to use of the automobile. Even for short trips walking is made difficult by the lack of connections in the street pattern and lack of sidewalks. Thus a suburban senior's everyday activities are constrained by land use and street patterns.[33] Increasing attention is being given to assisting seniors to maintain an active lifestyle both for physical health and social connectedness, and emphasis is being placed on modifying land use arrangements in the suburbs.[34] The underlying fact is that there are already considerable numbers of those aged 75 and older in suburbs and many more are to come. Among the strategies being propounded are:

· Identifying gaps in the sidewalk network and ensuring all sidewalks are wide enough to accommodate seniors with canes, walkers, and wheelchairs[35]
· Creating safe and comfortable walking and cycle routes
· Retrofitting existing street design and planning new sub-divisions so that there is more connectivity to community facilities for pedestrians and motorists[36]
· Revising land use regulations to allow accessory dwellings and shared dwellings in single-family neighbourhoods[37]
· Adding accessible routes and vehicles to the public transit system
· Providing home maintenance services
· Providing frequent benches and resting places for senior pedestrians
· Introducing small-scale health, social, and recreation facilities into neighbourhoods

Planning for Rural Seniors

For the most part, planning for rural seniors involves attention to the same sets of concerns and principles as for urban seniors, the major exception being communities of Aboriginal elders. The need to integrate the three community factors – housing, support services, and transportation – into seniors' planning applies equally to rural seniors.[38] The planning principles and process described above are appropriate as well. What differs is the nature of the rural community itself. First, the place is small in size and, second, it usually encompasses several towns and villages (and a nearby larger centre).

The resources rural seniors need are separated by many miles and are usually only accessible by automobile. Their everyday geography is spatially distended and their numbers small (although often large in terms of their concentration within the local population).

Add to this the fact that rural seniors vary in their values, social systems, and cultures, frequently from one small community to another in the same locale. As well, they may differ in their personal characteristics, as was found in a recent study that identified four groups: active community seniors, stoic seniors, marginalized seniors, and frail seniors.[39] These variations need to be taken into account because they affect the connections that seniors have both with services and with other people in the community. For example, the first type are largely independent, self-sufficient, and involved in community life, while the fourth type require considerable support and are prone to social isolation.[40] Needless to say, individual seniors may move between groups over time with increasing age and/or changing circumstances in income, marital status, and so forth.

Few towns and villages will experience additional population growth as the numbers of their seniors expand, the exception being places on the fringe of a metropolitan centre. The general implication is that demand for resources – resources already more scarce than are found in cities – will increase. Moreover, many rural communities are located within regions of economic decline, with the consequent reduction in younger populations to provide service and tax resources.[41] Solutions may have to be found on a regional basis involving the pooling of resources of several towns or a nearby city in order to achieve the scale necessary to provide infrastructure (e.g. medical clinics, housing) and services (e.g. transportation) efficiently.[42]

It is important, however, to recognize that the solutions have to be "rural": that is, built on local support systems, whether formal or informal.[43] They need to be small in scale and be based on values of reciprocity. A study of more than 200 Canadian rural communities identified five areas of need: housing, transportation, care facilities, recreation/social services and facilities, and home support services.[44] Solutions to filling these needs include:

- Providing housing in the form of self-contained units (that can be built as needed) for seniors no longer able to live in the family home and/or who are widowed
- Locating new housing within easy walking distance of local stores and services
- Organizing local volunteer drivers to provide rides to out-of-town services and facilities
- Providing a wheelchair-accessible van to transport physically impaired and other seniors to nearby services and events
- Providing sidewalks and street lighting
- Establishing an adult day centre
- Collaborating with the local school to provide recreation and education programs for seniors
- Funding small communities to construct seniors' social and recreational centres

Retirement Communities

Retirement communities are a feature of the Canadian landscape in rural regions, on the suburban edge of large cities, and even within cities. The coming surge of seniors will prompt their further growth, the development of new places, and the emergence of new types. It is not expected that the already-low inter- and intra-provincial migration rates of seniors (7.5%) will increase in the foreseeable future (see Table 2.8). However, the sheer growth in seniors' numbers will greatly expand interest in these places for those aged 65–74; the group most likely to decide to move from an old and familiar residence to a retirement setting.

"Retirement communities" encompass several different types of situations. Most retirement communities are purpose-built, like Arbutus Ridge on Vancouver Island, with housing arrayed around a golf course or other recreational resource. They aim to attract those who are still relatively young and are married, affluent, healthy, and active, at least when they move in. Such retirement "villages" may also include on-site health services, but residents are usually dependent upon nearby cities or towns for most other day-to-day services. Another type of retirement community is exemplified by

Elliot Lake in Ontario, which made a deliberate effort to attract retirees because of the decline in the community's mining fortunes and population.[45] In this situation, services and facilities for seniors were incorporated into the community. Yet another type is the existing community that has become the destination for retirees from other provinces or other places in the same province: Qualicum Beach, BC, and St Andrews, NB, are examples. They both have attracted amenity-seeking retirees because of their high-quality natural environments. Most other provinces have similar retirement destinations. Two more recent types of retirement situations are those occurring within cities either in the form of apartment complexes (sometimes called "campuses") or as "gated" enclaves of houses and garden apartments. Both these types have their own internal road system and, frequently, recreation facilities.

The principles of Senior-Smart planning should apply to all these types of retirement communities. Many began as a complex of residential units adjacent to recreation facilities such as a golf course, marina, or lake.[46] Usually, little thought was given to incorporating the neighbourhood attributes listed in Figure 9.3. More recently, planned retirement communities have included some of these features, including health services. Not unexpectedly, such retirement communities find, as all do, that residents age in place and their needs change, especially in regards to health, personal support, and transportation. Many of the towns and villages that become retirement destinations have the commercial and physical structure on which to build a more enabling community environment for seniors. Yet they too often have limits, when care for the very old looms as an issue and long-term care facilities cannot be made available, as Elliot Lake experienced. Not infrequently, it is found that as residents age there is a lack of amenities and services to support them. Their options then are either to move, or to remain somewhat isolated and dependent on others. Solutions that would allow for a high degree of "permeability" between the retirement community and its neighbouring town, include:

· Providing a community bus to nearby services and events
· Organizing residents to offer lifts to others who are less mobile

· Inviting health care and other professionals to schedule visits to the community

Planning for Transportation

Of the three community factors for seniors' independence (see Figure 7.1), transportation is the most ubiquitous in its effects. It applies to the well- and the ill-housed, to those needing support and those who do not. In seniors' lives transportation has a functional side (obtaining goods and services) and a psychological side (being able to get out and about). Clearly, fashioning options to meet such a wide range of needs is challenging, not least because the automobile is the transportation means of choice for seniors in Canada. Nonetheless, not all seniors have access to a car, or are able to drive even if one is available. Some have never driven, others cannot or choose not to drive because of health limitations, and still others cannot afford an auto: one-quarter or more of seniors are limited in their mobility in these ways.

All communities must face the fact that their seniors have been aging, and with increasing age come the physical and cognitive limitations that reduce a person's ability to drive safely. Alternative modes of transportation are needed so that older persons are able to stay connected to their community and maintain their sense of well-being.[47] The default option, so to speak, for those seniors who do not drive is public transit. However in its present form, public transit is often not a viable option, whether for "serious" or "discretionary" travel.[48] It may get a senior downtown or to a shopping centre, but for visiting friends or enjoying the natural environment it is problematic at best. For suburban seniors accessing bus service may be difficult, and in rural communities (including many retirement communities), there is usually no transit option at all.[49] Demand-response systems that provide door-to-door service, such as Paratransit, also often have limitations. Their use may be restricted to trips for health care and food shopping and/or require extensive advance booking for trips. As well, both these transit forms often have operating hours that do not include evenings, Sundays, and holidays, times when much discretionary travel occurs. Solutions in this vital area of seniors' independence include:

· Expanding the hours of operation of public transit
· Ensuring that transit stops and vehicles are accessible to seniors
· Encouraging seniors' organizations and other groups to offer lifts to seniors
· Providing demand-responsive transport systems that allow trips for all purposes and at all times
· Developing other transportation options such as "taxi vouchers" and "fuel vouchers"
· Encouraging businesses, both singly and collectively, to offer transport to and from their facilities and/or make deliveries

Planning for Ethnic Diversity

Canada's largest cities, in particular, are quickly becoming home to increasing numbers of seniors from visible minority cultures (see chapter 6). All indications are that most live in the ethnic "enclaves" that have been forming in Toronto, Vancouver, Montreal, and other large cities.[50] This tendency requires seniors' planners to be much more aware of the "people" dimensions discussed above, and of the neighbourhood attributes that might apply. Although it is likely that there will be similarities in the services and facilities required by ethnic seniors, it is important that their needs be met in "linguistically and culturally accessible ways," as has been expressed by these elders themselves.[51] Furthermore, since these are fairly new trends and knowledge about them is scarce, planners should approach such situations pragmatically rather than with a standard package of facilities and services. For example, it is often assumed that most visible minority seniors are cared for by their families, but there is considerable variation in the amount and kind of support that is provided by families.[52] There is "much more to learn ... about the needs of ethnic minority seniors," in the words of Canada's National Advisory Council on Aging who, in turn, make the following recommendations:[53]

· Provide housing options so that seniors have a choice whether or not to live with other family members

· Provide training to service agencies to ensure a better understanding of cultural and ethnic differences and how best to serve clients of various backgrounds
· Increase representation of ethnic minority seniors on community planning, policy, and program advisory bodies

Mapping for Seniors' Planning

Planning enabling environments for seniors is about matching the resources they need to where seniors live. This ranges from providing sidewalks to medical clinics to delivering meals to homebound seniors. It involves allocating facilities that are accessible to seniors (e.g. housing, seniors' centres, pharmacies) and/or delivering services to them (e.g. home support, meals-on-wheels). Beyond the qualitative aspects of the services and facilities that are provided, there remain questions about their spatial allocation. Resolving these issues is important both for seniors seeking access and for providers of service seeking to function effectively. So both clients and service providers will have locations on a map of the community.

The potential for using new geographical mapping tools to graphically portray and analyze seniors' planning issues is both great and underutilized.[54] Geographic Information Systems (GIS), combined with other spatial allocation models, allow planners to focus more discretely on their older populations and their relations to resource environments in a Senior-Smart way. At a basic level, GIS allow one to depict (on maps) such community features as where all seniors reside, where the very old among them live, where visible minority and Aboriginal seniors live and so forth. Against these features the location of community resources such as stores, health services and bus routes can be mapped. GIS have the ability to take the descriptive maps and combine them: for example, maps could be prepared that show both the location of older residents and the location of resources they need, thereby pointing up areas of deficiency.

In preparing the Seniors' Action Plan for Regina, planners mapped the location of physically impaired seniors requiring special transit and combined it with the location of younger impaired persons who also use this service to plan more effective use of vehicles (see chapter 8). GIS were applied in a U.S. situation (Connecticut) to develop a more efficient system for delivering meals to homebound seniors.[55] Routes were redesigned to take into account the number of delivery vehicles, the allocation of senior clients per delivery person, and the location of the central meal-preparation facility. Numerous other applications are possible, such as portraying the future size and distribution of the seniors' population among community neighbourhoods and using cohort-survival projections and assumptions about aging in place. The use of maps offers a means of sharing information about seniors and their needs in a format that can assist the complex planning task for all organizations and agencies. "Mapping sets the stage for coordination," is the way one study puts it in advocating GIS when planning for seniors.[56]

REFLECTIONS ON SUSTAINABLE SENIOR-SMART COMMUNITIES

Planning for enabling environments for seniors is no mean task. It poses major challenges for communities, their planners, other officials, and politicians to expand their focus from concerns over buildings and other physical infrastructure to include human well-being. Moreover, it will involve a degree of integration and coordination involving agencies within and outside local governments that is not frequently seen. The Senior-Smart planning and design guidelines proposed above parallel other recent broad-scale efforts to achieve more livable communities for seniors. For example, one tack advocates the need to create "lifecycle communities."[57] Another, as seen in the work of the American Association of Retired Persons (AARP), is to promote the development of communities that have "environments for successful aging."[58] And yet another, emanating from the collaboration of several U.S. organizations, presents a "blueprint" to help communities prepare for the aging of Baby Boom cohorts.[59] The common elements in these various approaches, as in our Senior-Smart proposals, are:

· A comprehensive view of the needs of seniors, both separately and in their interrelations, including housing, transportation, health and supportive services, public safety, and opportunities to engage in civic and volunteer activities

· An intentional, planned approach focused on the needs of seniors and how they may complement the needs of younger generations (and vice versa)
· Acceptance of the diversity of the seniors' population and the communities they live in, and the provision of choice for meeting diverse needs associated with age, gender, income, degree of frailty, and ethnicity
· Inclusion of seniors in the deliberations and decision-making at all stages in the planning process and subsequent policy-making and program development

There can be little disagreement with these tenets. They accept that communities comprise a diversity of people whose general needs overlap and often converge. The test of their strength, however, will come in their implementation. Will they, resolutely, treat seniors as *people,* not as a *"problem"* for planners to resolve? Will they see the limits of the now-popular urban planning paradigms, such as the New Urbanism and Smart Growth, when it comes to the everyday needs of a seniors' population aging in place? The principles of compact, walkable, transit-oriented neighbourhoods with protected open space and services close at hand are commendable and need to be incorporated in community planning and redevelopment.[60] But when it comes to planning for seniors, "the devil is in the details," or at least may be in regard to New Urbanism principles in neighbourhood development.[61] For example, in striving for compact development these neighbourhoods offer narrow, multi-level houses with several flights of stairs inside and steps to a porch outside, all of which present substantial barriers to accessibility for many seniors. And in the desire to minimize automobile use and visibility, autos are stored in the rear and can be difficult to access. These are not insurmountable issues, but they point up the need for planners to demand that dwelling units, properties, and their access are barrier-free. It is important not to be beguiled by design paradigms that result in many of the same barriers as existing neighbourhoods. This is not in the interest of current seniors who wish to age in place, or their juniors who follow them.

For a variety of reasons, the needs of seniors have been neglected in most communities in past decades. There is a large backlog of needs to be filled even before coping with the dramatic impact from the baby boom. Thus, planning to meet seniors' needs is a way to bring community environments into balance, a necessary step in transforming existing communities and neighbourhoods into communities for all ages. Success will require a profound change: can various public sectors, private interests and not-for-profit groups work collaboratively? Among the most promising developments are the efforts to provide social support to residential situations. More than two decades ago, it was observed that buildings, apartment complexes, neighbourhoods, and even entire towns not originally planned for seniors now housed large numbers of them. They were termed Naturally Occurring Retirement Communities or NORCs, and were the result of what we now call aging in place.[62] In the past decade, numerous clusters of seniors (now several hundred in the U.S) have organized themselves to provide needed services and security.[63] This indigenous and low-cost approach receives state financial and organizational support in New York, where these aging-in-place projects are called NORC-SSPs.[64]

Such efforts reflect seniors' desire for independence and offer two further advantages. First, they go far to sustain residential situations for those who desire to age in place by not forcing seniors to move from familiar surroundings because of lack of support and by conserving social cohesion for current and soon-to-be seniors.[65] Second, they are applicable to any type of residential area where seniors are clustered – city, suburb, small town, housing complex, or apartment building. Size of community need not be a concern: all that is needed is initiative, political will, and, not least, inclusion of senior residents. All the evidence indicates that seniors are ready.

Reflections on a Fall

GERALD HODGE

For more than two years I had been working on the book you're now looking at and writing about the various kinds of environmental press a senior might encounter in a community, especially a frail senior. Then, on a Tuesday morning late in May, I slipped on a grassy slope and broke my left ankle and, suddenly, I was an example of one of the senior statistics I'd been citing: over one-half of seniors who enter a hospital's emergency ward do so because of a fall.

After three days in the hospital I was allowed to go home with a cast on my lower leg, and then I became another version of a senior – a physically impaired community-living senior. More particularly, I could neither drive nor walk, the only two modes of mobility available to me in this small island community on the British Columbia coast. It was soon clear that my everyday geography was going to be changed dramatically. I came home from the hospital with a walker which, because I had only one good foot, was really a "hopper," that would allow me to move around inside the house in which I live with my partner, Sharron. Going beyond the house meant first getting help to get down four steps seat-first from our deck to the gravel walkway, and then hopping 30 feet to our car. At our destination, anything other than a flat surface for the walker or a wheelchair proved to be inaccessible. Further, these movements required considerable stamina, which I was badly lacking due to the injury, surgery, and my mostly sedentary situation. This prevailed for more than six weeks.

Compare now an ordinary a weekday in my life up to then, which involved a walk late each afternoon to the tier of green mailboxes at Sandpiper Road, about three-quarters of mile there and back. Since I'm not very good at routinely walking for exercise, this gets a useful task done and allows me to get a daily constitutional. But more than just a walk, this outing provides me the opportunity to check out the neighbourhood to see what's happening. Isn't that a new "for sale" sign down road? What is the small shed for next to Arnie's driveway? Maybe all those cars mean the summer people are having another party? Occasionally at the mailboxes I encounter Tom and exchange views on the weather or a word on jazz, or I wave at April whizzing by on her bike. This simple walk means that I see my community and take part in it.

As long as my leg was in a fiberglass cast, driving was out also. This further reduced my contact with the community: no Co-op store or library where one was always bound to meet friends and neighbours and get caught up with community happenings. Finding out about such things depended upon people bringing news to me, or me seeking them out by telephone and email. Several friends, seniors like me, stopped by for a chat, providing a sort of vicarious community geography. After what seemed like an age but was really only six weeks, my cast was removed. I had eagerly waited the day when I would be able to drive again. However, though I could now cover larger distances, I still had to face walking on my still-not-fully-healed foot when I got to my destination. Climbing stairs proved difficult, as did walking on uneven ground. Even ramps for the handicapped proved difficult on the downward slope. Needless to say, no stroll to nearby beaches nor hikes in the forest were possible.

Three months after the fall I have to limit the amount I walk, and I haven't been able to resume my daily constitutional to the mailbox – maybe I will be able to a month from now. I've resumed a number of household chores such as shopping and taking out the recyclables that had fallen to Sharron during my convalescence but some, such as mowing the lawn, are still beyond my capability. I was not a frail senior when I started writing this book, but now I am much more aware of the realities that underlie the statistics and situations I've written about. I'm aware how easily everyday activities that give much meaning to an older person's life can be disrupted by a simple fall. I'm also aware of what this kind of event might mean for those who live alone (it is not uncommon for the lone senior to be sent to a nursing home in such situations). Not least, I can verify that the strongly held value that seniors place on independence – "to be able to carry out life's activities within a normal community setting, to be able to make choices about these activities and to have a degree of control over one's life" – is as important as they say.*

* Blossom T. Wigdor and Louise Plouffe, *Seniors' Independence: Whose Responsibility?* (Ottawa: National Advisory Council on Aging, 1992). 8.

Appendix

Internet Resources on Aging and Community Environments

The internet provides a valuable source of information and experience regarding seniors and their environments. The list of sites below represents a selection of these Web resources and is not meant to be exhaustive. Readers are encouraged to pursue links to additional sites. URL addresses are current as of mid-2008; in some cases one may encounter changes. Readers are also reminded that there may be instances when one may need to revert to the main site address (before the "/" slashes) and follow appropriate links to the desired site.

GATEWAY SITES

There are several notable Web sites that provide and an array of links to other sites on aging and community environments as well as being important in and of themselves.

Canadian Association
on Gerontology
http://www.cagacg.ca/

LIENS Canadian Web Sites
http://www.phac-aspc.gc.ca/
seniors-aines/cgi-bin/daslinks/
linkerviewer.pl?mode=
view&Submit=can

National Seniors' Council
(Canada)
http://www.seniorscouncil.gc.ca/
en/about_us/

Health Care Information – Aging
Links (McMaster Univ.)
http://hsl.mcmaster.ca/tomflem/
aging.html

Canadian Association of
Retired Persons
www.carp.ca

American Association of Retired
Persons (US)
http://www.aarp.org/
internetresources/

Administration on Aging (US)
http://www.aoa.gov/about/
about.asp

National Academy on an Aging
Society (US)
http://www.agingsociety.org/
agingsociety/

Centre for Policy on Ageing (UK)
http://www.cpa.org.uk/cpa/
about_cpa.html

RESEARCH RESOURCES

Statistics Canada
http://www.statcan.ca/

Canada Mortgage and Housing
Corporation
http://www.cmhc-schl.gc.ca/
en/inpr/

Canadian Institute for Health
Information
http://secure.cihi.ca/cihiweb/
splash.html

Canadian Seniors' Directory
http://www.seniors.ca/index.html

British Columbia Network of
Aging Research
http://bcnar.ca/

United Nations Population
Statistics
http://unstats.un.org/unsd/
default.htm

US National Archive of
Computerized Data on Aging
http://www.icpsr.umich.edu/
NACDA/index.html

Retirement Research Foundation
(US)
http://www.rrf.org/index.html

SeniorResource (US)
http://www.seniorresource.com/

PROVINCIAL AGENCIES
FOR AGING

British Columbia Active Aging
http://www.healthservices.gov.
bc.ca/seniors/

Alberta Seniors and
Community Supports
http://www.seniors.gov.ab.ca/

Alberta Council on Aging
http://www.seniorfriendly.ca/

Saskatchewan Services to Seniors
http://www.socialservices.gov.
sk.ca/seniors/

Manitoba Seniors' Secretariat
http://www.gov.mb.ca/shas/

Ontario Seniors' Secretariat
http://www.citizenship.gov.on.ca/
seniors/english/

Quebec RVCD
http://wpp01.msss.gouv.qc.ca/
appl/k30/K30Mission.asp

New Brunswick Seniors
and Housing
http://www.gnb.ca/0017/Seniors/
index-e.asp

Nova Scotia Dept. of Seniors
http://www.gov.ns.ca/scs/
positiveaging.asp

Prince Edward Island Seniors'
Secretariat
http://www.gov.pe.ca/infopei/
index.php3?number=3283&lang=

Newfoundland/Labrador Health
and Community Services
http://www.health.gov.nl.ca/
health/

UNIVERSITY RESEARCH
CENTRES ON AGING

University of Victoria
http://www.coag.uvic.ca/

University of British Columbia
http://www.crpd.ubc.ca/

Simon Fraser University
http://www.sfu.ca/grc/

Thompson Rivers University (BC)
http://research.tru.ca/centres.php

University of Alberta
http://www.ales2.ualberta.ca/
hecol/rapp/

University of Calgary
http://www.psych.ucalgary.ca/
PACE/PCA-Lab/index.html

University of Regina
http://uregina.ca/hadjistt/
centre_index.htm

University of Manitoba
http://www.umanitoba.ca/centres/
aging/

Lakehead University
http://cerah.lakeheadu.ca/

McMaster University
http://www.fhs.mcmaster.ca/
mcah/

Social and Economic Dimensions
of an Aging Population
(McMaster)
http://ideas.repec.org/s/mcm/
sedapp.html

Nipissing University
http://nipissingu.ca/ageresearch/

University of Toronto
http://www.aging.utoronto.ca/

Waterloo University
http://www.ahs.uwaterloo.ca/hsg/
research/

McGill University
http://aging.mcgill.ca/

universitè de Laval
http://www.ivpsa.ulaval.ca/cms/
index.php

universitè de Montrèal
http://www.criugm.qc.ca/

universitè de Sherbrooke
http://www.cdrv.ca/FR/400/

St Thomas University
http://www.stu.ca/research/
3rdage/index.htm

universitè de Moncton
http://www.umoncton.ca/udem/
larecherche/Recherche/
Centres.html

University of Prince Edward Island
http://www.upei.ca/~csha/
index.html

Mt. St Vincent University
http://www.msvu.ca/nsca/
index.asp

Memorial University
http://www.nlcahr.mun.ca/

COMMUNITY ENVIRONMENTS
FOR SENIORS

Aging in Place
http://www.seniorresource.com/
ageinpl.htm
http://www.aginginplace.org/
http://www.smartgrowthamerica.
org/aging4.04.html
http://www.seniorsservingseniors.
bc.ca/resources.asp

Age-friendly Cities (World Health
Organization)
http://www.who.int/ageing/
publications/Global_age_friendly_
cities_Guide_English.pdf
http://www.who.int/ageing/
publications/Age_friendly_cities_
checklist.pdf

Elderly drivers
http://www.tsfbcaa.com/
mature_drivers
http://www.tsfbcaa.com/
assess_your_driving_performance

Everyday Neighborhoods
http://www.cqgrd.gatech.edu/
conf/3-sessions.php
http://www.smartgrowth.org/
default.asp

Multicultural Environments
http://canada.metropolis.net/
index_e.html

NORCs
http://www.nyarm.com/
march99/0113.html
http://www.albany.edu/aging/
norc.htm
http://www.beaconhillvillage.org/

Physical Activity and Aging
http://www.uwo.ca/actage/

Rural Seniors
http://www.phac-aspc.gc.ca/
seniors-aines/pubs/age_friendly_
rural/index_e.htm

Seniors' Housing
http://www.iog.wayne.edu/
http://www.cmhc-schl.gc.ca/en/co/
maho/adse/masein/index.cfm
http://cms.city.richmond.bc.ca/
Page2035.aspx
http://www.okotoks.ca/sustain-
able/Soul/housing.asp

Notes

1 Lawton, M. Powell, *Environment and Aging* (Monterey, CA: Brooks/Cole Publishing, 1980), x.

2 Three worthy examples are Northcott, H.C. *Changing Residence: The Geographic Mobility of Elderly Canadians* (Toronto: Butterworths, 1988), Stone, Leroy O. and Frenken, Hubert, *Canada's Seniors* (Ottawa: Statistics Canada, 1988), and Moore, Eric G. and Rosenberg, Mark W. *Growing Old in Canada: Demographic and Geographic Perspectives* (Toronto: Nelson Canada, in conjunction with Statistics Canada, 1997), Cat. No. 96321-MPE, No. 1.

3 Blytheway, Bill ed. *Everyday Living in Later Life* (London: Centre for Policy on Ageing, 2003) and Gubrium, Jaber F. and Holstein, James A. eds. *Aging and Everyday Life* (Malden, MA: Blackwell, 2000).

4 Cvitkovich, Yuri and Wister, Andrew, "The Importance of Transportation and Prioritization of Environmental Needs to Sustain Well-Being Among Older Adults," *Environment and Behavior* 33:6 (2001), 808–29.

5 Kunkel, Suzanne, "Mapping the Field: Shifting Contours of Social Gerontology," *The Gerontologist* 43:1 (2003), 128–32.

6 In many European countries gerontologists use age 60, a norm that the United Nations also applies in its international comparisons of population aging.

7 Cf. McDaniel, Susan A. *Canada's Aging Population* (Toronto: Butterworths, 1986).

8 Many people today are retiring earlier than age 65 according to Statistics Canada. See *Canada's Changing Retirement Patterns: Findings from the General Social Survey* (Ottawa, 1996), Cat. No. 89-546-XPE.

9 Both the Canada and Quebec Pension Plans can be accessed today as early as age 60.

10   McDaniel, *Canada's Aging Population.*

11   Demographers have made much of such age dynamics to predict social and economic trends. One of the first was Richard Easterlin in *Birth and Fortune: The Impact of Numbers on Personal Welfare* (New York: Basic Books, 1980). The popular Canadian rendering of this theme, by David Foot in *Boom, Bust and Echo: Profiting from the Demographic Shift in the 21st Century* (Toronto: McFarlane and Ross, 1996), shows how the Canadian economy will be affected by changing cohorts.

12   Weiss, Robert S. and Bass, Scott A. *Challenges of the Third Age: Meaning and Purpose in Later Life* (New York: Oxford University Press, 2002).

13   To these types of aging one may add simple chronological aging, according to McPherson, Barry D. *Aging as a Social Process* (Toronto: Butterworths, 1983).

14   Kunkel, "Mapping the Field."

15   Kornman, John M. and Kingson, Eric R. "Trends, Issues, Perspectives and Values for the Aging of the Baby Boom Cohorts," *The Gerontologist* 36:1 (1996), 15–26.

16   Statistics Canada, *Health Reports: Health at Older Ages* (Special Issue, Supplement to Vol. 16, Ottawa: 2006), Cat. No. 82-003-SIE, 10.

17   Statistics Canada, *Health and Activity Limitation Survey, 1991* (Ottawa), Cat. No. 82-E0011 GBD.

18   National Advisory Council on Aging, "Seniors and Disabilities," *Expression* 11:1 (1996).

19   A recent and comprehensive review of this literature is found in Raina, Parminder, Chambers, Larry W. et al. "Income, Health, Disability, and the Functional Independence of the Elderly," in Frank T. Denton et al. eds. *Independence and Economic Security in Old Age* (Vancouver: UBC Press, 2000), 112–35.

20   Statistics Canada, *Health at Older Ages* (2006), Table 2.

21   McDonald, Lynn and Robb, Leslie A. *The Economic Legacy of Divorced and Separated Women in Old Age,* Research Paper No. 104, Program for Research on Social and Economic Dimensions of an Aging Population [SEDAP] (Hamilton, ON: McMaster University, 2003).

22   The statistics in the preceding sentences are from the 2001 census.

23   Finlayson, Marcia and Kaufert, Joseph, "Older Women's Community Mobility: a Qualitative Exploration," *Canadian Journal on Aging* 21:1 (2002), 75–84.

24   Buchignani, Norman and Strong-Esther, Christopher, "Informal Care and Older Native Canadians," *Ageing and Society* 19 (1999), 3–32.

25   Mack, Ruthanna, Salmoni, Alan, et al. "Perceived Risks to Independent Living: The Views of Older Community-Dwelling Adults," *The Gerontologist* 17:6 (1997), 729–36.

26 Statistics Canada, *A Portrait of Seniors in Canada*, 3rd edn. (Ottawa, 1999), Cat. No. 89-19 XPE.

27 Wahl, Hans-Werner and Weisman, Gerald, "Environmental Gerontology at the Beginning of the New Millennium: Reflections on its Historical, Empirical, and Theoretical Development," *The Gerontologist* 43:5 (2003), 616–27.

28 Föbker, S. and Grotz, R. "Everyday Mobility of Elderly People in Different Urban Settings: The Example of the City of Bonn, Germany," *Urban Studies* 43:1 (2006), 99–118.

29 As cited in McDaniel, *Canada's Aging Population*, 2.

30 Moore, Eric G. and Pacey, Michael, "Geographic Dimensions of Aging in Canada, 1991–2001," *Canadian Journal on Aging* 23 (2004 Supplement), S5–21.

31 Hou, Feng and Picot, Garnett, "Visible Minority Neighborhoods in Toronto, Montreal, and Vancouver," *Canadian Social Trends* 72 (2004), 8–13.

32 Litwak, E. and Longino, C.F. "Migration Patterns among the Elderly: A Developmental Perspective," *The Gerontologist* 27:2 (1987), 266–72.

33 Golant, Stephen M. "Factors Influencing the Locational Context of Old People's Activities," *Research on Aging* 6:4 (1984), 528–48.

34 Among the most important are Lawton, Note 1 *supra,* Rowles, Graham, D. *Prisoners of Space? Exploring the Geographical Experience of Older People* (Boulder, CO: Westview Press, 1978); and Golant, Stephen M. *A Place to Grow Old: The Meaning of Environment in Old Age* (New York: Columbia University Press, 1984).

35 Wahl and Weisman, "Environmental Gerontology at the Beginning of the New Millennium."

36 Lawton, M. Powell and Nahemow, Lucille, "Ecology and the Aging Process," Eisdorfer, C. and Lawton, M.P. eds. *Psychology of Adult Development and Aging* (Washington DC: American Psychological Association, 1973), 619–74.

37 Nahemow, Lucille, "The Ecological Theory of Aging: Powell Lawton's Legacy," in Rubinstein, Robert L. et al. eds. *The Many Dimensions of Aging* (New York: Springer, 2000), 22–40.

38 Wigdor, Blossom T. and Plouffe, Louise, *Seniors' Independence: Whose Responsibility?* (Ottawa: Forum Collection, National Advisory Council on Aging, 1992), 8.

39 British Columbia Task Force on Issues of Concern to Seniors, *Toward a Better Age* (Victoria, 1990).

40 Mack, Ruthanna, et al. "Perceived Risks to Independent Living."

41 Canada, National Advisory Council on Aging "Transportation – The Key to It All," *Expression* 2:4 (1985).

42 Rowles, Graham D. "Toward a Geography of Growing Old," in Butt-imer, A. and Seamon, D. eds. *The Human Experience of Space and Place* (London: Croom Helm, 1980), 55–72.

43 Rowles, Graham D. "The Surveillance Zone as Meaningful Space for the Aged," *The Gerontologist* 21:3 (1981), 304–11.

44 Rowles, Graham D. "Geographical Dimensions of Social Support in Rural Appalachia," in Rowles, Graham D. and Ohta, Russell J. eds. *Aging and Milieu: Environmental Perspectives on Growing Old* (New York: Academic Press, 1983), 111–30.

45 National Advisory Council on Aging, *Understanding Seniors' Independence: The Barriers and Suggestions for Action*, Report No. 1 (Ottawa, 1989).

46 Much of the content of this section has been suggested by the National Advisory Council on Aging's report *1999 and Beyond: Challenges of an Aging Canadian Society* (Ottawa, 1999).

CHAPTER TWO

1 Statistics Canada, *Health Reports: Health at Older Ages* (Special Issue, Supplement to Vol. 16: Ottawa, 2006), Cat. No. 82-003-SIE, 10.

2 Statistics Canada, *Canada's Retirement Income Programs: A Statistical Overview* (Ottawa, 2003), Cat. No. 74-507-XIE.

3 Clark, Warren, "What Do Seniors Spend on Housing?" *Canadian Social Trends* 78 (2005), 4–9.

4 Ibid.

5 Moore, Eric G. and Rosenberg, Mark W. *Growing Old in Canada: Demographic and Geographic Perspectives* (Toronto: Nelson Canada in conjunction with Statistics Canada, 1997), Cat. No. 96321-MPE, No. 1, 8ff.

6 Moore, Eric G. and Pacey, Michael, "Geographic Dimensions of Aging in Canada, 1991–2001," *Canadian Journal on Aging* 23 (Supplement 2004), S5–21.

7 A number of offsetting factors account for this stability in gender levels, not least being the slightly faster rate of increase of life expectancy for men.

8 Statistics Canada, *Canada's Ethnocultural Portrait: the Changing Mosaic* (2001 Census Analysis Series: Ottawa, 2003), Cat. No. 96F0030XIE-2001008, 39.

9 Statistics Canada Employment Equity Data Program, *Projections of Visible Minority Population Groups, Canada, Provinces and Regions, 1991–2016* (Minister of Industry: Ottawa, 1996), Cat. No. 91-541-XPE, 10.

10 Ibid, 68.

11 Hou, Feng and Picot, Garnett, "Visible minority neighborhoods in Toronto, Montreal and Vancouver," *Canadian Social Trends* 72 (2004), 8–13.

12 United Nations Economic and Social Affairs, *World Population Prospects: The 2004 Revision* (New York: 2005). Retrieved from http://www.un.org/popin/data.html.

13 The difference between this higher share for Canada and the nearly 13 percent shown in Tables 2.1 and 2.2 is due to the inclusion of seniors aged 60–64, and the fact that the UN figures are for 2004.

14 This tendency was also noted in the 1991 census data by Moore and Rosenberg, *Growing Old in Canada,* 70ff.

15 Statistics Canada, *A Portrait of Seniors in Canada* (Ottawa: 1999), Cat. No. 89-19 XPE, 3rd edn. Table 4.1.

16 Statistics Canada, *Profile of the Canadian Population by Age and Sex: Canada Ages* (2001 Census Analysis Series: Ottawa, 2002), Cat. No. 96F0030XIE2001002, 15.

17 Moore and Rosenberg make this point forcefully in their study of the elderly in the 1991 census in *Growing Old in Canada,* 90.

18 Morrison, P.A. "Demographic Factors Reshaping Ties to Family and Place," *Research on Aging* 12:4 (1979), 399–408.

19 Moore and Rosenberg, *Growing Old in Canada,* 99ff.

20 Statistics Canada, *Profile of the Canadian Population by Mobility Status: Canada, a Nation on the Move* (2001 Census Analysis Series 5: Ottawa, 2002) 96F0030XIE2001006.

21 Moore and Rosenberg, *Growing Old in Canada,* 105.

22 Ibid, 93–9.

23 Moore and Pacey, "Geographic Dimensions of Aging in Canada."

24 Biggar, J.C. "Who Moved among the Elderly, 1965–1970: A Comparison of Types of Older Movers," *Research on Aging* 2 (1980), 73–91.

25 Wiseman, R.F. "Why Older People Move," *Research on Aging* 2:2 (1980), 141–54, and Longino, C.F. Jr. "Going Home: Aged Return Migration in the United States 1965–1970," *Journal of Gerontology* 34 (1979), 736–45.

26 Longino, C.F. Jr. "The Forest and the Trees: Micro-level Considerations in the Study of Geographic Mobility in Old Age," in A. Rogers, ed. *Elderly Migration and Population Redistribution* (London: Bellhaven Press, 1992), 22–34.

27 Longino, C.F. Jr and Marshall, V.W. "North American Research on Seasonal Migration," *Ageing and Society* 10 (1990), 229–35, McHugh, K.E. and Mings, R.C. "On the Road Again: Seasonal Migration to a Sunbelt Metropolis," *Urban Geography* 12 (1991), 1–18, and Martin, H.W.,

Hoppe, S.K. et al. "Socioeconomic and Health Characteristics of Anglophone Canadian and U.S. Snowbirds," *Journal of Aging and Health* 4 (1992), 500–13.

28 McHugh, K.E. and Mings, R.C. "The Circle of Migration: Attachment to Place in Aging," *Annals of the Association of American Geographers* 86:3 (1996), 530–50.

29 Tucker, R.D., Mullins, L.C. et al. "Older Canadians in Florida: A Comparison of Anglophone and Francophone Seasonal Migrants," *Canadian Journal on Aging* 11:3 (1992), 281–97.

30 This section follows the approach taken by C.F. Longino Jr in "Geographical Distribution and Migration," in Binstock, R.H. and George, L.K. eds. *Handbook of Aging and the Social Sciences,* 5th edn. (San Diego: Academic Press, 2001), 103–24.

31 Wiseman, "Why Older People Move."

32 Cuba, L.J. "Models of Migration Decision-Making Reexamined: The Destination Search of Older Migrants to Cape Cod," *The Gerontologist* 31:2 (1991), 204–9.

33 Haas, W.H. III and Serow, W.J. "Amenity Retirement Migration Process: A Model and Preliminary Evidence," *The Gerontologist* 33:2 (1993) 212–20, and Carlson, J.E., Junk, V.A. et al. "Factors Affecting Retirement Migration to Idaho: An Adaptation of the Amenity Migration Model," *The Gerontologist* 38:1 (1998), 18–24.

34 Warnes, A.M. "Migration and the Life Course," in Champion, T. and Fielding, T. eds. *Migration Processes and Patterns* (London: Bellhaven Press, 1992), 175–87.

35 Litwak, E. and Longino, C.F. Jr. "Migration Patterns Among the Elderly: A Developmental Perspective," *The Gerontologist* 27:3 (1987), 266–72.

36 Fournier, G.M., Rasmussen, D.W., and Serow, W.J. "Elderly Migration as a Response to Economic Incentives," *Social Science Quarterly* 69 (1988), 245–60.

37 Rowles, G. and Ravdal, H. "Aging, Place and Meaning in the Face of Changing Circumstances," in Weiss, R.S. and Bass, S.A. eds. *Challenges of the Third Age* (New York: Oxford University Press, 2002), 81–114, and Rowles, G. "A Place to Call Home," in Carstensen, L.L. and Edelstein, B.A. eds. *Handbook of Clinical Gerontology* (New York: Pergamon, 1987), 335–53.

38 Cuba, L.J. "Retiring from Vacationland: From Visitor to Resident," *Generations* 13:2 (1989), 63–7.

39 Lawton, M. Powell, *Environment and Aging* (Monterey, CA: Brooks/Cole Publishing, 1980), 17.

40 Cutchin, M. "Deweyan Integration: Moving Beyond Place Attachment in Elderly Migration Theory," *International Journal of Aging and Human Development* 52:1 (2001), 29–44.

41 Tucker, R.D., Mullins, L.C. et al. "Older Canadians in Florida."

42 Martin, H.W., Hoppe, S.K. et al. "Socioeconomic and Health Characteristics."

43 Northcott, H.C. *Changing Residence: The Geographic Mobility of Elderly Canadians* (Toronto: Butterworths, 1988).

44 Hodge, G. *Seniors in Small Town British Columbia* (Vancouver: Simon Fraser University Gerontology Research Centre and University of British Columbia Centre for Human Settlements, 1991).

45 Ibid, 10.

46 Hunt, M.E. and Hunt, G. "Naturally Occurring Retirement Communities," *Journal of Housing for the Elderly* 3:3/4 (1985), 3–21.

47 Lin, Jane, "The Housing Transitions of Seniors," *Canadian Social Trends* 79 (Winter 2005), 22–6.

48 The term "holon" originated in Arthur Koestler's book *The Ghost in the Machine* (New York: Random House, 1967). It has been elaborated by Ken Wilber in *The Eye of Spirit* (Boston: Shambhala, 1997), esp. 99–100.

CHAPTER THREE

1 Hanson, S. and Hanson, P. "The Geography of Everyday Life," in Gärling, T. and Golledge, R. eds. *Behavior and Environment: Psychological and Geographical Approaches* (Amsterdam: Elsevier, 1993), 249–69.

2 There were a total of 5,600 census subdivisions (CSDs) used in the 2001 Census, covering the entire country. They apply to several types of settlement such as municipalities (both urban and rural) and Indian reserves as well as unorganized (mostly rural) territories. See www.statcan.ca/english/Subjects/Standard/sgc/2001 for full definitions.

3 An "urban area" is defined by Statistics Canada for census purposes as "an area with a population of at least 1,000 and no fewer than 400 persons per square kilometre." However, in most Canadian studies, places with populations up to 10,000 are defined as "rural" by virtue of their role in servicing outlying regions; see, for example, Gerald Hodge and M.A. Qadeer, *Towns and Villages in Canada: The Importance of Being Unimportant* (Toronto: Butterworths, 1983). A variation on this construct is found in Rothwell, N., Bollman, R.D. et al. "Migration to and from Rural and Small Town Canada," *Rural and Small Town Canada Analysis Bulletin* 3:6 (March 2002), Statistics Canada Cat. No. 21-006-XIE.

4 Hodge, Gerald, *The Graying of Canadian Suburbs: Patterns, Pace and Prospects* (Ottawa: Canada Mortgage and Housing Corporation, 1994).

5 Golant, Stephen M. "The Metropolitanization and Suburbanization of the U.S. Elderly Population: 1970–1988," *The Gerontologist* 30:1 (1990), 80–5.

6 Ibid, Table 1, 82.

7 Moore, Eric G. and Pacey, Michael, "Geographic Dimensions of Aging in Canada, 1991–2001," *Canadian Journal on Aging* 23 (2004 Supplement), S5–21.

8 One of the earliest renderings of metropolitan growth was the Concentric Zone Theory of Burgess, E.W. "The Growth of the City," in Park, R.E., Burgess, E.W. and McKenzie, R.D. eds. *The City* (Chicago: University of Chicago Press, 1925). More recent concepts include the "polycentric city" and "urban realms" as in Gordon, P., Richardson, H.W., and Wong, H.L. "The Distribution of Population and Employment in a Polycentric City: The Case of Los Angeles," *Environment and Planning A*, 18 (1986), 161–73; and Vance, James E. Jr. *The Continuing City: Urban Morphology in Western Civilization* (Baltimore: Johns Hopkins University Press, 1990), 502ff.

9 Hodge, Gerald and Gordon, David L.A. *Planning Canadian Communities*, 5th ed. (Toronto: Nelson Canada, 2007), 110–12.

10 Golant, Stephen M. *The Residential Location and Behaviour of the Elderly* (Chicago: University of Chicago Dept. of Geography Research Paper 143, 1972).

11 Golant, Stephen M. "The Metropolitanization and Suburbanization," and Hodge, Gerald, *The Graying of Canadian Suburbs*.

12 This is known as the "historic-cohort" explanation and is found in Golant, Stephen M. "The Suburbanization of the American Elderly," in Rogers, A. ed. *Elderly Migration and Population Redistribution* (London: Bellhaven Press, 1992), 163–80.

13 Amalgamations of core cities and adjacent municipalities occurred in Toronto, Ottawa-Hull, London, Greater Sudbury, and Hamilton in Ontario, and Halifax, Nova Scotia, between the 1991 and 2001 censuses. For maps see Peter Murphy, *Census Metropolitan Areas and Census Agglomerations with Census Tracts for the 2001 Census*, Geography Working Paper Series (Ottawa: Statistics Canada, 2002), Cat. No. 92F0138MIE2002001.

14 Much of the material in this and the following section is drawn from the author's 1994 study, *The Graying of Canadian Suburbs*. The study examined seniors' populations in the 25 extant CMAs in 1991.

15 In censuses prior to 1991, data on seniors concluded with the age group 75+.

16 This variation on the "concentric zone" theory of urban development, referred to in Note 9 *supra,* was used by Canadian demographer Leroy Stone to distinguish shifts of older populations in CMAs in Western Canada. See Stone, Leroy O. "Settlement Pattern Shifts of the Older Population in and around Western Canada Metropolitan Areas," in *Aging Households: Demographic Trends and Implications for Service Provision at Home and Abroad* (Vancouver: University of British Columbia Centre for Human Settlements, Occasional Paper 27, 1983), 3–37.

17 For detailed maps see Note 14, *supra.*

18 A more detailed rendering is possible utilizing Statistics Canada public access tapes; however, their use was beyond the resources available here.

19 Hodge, Gerald, "(Rural) Canada," in Cloke, Paul, ed. *Policies and Plans for Rural People* (London: Unwin Hyman, 1988), 166–91.

20 Hodge, Gerald, *The Elderly in Canada's Small Towns: Recent Trends and their Implications* (Vancouver: University of British Columbia Centre for Human Settlements, 1987), Table 4.8.

21 Hodge, Gerald, *Canada's Aging Rural Population: The Role and Response of Local Government* (Toronto: ICURR Press, 1993).

22 Marshall, Linda J. and Hunt, Michael, "Rural Naturally Occurring Retirement Communities: A Community Assessment Procedure," *Journal of Housing for the Elderly* 13:1–2 (1999), 19–34.

23 Ormond, Barbara A., Black, Kirsten J. et al. *Supportive Services Programs in Naturally Occurring Retirement Communities* (Washington: U.S. Department of Health and Human Services, 2004).

24 Cf. Hodge, *The Elderly in Canada's Small Towns.*

25 McNiven, C, Puderer, H., and Janes, D. "Census Metropolitan Area and Census Agglomeration Influenced Zones (MIZ): A Description of the Methodology," *Geography Working Paper Series* No. 2000-2 (January 2000), Statistics Canada, Cat. No. 92F0138MIE.

26 A total of 4,608 CSDs are included in the four MIZ categories. All 97 CSDs in the three northern territories are excluded; the total 2001 population excluded is 92,660 including 3,885 seniors. Statistics Canada, "Introduction to the Dictionary: Geographic Classifications, *2001 Census Dictionary*" (Ottawa: 2002) Table 3. Cat. No. 92-378-XIE.

27 McNiven, et al. "Census Metropolitan Area and Census Agglomeration Influenced Zones," 7ff.

28 For the several Canadian approaches see Du Plessis, V., Beshiri, R., and Bollman, R.D. "Definitions of Rural," *Rural and Small Town Canada*

Analysis Bulletin 3:3 (November 2001), Statistics Canada Cat. No. 21-006-XIE.

29 For further definition see note 3 *supra*.

30 Wigdor, Blossom T. and Plouffe, Louise, *Seniors' Independence: Whose Responsibility?* (Ottawa: Forum Collection, National Advisory Council on Aging, 1992), 8.

31 Lawton, M. Powell, "Planning Environments for the Elderly," *Journal of the American Institute of Planners* 36 (1970), 124–9.

32 Wilson, J.W. *Cast Me Not Off: Location Policy for Homes for the Elderly* (Burnaby, BC: Simon Fraser University Department of Geography, 1980).

33 Yeates, Maurice, "The Need for Environmental Perspectives on Issues facing Older People," in Golant, Stephen M. ed. *Location and Environment of Elderly Population* (Washington: Winston and Sons/Wiley, 1979), 71–80.

34 National Advisory Council on Aging, *Understanding Seniors' Independence: The Barriers and Suggestions for Action* (Ottawa, 1989).

35 Nahemow, Lucille, "The Ecological Theory of Aging: Powell Lawton's Legacy," in Rubinstein, Robert L. et al. eds. *The Many Dimensions of Aging* (New York: Springer, 2000), 22–40.

36 Secker, Jenny, et al. "Promoting Independence: But Promoting What and How?" *Ageing and Society* 23 (2003), 375–91.

CHAPTER FOUR

1 The title of this chapter is suggested by Altergott, Karen, ed. *Daily Life in Later Life: Comparative Perspectives* (Beverly Hills: Sage, 1988).

2 Zuzanek, Juri and Box, Sheila, "Life Course and the Daily Lives of Older Adults in Canada," in *Daily Life in Later Life*, 147–85.

3 Seamon, David, *A Geography of the Lifeworld* (London: Croon Helm, 1979).

4 Wahl, Hans-Werner and Weisman, Gerald, "Environmental Gerontology at the Beginning of the New Millennium: Reflections on its Historical, Empirical, and Theoretical Development," *The Gerontologist* 43:5 (2003), 616–27.

5 Kendig, Hal, "Directions in Environmental Gerontology: A Multidisciplinary Field," *The Gerontologist* 43:5 (2003), 611–15.

6 Cf. Rubinstein, Robert L. et al. eds. *The Many Dimensions of Aging* (New York: Springer, 2000), and Weiss, Robert S. and Bass, Scott A. eds. *Challenges of the Third Age: Meaning and Purpose in Later Life* (New York: Oxford University Press, 2002).

7 Cf. Cummings, E. and Henry, H.W. *Growing Old: The Process of Disengagement* (New York: Basic Books, 1961).

8 Cf. Maddox, G.L. "Persistence of Life Style Among the Elderly: A Longitudinal Study of Patterns of Social Activity in Relation to Life Satisfaction," in Neugarten, B.L. ed. *Middle Age and Aging* (Chicago: University of Chicago Press, 1968), 181–3.

9 Cf. Cavan, R.S. "Self and Role in Adjustment During Old Age," in Rose, A.M. ed. *Human Behavior and Social Process* (Boston: Houghton Mifflin, 1962), 526–36.

10 Cf. Havighurst, R.J., Neugarten, B.L., and Tobin, S.S. "Disengagement and Patterns of Aging," in *Middle Age and Aging*, 161–72.

11 Lawton, M.P. and Nahemow, L. "Ecology and the Aging Process," in Eisdorfer, C. and Lawton, M.P. eds. *Psychology of Adult Development and Aging* (Washington: American Psychological Association, 1973), 619–74.

12 Lawton, M.P. "Assessing the Competence of Older People," in Kent, D., Kastenbaum, R., and Sherwood, S. eds. *Research, Planning and Action for the Elderly* (New York: Behavioral Publications, 1972), 122–43.

13 Nahemow, Lucille, "The Ecological Theory of Aging: Powell Lawton's Legacy," in *The Many Dimensions of Aging*, 22–40.

14 Weisman, G.D., Chaudhury, H., and Moore, K.D. "Theory and Practice of Place: Toward an Integrative Model," in *The Many Dimensions of Aging*, 3–21.

15 Lawton, M.P. "Time, Space and Activity," in Rowles, G.D. and Ohta, R.J. eds. *Aging and Milieu: Environmental Perspectives on Growing Old* (New York: Academic Press, 1983), 41–61.

16 Gärling, T. and Garvill, J. "Psychological Explanation of Participation in Everyday Activities," in Gärling, T. and Golledge, R. eds. *Behavior and Environment: Psychological and Geographical Approaches* (Amsterdam: Elsevier, 1993), 290–7.

17 Horgas, A.L., Wilms, H-U., and Baites, M.M. "Daily Life in Very Old Age: Everyday Activities as Expression of Successful Living," *The Gerontologist* 38:5 (1998), 556–68.

18 Hanson, S. and Hanson, P. "The Geography of Everyday Life," in *Behavior and Environment: Psychological and Geographical Approaches*, 249–69.

19 Victorino, C.C. and Gauthier, A.H. "Are Canadian Seniors Becoming More Active? Empirical Evidence Based on Time-Use Data," *Canadian Journal on Aging* 24:1 (2005), 45–56.

20 Lawton, "Time, Space and Activity," and others.

21 Rowles, G.D. *Prisoners of Space? Exploring the Geographical Experience of Older People* (Boulder, CO: Westview Press, 1978).

22 Golant, S.M. "Factors Influencing the Locational Context of Old People's Activities," *Research on Aging,* 6:4 (1984), 528–48; Horgas et al. "Daily Life in Very Old Age," and several other studies.

23 Carp, F. "Walking as a Means of Transportation for Retired People," *Gerontologist* 11 (1971), 104–11.

24 Cf. Golant, "Factors Influencing the Locational Context," and Cutler, S.J. and Coward, R.T. "Availability of Personal Transportation in Households of Elders," *The Gerontologist* 15 (1992), 155–9.

25 Finlayson, M. and Kaufert, J. "Older Women's Community Mobility: A Qualitative Exploration," *Canadian Journal on Aging* 21:1 (2002), 75–84.

26 Gallo, J.J., Rebok, G.W., and Lesikar, S.E. "Driving Habits of Adults Aged 60 Years and Older," *Journal of American Geriatrics Society* 47:3 (1999), 335–41.

27 Golant, S.M. "Factors Influencing the Nighttime Activity of Old Persons in Their Community," *Journal of Gerontology* 39:4 (1984), 485–91.

28 Fobker, Stafanie and Grotz, Reinhold, "Everyday Mobility of Elderly People in Different Urban Settings: The Example of the City of Bonn, Germany," *Urban Studies* 43:1 (2006), 99–118.

29 Pastalan, L.A. "Sensory Changes and Environmental Behavior," in Byerts, T.O., Howell, S.C., and Pastalan, L.A. eds. *Environmental Context of Aging: Lifestyles, Environmental Quality and Living Arrangements* (New York: Garland STPM Press, 1979), 118–26.

30 Lawton, "Time, Space and Activity."

31 Stobert, Susan, Dosman, Donna, and Keating, Norah, *Aging Well: Time Use Patterns of Older Canadians* (Ottawa: Statistics Canada, 2006). Cat. No. 89-622-XIE, no. 2.

32 Victorino and Gauthier, "Are Canadian Seniors Becoming More Active?"

33 Zuzanek and Box, "Life Course and the Daily Lives of Older Adults."

34 Finlayson and Kaufert, "Older Women's Community Mobility."

35 Cf. Cantor, M.H. "Life Space and Social Support," in *Environmental Context of Aging: Lifestyles, Environmental Quality and Living Arrangements,* 33–61, and Hodge, Gerald, *Shelter and Services for the Small Town Elderly* (Ottawa: Canada Mortgage and Housing Corporation, 1984).

36 Cf. Wilson, J.W. *Cast Me Not Off: Location Policy for Homes for the Elderly* (Burnaby, BC: Simon Fraser University Department of Geography, 1980) and Ontario Ministry of Municipal Affairs and Housing, *Towards Community Planning for an Aging Society* (Toronto: Queen's Printer, 1983).

37 Regnier, V. "Urban Neighborhood Cognition: Relationships Between Functional and Symbolic Community Elements," in *Aging and Milieu: Environmental Perspectives on Growing Old,* 62–82.

38 Wilson, *Cast Me Not Off.*

39 King, E.C. et al. "Physical Activity Interventions Targeting Older Adults: A Critical Review and Recommendations," *Preventive Medicine* 15:4 (1998), 316–33.

40 Loukaitou-Sideris, Anastasia, "Is It Safe to Walk? Neighbourhood Safety and Security Considerations and Their Effect on Walking," *Journal of Planning Literature* 20:3 (2006), 219–32.

41 Fletcher, P.C. and Hirdes, J.P. "Risk Factors for Serious Falls Among Community-Based Seniors: Results from the National Population Health Survey," *Canadian Journal on Aging* 21:1 (2002), 103–16, and Langlois, J.A. et al. "Dependence in Activities of Daily Living as a Risk Factor for Fall Injury Events Among Older People Living in the Community," *Journal of the American Geriatric Society* 43:3 (1995), 275–8.

42 Steinberg, Shawna, "Canada's Safest Cities," *Chatelaine* (April 1999), 70–81.

43 Gallagher, E.M. and Brunt, H. "Head Over Heels: Impact of a Health Promotion Program to Reduce Falls in the Elderly," *Canadian Journal on Aging* 15:4 (1994), 84–96.

44 Gallagher, E.M. and Scott, V. *The STEPS Project: A Project to Reduce Falls in Public Places Among Seniors and People With Disabilities* (Victoria, BC: University of Victoria School of Nursing, 1995), 13.

45 Clarke, P. and Colantonio, A. "Wheelchair Use Among Community-Dwelling Older Adults: Prevalence and Risk Factors in a National Sample," *Canadian Journal on Aging* 24:2 (2005), 191–8.

46 Golant, "Factors Influencing the Nighttime Activity."

47 Ibid.

48 Lebowitz, B.D. "Age and Fearfulness: Personal and Situational Factors," *Journal of Gerontology* 30 (1975), 696–700; and Lawton, M.P. et al. "Psychological Aspects of Crime and Fear of Crime," in Goldsmith, J. and Goldsmith, S.S. eds. *Crime and the Elderly* (Lexington, MA: Heath, 1976), 21–9.

49 Steinberg, "Canada's Safest Cities."

50 Hale, C. "Fear of Crime: A Review of the Literature," *International Review of Victimology* 4 (1996), 79–150, and Bannister, J. and Fyfe, N. "Fear and the City," *Urban Studies* 38:5 (2001), 807–13.

51 Wilson, J.W. "Planning Safer Communities," *Plan Canada* 26:3 (1985), 64–82, and Loukaitou-Sideris, A. "Hot Spots of Bus Stop Crime: The Importance of Environmental Attributes," *Journal of the American Planning Association* 65:4 (1999), 385–408.

52 Finlayson and Kaufert, "Older Women's Community Mobility."

53 Mack, Ruthanna et al. "Perceived Risks to Independent Living: The Views of Older, Community-Dwelling Adults," *The Gerontologist* 37:6 (1997),

729–36; and Bonnel, W.B. "Giving Up the Care: Older Women's Losses and Experiences," *Journal of Psychosocial Nursing* 37:5 (1999), 10–15.

54 Finlayson and Kaufert, "Older Women's Community Mobility."

55 Tuan, Y.F. *Space and Place* (Minneapolis: University of Minnesota Press, 1977).

56 McHugh, K.E. and Mings, R.C. "The Circle of Migration: Attachment to Place in Aging," *Annals of the Association of American Geographers* 86:3 (1996), 530–50.

57 Rowles, G.D. and Ravdal, H. "Aging, Place, and Meaning in the Face of Changing Circumstances," in *Challenges of the Third Age: Meaning and Purpose in Later Life,* 81–114.

58 Lawton, M.P. "Knowledge Resources and Gaps in Housing the Aged," in Tilson, D. ed. *Aging in Place* (Glenview, IL: Scott, Foresman, 1990), 287–309.

59 Rubenstein, R.L. and Parmalee, P.A. "Attachment to Place and the Representation of the Life Course of the Elderly," in Altman, I. and Low, S.M. eds. *Place Attachment* (New York: Plenum Press, 1992), 139–63.

60 Golant, S.M. "Conceptualizing Time and Behavior, in Environmental Gerontology: A Pair of Old Issues Deserving New Thought,' *The Gerontologist* 43:5 (2003), 638–48.

61 Buttimer, Anne, "Home, Reach and the Sense of Place," in Buttimer, A. and Seamon, D. eds. *The Human Experience of Space and Place* (New York: St. Martin's Press, 1980), 166–87.

62 Maddox, G.L. "If You Want to Understand Something, Try to Change It: An Essay Honoring Powell Lawton," in *The Many Dimensions of Aging,* 231–8.

CHAPTER FIVE

1 Rowles, G.D. "Toward a Geography of Growing Old," in Buttimer, A. and Seamon, D. eds. *The Human Experience of Space and Place* (London: Croon Helm, 1980), 15–72.

2 Lawton, M.P. "The Impact of Environment on Aging and Behavior," in Birren, J. and Shaie, K. eds. *Handbook on the Psychology of Aging* (New York: Van Nostrand, 1977), 276–301.

3 Hodge, G. *Shelter and Services for the Small Town Elderly: The Role of Assisted Housing* (Ottawa: Canada Mortgage and Housing Corporation, 1984), 56ff.

4 Cantor, M.H. "Life Space and Social Support," in Byerts, T., Howell, C., and Pastalan, L. eds. *Environmental Context of Aging: Life-Styles,*